STUDENT GUIDE

Introduction to

MANAGEMENT

ACCOUNTING

Frank H. Selto
Ph.D., University of Colorado at Boulder

Dudley W. Curry
Ph.D., C.P.A., Southern Methodist University

STUDENT GUIDE

Introduction to MANAGEMENT ACCOUNTING

9th Edition
Charles T. Horngren
Gary L. Sundem

Prentice Hall, Englewood Cliffs, New Jersey 07632

Editorial production/supervision: *Carolyn Del Corso*
Prepress buyer: *Trudy Pisciotti*
Manufacturing buyer: *Patrice Fraccio*
Supplement acquisitions editor: *Lisamarie Brassini*
Acquisitions editor: *Terri Daly*

©1993 by Prentice-Hall, Inc.
A Simon & Schuster Company
Englewood Cliffs, New Jersey 07632

All rights reserved. No part of this book may be
reproduced, in any form or by any means,
without permission in writing from the publisher.

Printed in the United States of America

10 9 8 7 6 5 4 3 2 1

ISBN 0-13-482167-X

Prentice-Hall International (UK) Limited, *London*
Prentice-Hall of Australia Pty. Limited, *Sydney*
Prentice-Hall Canada Inc. *Toronto*
Prentice-Hall Hispanoamericana, S.A., *Mexico*
Prentice-Hall of India Private Limited, *New Delhi*
Prentice-Hall of Japan, Inc., *Tokyo*
Simon & Schuster Asia Pte. Ltd., *Singapore*
Editora Prentice-Hall do Brasil, Ltda., *Rio de Janeiro*

Contents

	TO THE STUDENT	vii
CHAPTER 1	PERSPECTIVE: SCOREKEEPING, ATTENTION DIRECTING, AND PROBLEM SOLVING	1
CHAPTER 2	INTRODUCTION TO COST-VOLUME RELATIONSHIPS	15
CHAPTER 3	VARIATIONS OF COST BEHAVIOR	33
CHAPTER 4	INTRODUCTION TO COST SYSTEMS	46
CHAPTER 5	RELEVANT INFORMATION AND DECISION MAKING-PART ONE	63
CHAPTER 6	RELEVANT INFORMATION AND DECISION MAKING-PART TWO	81
CHAPTER 7	THE MASTER BUDGET: THE OVERALL PLAN	96
CHAPTER 8	FLEXIBLE BUDGETS AND STANDARDS FOR CONTROL	115
CHAPTER 9	MANAGEMENT CONTROL SYSTEMS AND RESPONSIBILITY ACCOUNTING	130
CHAPTER 10	MANAGEMENT CONTROL IN DECENTRALIZED ORGANIZATIONS	145
CHAPTER 11	CAPITAL BUDGETING: AN INTRODUCTION	159
CHAPTER 12	CAPITAL BUDGETING: TAXES AND INFLATION	175
CHAPTER 13	COST ALLOCATION AND ACTIVITY-BASED COSTING	190
CHAPTER 14	JOB COSTING SYSTEMS, OVERHEAD APPLICATION, SERVICE INDUSTRIES	204
CHAPTER 15	PROCESS-COSTING SYSTEMS	217
CHAPTER 16	OVERHEAD APPLICATION: DIRECT AND ABSORPTION COSTING	233
CHAPTER 17	QUANTITATIVE TECHNIQUES USED IN MANAGEMENT ACCOUNTING	248
CHAPTER 18	BASIC ACCOUNTING: CONCEPTS, TECHNIQUES, AND CONVENTIONS	264
CHAPTER 19	UNDERSTANDING CORPORATE ANNUAL REPORTS: BASIC FINANCIAL STATEMENTS	282
CHAPTER 20	MORE ON UNDERSTANDING CORPORATE ANNUAL REPORTS	295
CHAPTER 21	DIFFICULTIES IN MEASURING NET INCOME	310
APPENDIX	INTRODUCTION TO JOURNAL ENTRIES AND T-ACCOUNTS	322

To the Student

This student guide is designed for use with the ninth edition of *Introduction to Management Accounting* by Horngren and Sundem. For each textbook chapter there is a corresponding guide chapter that presents the main focus and objectives and contains a detailed review of key concepts, plus a comprehensive set of practice test questions and problems. The solutions, which appear immediately after each practice test, can provide useful feedback to reinforce your learning.

HOW TO USE YOUR TEXTBOOK AND STUDENT GUIDE

Have you already developed a general study system or learning style that is most effective for you? Whether your answer is yes or no, please consider some time-tested ideas and procedures for the successful use of these materials in the study of management accounting.

1. First, this study requires more than the mere memorization of a few rules and definitions. Actually, it is essential that you develop for each chapter a clear understanding of the main concepts and their logical relationships. Remember that many of the chapters depend heavily on the earlier chapters in the textbook.
2. Don't try to digest an entire assignment in one long study session. This approach can be tiring, frustrating, and ineffective -- or at least an inefficient way to use your time. Instead, profitably divide your study time into several shorter periods:
    (a) If an entire textbook chapter has been assigned for a class meeting, you may want first to read the chapter from beginning to end without interruption. Next, study the chapter in detail.
    (b) During this second study, carefully proceed through each step of all the examples and illustrations. Note particularly the "Summary Problems for Your Review." These cover the most important ideas in the chapter. Conscientiously trace each step in these problems to their solutions until your understanding is complete.
3. After your textbook study of a chapter, read the corresponding chapter in this student guide:
    (a) The "Review of Key Concepts" is a descriptive outline that can aid your retention of the most important concepts and relationships presented by the textbook chapter.
    (b) Solve the "Practice Test Questions and Problems." By checking your answers with the solutions, you can generate valuable feedback for mastering the chapter contents. At this point, don't hesitate to refer to your textbook as needed for more complete understanding.
4. Next, solve the textbook problems that have been assigned as homework by your instructor. *Work alone*, at least initially, and not with a "study buddy." Try to develop reliance on yourself, not on somebody else.
5. After the class discussion of the assigned problems, you can decide whether to restudy selected parts of the textbook.

REVIEWING FOR TESTS AND EXAMS

1. If you have regularly completed all of your study and written assignments on time, the necessary review for an exam probably will be minimal. In any case, you will find it not feasible to cover everything in detail. Be selective. Concentrate your review on either the most important matters or the textbook sections that seem most difficult for you.
2. You may find it helpful to "top off" your review by rereading selected parts of the student guide and reworking some of the practice test questions and problems.

Good luck!

Frank H. Selto
University of Colorado at Boulder

Dudley W. Curry
Southern Methodist University

CHAPTER 1

Perspective: Scorekeeping, Attention Directing, and Problem Solving

---

MAIN FOCUS AND OBJECTIVES

This preview chapter emphasizes the partnership roles of managers and accountants in planning and controlling the operations of an organization. Our broad aim is to understand how accounting systems can aid management decisions. The chapter presents the three themes that govern the practice of management accounting: *the concept of cost-benefit analysis, the behavioral focus, and adaptation to change.* Specific learning targets for this chapter are to:

- Describe the different users of accounting information

- Name the questions accounting helps answer

- Distinguish service from manufacturing organizations

- Explain cost-benefit and behavioral issues

- Explain the role of budgets and performance reports in planning and control

- Discuss effects of product life cycles

- Distinguish line and staff authority and roles of controllers and treasurers

- Identify current trends in management accounting and the ethical responsibilities of management accountants

---

REVIEW OF KEY CONCEPTS

A. All accounting information is prepared to help someone make decisions. In many cases, accounting information is absolutely critical to making good decisions. Users of accounting information and their decisions include:

  1. Internal managers making short-term planning and control decisions

  2. Internal managers making investment and long-term planning decisions

3. External parties, such as investors who decide whether to invest in the company and government authorities who decide on various policy and regulatory matters

B. Note how the primary users and decisions of accounting information are different:

1. The first two categories deal with the internal use of information by managers: this is *management accounting*, and the focus of this text and study guide.

2. The third category is concerned mainly with the use of information by individuals who are external to the organization: this is *financial accounting*.

3. Different needs and different users indicate either different accounting *systems* for each category or a complex, multi-purpose accounting *system* that serves all.

> See textbook Exhibit 1-1

C. Income tax and other regulatory authorities set allowable accounting practices for external, financial accounting (e.g., GAAP). There are no similar constraints on management accounting.

> Before going on to the next section, be sure that you understand the different users of accounting information and how different accounting systems provide information for their decision-making needs.

D. Three major themes govern the design of management accounting systems:

1. The **cost-benefit** theme of choosing among accounting systems and methods:
   a. All accounting information and systems are economic goods available at various *costs*.
   b. More extensive management accounting information is desirable only if the *benefits* (through improved decision-making) exceed the costs of the information.
   c. Often it is easier to identify the costs of new information (e.g., computer hardware, software, and personnel) than the benefits.

2. **Behavioral implications** of operating a management accounting system:
   a. The use of budgets stimulates planning activities -- this is a beneficial behavioral effect.
   b. Individual motivations are strongly influenced by performance reports and incentives that are used to appraise both decisions and managers -- this can be a favorable behavioral effect **if** the performance reports and incentives are designed properly. Otherwise, adverse behavioral effects may result.

3. **Adaptation to change:**
   a. External environments and internal decision-making change over time.
   b. Management accounting systems will provide useful information in the future only if they evolve along with the environment and the organization. Many accountants, managers, and academics have criticized accounting systems for not evolving and, therefore, for impeding good decision-making.

        c.   Current changes include: (1) increased emphasis on service, (2) increased global competition, (3) advances in technology, and (4) advances in manufacturing practices (e.g., JIT and CIM).
        d.   Management accountants themselves must be willing and able to learn and evolve.

> Can you explain the three major influences on management accounting systems?

E. The basic ideas of management accounting apply to service organizations as well as to manufacturing organizations.
   1.   Service organizations produce a service instead of a tangible product.
        a.   They include banks, insurance companies, railroads, theaters, and medical clinics.
        b.   Nearly all nonprofit organizations are engaged in service activities -- for example, universities, public libraries, churches, charitable organizations, and government agencies.
   2.   The main distinctive characteristics of service organizations are:
        a.   They are **labor-intensive** and not capital-intensive.
        b.   Their outputs are **difficult to define and measure.**
        c.   Their major inputs and outputs are **intangible** and therefore **cannot be stored.**
   3.   The last two items are the reasons why management accounting in service organizations (1) is especially challenging and (2) may have the most opportunity for improving decision-making.

F. Accounting systems produce three kinds of information:
   1.   **Scorekeeping information** helps in the routine evaluation of performance and position (How well are we doing?).
   2.   **Attention-directing information** aids in identifying problems and opportunities worth further investigation (Where should I be directing my management effort?).
   3.   **Problem-solving information** is useful for long-range planning and for making special, nonrecurring decisions (What are my opportunities and constraints?).

G. Note that management accounting is patterned after the management process.

> See textbook Exhibit 1-2

   1.   Management decision making is composed of two basic functions:
        a.   **Planning:** deciding on objectives and ways to attain them.
        b.   **Controlling:** evaluating performance through **feedback,** modifying plans if necessary, and implementing plans.

> See textbook Exhibits 1-3 and 1-5

   2.   **Budgets** are the main type of planning information.
   3.   **Performance reports** are the main type of controlling information.

4. Performance reports that periodically compare actual outcomes with budgets provide **feedback** to employees on the quality of plans and implementation of plans.

5. **Management by exception** means focusing attention and effort on the more significant deviations from expected results. In accounting these deviations are called **variances**.

> See textbook Exhibits 1-4 and 1-6

> Before going on, be sure that you understand the different types of information that accounting systems provide and how this information is consistent with the management process.

H. The development stage of the **product life cycle** determines most of the costs of products and programs.

> See textbook Exhibit 1-7

1. During the production or delivery stages, typical accounting systems do not report past development costs or future phase-out costs.

2. Thus, product costs over the entire life cycle may be understated by ignoring development and phase-out costs.

3. Proper decision-making for current products (and importantly for planning future products) requires that managers consider the costs over the entire product life cycle.

I. The chief accounting executive, or chief management accountant, is often called the **controller** (or *comptroller* in government organizations).

1. The controller's authority is basically of the **staff type**, that is, giving advice and service to other departments.

> See textbook Exhibit 1-8

2. The controller has direct control, called **line authority**, only over personnel of the controller's department, such as staff accountants (sometimes called financial analysts), internal auditors, cost clerks, and the general ledger bookkeeper.

> See textbook Exhibit 1-9

3. The main functions of the controller are preparing information for planning and reporting, and interpreting and evaluating information in consultation with other managers.

4. In contrast to the controller's functions, the **treasurer** of a company is concerned mainly with such financial activities as investor relations, banking, long and short-term borrowing, and investments.

J. The study of management accounting is rewarding because:

1. Management accounting is a major source of information throughout the organization. Management accountants, therefore, have the opportunity to learn the detailed workings of the organization perhaps better than anyone else.
2. As a result, many top management officers have been managment accountants.
2. Professional recognition is available as a Certified Management Accountant (CMA).

K. High standards of ethical conduct are essential to the practice of management accounting.
1. Without acknowledged ethical behavior, accountants and their information are not credible.
2. Accountants are recognized by the public as adhering to high ethical standards.
3. To a large degree, the accounting profession's ethical reputation is responsible for its high social status.
4. The Institute of Management Accountants has developed standards of ethical behavior that address:
   a. Professional competence
   b. Confidentiality of information
   c. Integrity
   d. Objectivity

See textbook Exhibit 1-10

The previous sections described the organizational and professional roles of management accountants. Can you describe the practice and profession of management accounting?

PRACTICE TEST QUESTIONS AND PROBLEMS WITH SOLUTIONS

This section will help you find out how well you have absorbed the content of the textbook. Try to answer all of these questions and problems *with your textbook closed*. Then, check your answers with the solutions that immediately follow this practice test. In this way, you can determine which parts of the textbook chapter to restudy.

True-False Statements

Determine whether each of the following statements is True (T) or False (F) and enter your answer, T or F, in the space provided.

_____1. Management control refers primarily to the setting of maximum limits on expenditures.

_____2. The treasurer of a company is concerned mainly with planning, reporting, evaluating, and interpreting.

_____3. The U.S. Foreign Corrupt Practices Act pertains to the operations of all U.S. companies that conduct business in foreign countries.

_____4. Compared with the typical management accounting reports, financial accounting reports are more likely to focus only on the actual results of the preceding period.

_____5. One feature common to both financial and managerial accounting is that the methods and practices of both are strictly constrained by external authorities.

_____6. There are essentially no conceptual differences between management accounting for service and for manufacturing organizations.

_____7. The Foreign Corrupt Practices Act requires that internal accounting controls of all publicly owned U.S. firms be documented by independent, external auditors.

_____8. Management accounting is more likely than financial accounting to depend on economics and decision sciences.

_____9. Management by exception refers to assigning the most difficult management control tasks only to exceptional managers, who are identified by accounting performance reports.

_____10. It is important to understand a product's life cycle so that costs from one stage of the cycle are not mixed with costs from another stage.

_____11. The controller of an organization exercises both line and staff authority.

_____12. Risk management is one of the usual duties of the controller.

_____13. One of the objectives of the IMA is to establish management accounting as a recognized profession.

_____14. One of the drawbacks of being a professional management accountant is that, because the job is so narrowly focused, few accountants are considered for top management positions.

_____15. One of the advantages of being a professional management accountant is that the field is one of the few stable fields, where techniques learned today are likely to be useful even decades from now.

Multiple Choice Questions

For the following multiple-choice questions, select the best answer(s) and enter identification letters in the spaces provided:

____1. Management accounting for an organization is aimed mainly at the decision needs of: (a) its stockholders, (b) its creditors, (c) government regulators, (d) internal managers.

____2. Analyzing variances from the budget of the cost of materials used in making a particular product should be classified as: (a) problem solving, (b) attention directing, (c) scorekeeping, (d) financial auditing.

____3. Controlling is done by: (a) accountants, (b) managers, (c) internal auditors, (d) accounting systems.

____4. The controller has direct, line authority over: (a) line departments, (b) staff accountants, (c) staff departments, (d) executives.

____5. The management controlling function includes: (a) formulating plans, (b) implementing plans, (c) evaluating results, (d) providing feedback.

____6. Performance reports primarily serve: (a) the planning function, (b) the evaluation function, (c) the feedback function, (d) the audit function.

____7. Budgets primarily serve: (a) the financial reporting function, (b) the feedback function, (c) the planning function, (d) the controlling function.

____8. Unique difficulties of management accounting in service organizations *do not* include: (a) labor intensity, (b) diverse output, (c) ill-defined output, (d) perishability of output.

____9. The controller is likened most aptly to a ship's: (a) captain, (b) engineer, (c) cook, (d) navigator, (e) executive officer.

____10. The effective restrictions on measurements that can be reported by a management accounting system *do not* include: (a) GAAP, (b) the cost-benefit philosophy, (c) behavioral impacts, (d) adaptation to change.

____11. The most useful scorekeeping information is the evaluation of performance made by comparing actual results for a month with: (a) the budget for that month, (b) actual results of the preceding month, (c) actual results of the same month a year ago, (d) actual results with results of a competitor.

Completion

Fill in the blanks to complete each of the following statements and requirements:

1. The two basic functions of the management process are _____ and _____.

2. Management planning is deciding on _____ and _____.

3. The three main types of useful information that the management accountant should supply are:

   _____-keeping information,
   _____-directing information, and

_____-solving information.

4. The concentration of the executive's attention and effort on the more significant deviations from expected results is called _____.

5. The three distinctive features of service organizations are:

(a)_____
(b)_____
(c)_____

6. The chief accounting executive, or chief management accountant, is often called the_____.

7. Interpreting and evaluating information in consultation with operating managers is an example of the exercise of the controller's _____ authority.

8. Comparison of this year's actual results with this year's budget is an example of a _____.

9. Write out in full the words for each of the following initials:

(a) AICPA:_____
(b) CMA:_____
(c) GAAP:_____
(d) GAO:_____
(e) IMA:_____

10. The major areas of responsibility for ethical conduct by management accountants are:

(a)_____
(b)_____
(c)_____
(d)_____

11. Identify each of the following features as being *more* identified with management accounting (MA) or with financial accounting (FA):

_____1. Measuring actual performance against actual results of preceding period
_____2. Less freedom in choosing measurement methods and principles
_____3. Flexible time-span
_____4. Detailed reports on subunits of an organization
_____5. Stronger orientation to investors
_____6. Constrained by GAAP
_____7. Affects employees' daily behavior
_____8. Focus on prior period's results

12. For each of the following activities within a company, identify the main function that is being performed: SK = scorekeeping; PS = problem solving; AD = attention directing.

_____1. Preparing the variance of actual dollar sales from budgeted sales by type of product and by name of salesperson.
_____2. Tabulating spoiled rejected product units at the end of a manufacturing process.
_____3. Entering checks in the cash disbursements journal.
_____4. Estimating future cash inflows and cash outflows relating to the contemplated acquisition of specialized manufacturing machinery.
_____5. Computing and recording end-of-year adjustments for accrued wages and salaries.

13. For each of the following pairs, use the code shown below to indicate the usual type of authority of the first-named party over the second-named party: L = line authority; S = staff authority; N = no authority

_____1. controller/payroll clerks
_____2. production superintendent/accounts payable bookkeeper
_____3. engineering vice-president/storekeeper
_____4. controller/production superintendent
_____5. president/chairman of the board
_____6. chief inspector/controller
_____7. manufacturing vice-president/receiving clerk
_____8. assistant controller/accounts receivable bookkeeper
_____9. controller/purchasing officer
_____10. internal auditor/assistant controller

Problems

Prepare solutions for each of the following problems in the spaces provided.

1. The Parent Teacher Organization (PTO) of Eisenhower Elementary School held a fund-raising fair in the school gynasium. The PTO president had prepared the following budget assuming 200 attendees who spend an average of $20 each and donations of all other resources:

Revenues	$4,000
Costs:	
Food and beverages	800
Prizes	500
Supplies	300
Custodial services	200
Total costs	$1,800
Income	$2,200

Afterwards, the PTO treasurer (the PTO has no controller) determined that 150 people had attended the fair, and total revenues were $2,250. Cost of food and beverages was $750. All prizes were awarded. Supplies cost $180, and custodial services were $500 due to damage of the gymnasium floor.

Prepare a performance report that shows how actual results differ from budgeted results. Which variances deserve further examination?

Item	Actual results	Budgeted results	Variance	Explanation
Revenues		$4,000		
Costs:				
Food and beverages		800		
Prizes		500		
Supplies		300		
Custodial services		200		
Total costs		$1,800		
Income		$2,200		

2. The Evergreen Chamber of Commerce prepared the following budget for its annual Fourth of July concert and fireworks show.

Sources of revenue:	
Merchant donations	$10,000
Public donations	5,000
Total revenue	$15,000
Costs:	
Fireworks	$12,000
Rentals (band tent, audio equipment, portable toilets, barricades)	2,000
Police and fire protection services	3,000
Total costs	$15,000
Budgeted loss	$ (2,000)

Donations totaled $13,000. Due to an unusually wet first week of July, police and fire protection services cost $1,000 less than expected. Some fireworks did not ignite, and the distributor issued a $500 refund. One of the portable toilets was destroyed by members of the public and had to be replaced for $400.

Prepare a performance report that shows how actual results differ from budgeted results. Which variances deserve further examination?

CHAPTER 1 SOLUTIONS TO PRACTICE TEST QUESTIONS AND PROBLEMS

True or False Statements

1. False — This is spending control. Management control is exercised by coordinating planning, evaluation, and feedback.

2. False — These are controller's duties. The treasurer is concerned with financing activities, investor relations, and so on.

3. False — The Act affects only publicly-held companies **and** affects them whether or not they conduct international business.

4. True — Though both types of accounting reports contain past results, management accounting reports also focus on future outcomes (e.g., through budgets).

5. False — In general, management accounting practices are not constrained by external authorities.

6. True — In concept, they are the same, though in practice management control is likely to be more difficult in service organizations.

7. False — The Act requires management to document its internal accounting controls.

8. True — The planning and control activities of management accounting are more likely to depend on other management disciplines.

9. False — Management by exception refers to focusing efforts on exceptionally large variances.

10. False — Consideration of the product life cycle is important for consideration of total product costs, from development to phase-out.

11. True — The controller has staff authority with other staff line departments and has line authority over the accounting department.

12. False — Risk management (insurance) is usually a treasurer function.

13. True — This is an objective of the Institute of Management Accountants (IMA). The AICPA is concerned primarily with independent auditors and tax practitioners.

14. False — Management accounting is a broad-based job, and many management accountants have become top executives of large organizations.

15. False — Management accounting is rapidly changing field, and techniques learned today may be obsolete soon. Basic principles are likely to remain valid, however.

Multiple Choice Questions

1. d — Though management accountants are involved with providing information for stockholders, creditors, and government regulators, the primary focus is providing information for internal managers.

2. b — Identifying causes for variances directs attention to problem areas. Preparing the performance report (variances) is scorekeeping. Financial auditing is concerned with assessing the effectiveness of internal controls and determining whether financial statements have been prepared in accordance with GAAP.

3. b   The actual task of controlling operations is a management task. Accounting systems provide information as designed by accountants. Internal auditors give guidance to managers about internal and management control strengths and weaknesses.

4. b   The controller directs and is responsible for the activities of staff accountants. The controller has staff authority to advise line and staff departments and executives.

5. b, c, d   Control encompasses all these activities; whereas formulating plans is a planning activity.

6. b,c   Performance reports are scorekeeping information that aid in control of operations; thus, they primarily aid evaluation and feedback. Through feedback, managers may learn from these reports, however, and use them as input for planning.

7. c   Budgets are one of the primary planning tools because they quantify the resources needed to attain organizational objectives. Budgets are used as part of performance reports, so they also serve the controlling and feedback functions. Financial reporting for the most part is not concerned with budgets.

8. b   Any type of organization may have diverse products (and services). Service organizations, however, are more labor intensive and their output is less well-defined and is more perishable than other (manufacturing) organizations.

9. d   The controller helps to chart the organization's operational and financial path and is so more like a navigator.

10. a   GAAP technically does not apply to management accounting, though management accounting systems may rely on financial accounting systems that do comply with GAAP. Management accounting must meet cost-benefit and behavioral criteria, and adapt to changing conditions.

11. a   The budget for the current month is the best benchmark for comparing actual current performance. The results of the preceding month and the same month a year earlier may be irrelevant to current performance; they may help identify trends, however. Comparisons to competitors' results are difficult, but may be useful if enough is known about them to make comparing their results meaningful.

Completion

1. planning and controlling
2. objectives and ways to achieve them
3. scorekeeping, attention-directing, and problem-solving
4. management by exception
5. (a) highest costs are related to payroll (labor is intensive), (b) output is hard to define and measure, (c) major inputs and outputs cannot be stored,
6. controller
7. staff

8.   performance report or scorekeeping activity

9.   American Institute of Certified Public Accountants, Certified Management Accountant, Generally Accepted Accounting Principles, General Accounting Office, Institute of Management Accountants

10.   professional competence, confidentiality of information, integrity, objectivity.

11.   1 FA, 2 MA, 3 FA, 4 MA, 5 MA, 6 FA, 7 MA, 8 FA

12.   1 AD, 2 SK, 3 SK, 4 PS, 5 SK

13.   1 L, 2 N, 3 N, 4 S, 5 N, 6 N, 7 L , 8 L, 9 S, 10 N

Problems

Item	Actual results	Budgeted results	Variance	Explanation
Revenues	$2,250	$4,000	$1,750 U	Fewer attendees who spent less per person than expected
Costs:				
Food and beverages	750	800	50 F	Less consumption in total, but greater per person
Prizes	500	500	0	
Supplies	180	300	120 F	Probably due to fewer attendees
Custodial services	500	200	300 U	Due to damage to gymnasium floor
Total costs	$1,930	$1,800	$ 130 U	
Income	$ 320	$2,200	$1,880 U	

The revenue and custodial services variances probably deserve the most attention. Why did so many fewer people attend the fair and spend less than expected per person? How was the floor damaged, and can damage be avoided in the future?

2.

Item	Actual	Budget	Variance	Explanation
Sources of revenue:				
Merchant donations		$10,000		
Public donations		5,000		
Total	$13,000	$15,000	$ 2,000 U	Merchants or public?
Costs:				
Fireworks	$11,500	$12,000	$ 500 F	Refund for defective fireworks
Rentals (band tent, audio equipment, portable toilets, barricades)	2,400	2,000	400 U	Replacement of portable toilet
Police and fire protection services	2,000	3,000	1,000 F	Lower staffing due to weather
Total	$15,900	$17,000	$ 1,100 F	
Loss	$ 2,900	$(2,000)	$ 900 U	

Though the total variance is relatively small, the Chamber of Commerce might consider whether the defective fireworks, lower police staffing (and resulting vandalism?) could affect future attendance and financial support. The Chamber also should determine the source of the shortfall in donations (merchants or public). Support for the activity may be diminishing from both.

CHAPTER **2**

Introduction to Cost Behavior and Cost-Volume Relationships

MAIN FOCUS AND OBJECTIVES

This chapter presents a powerful planning model to assist decision-making. It is called *cost-volume-profit analysis or breakeven analysis.* To use this model, you must have a clear understanding of:

- How cost drivers affect cost behavior
- How changes in cost drivers affect variable costs and fixed costs
- Breakeven and target volumes in dollars and units
- Cost-volume-profit graphs
- The limiting assumptions of cost-volume-profit analysis
- The difference between contribution margin and gross margin
- Effect of taxes and sales mix on cost-volume-profit models

Be sure that, through practice in solving problems, you are comfortable using the two equivalent methods for making a cost-volume-profit analysis: the *contribution-margin technique* and the *equation technique.*

REVIEW OF KEY CONCEPTS

A. Suppose a computer manufacturing company changes its levels of various activities (orders taken, computers produced, labor hours worked, material used, etc.).

    1. Costs may be affected by these changes in activity. **Cost drivers are activities that affect costs.**

2. Changes in cost driver activity affect fixed costs and variable costs as follows:

Cost Type	Total Cost	Unit Cost
Variable	Increase or decrease	No Change
Fixed	No Change	Increase or decrease

3. The logic that supports these effects is tied directly to the definitions of these two basic types of costs:

4. **Variable costs** are costs (expenses) that *change in total* in direct proportion to changes in the related level of cost driver activity.
   a. Therefore, variable costs stay the same per unit of activity, but increase in total as activity increases.

   > See textbook Exhibit 2-1

   b. *Example*: Assume that activity increases. Each unit of activity causes total costs to increase by the variable cost per unit of activity. If the computer company has variable material cost of $500 per computer and makes 10,000 computers, the total variable materials cost is $500 × 10,000 = $5,000,000. Making one more computer would raise total variable material cost to $5,000,500 because the variable material cost per unit is constant at $500 per computer.
   c. Other examples of variable costs include sales commissions and most kinds of purchased merchandise, supplies, and parts.

5. **Fixed costs** are the costs that *are not affected in total* by changes in cost driver activity over a given time span.
   a. Therefore, fixed costs *do not stay the same per unit of cost driver activity*: fixed costs on a per-unit basis vary *inversely* with changes in activity volume.
   b. *Example*: Assume that activity increases. There will be more activity supported by the same total fixed costs. If the computer company has $1 million of fixed costs to make 10,000 computers in one year, the fixed cost per computer is $1,000,000 ÷ 10,000 = $100. Next year, if 20,000 computers are made with no change in total fixed costs, the fixed cost per computer is reduced to $1,000,000 ÷ 20,000 = $50. Thus, when activity increases, fixed costs on a per-unit basis decrease.
   c. Other examples of fixed-cost items per period include factory rent, executive salaries, and periodic depreciation.
   d. A fixed cost is fixed only in relationship to a given planning period for the expected band of activity level, which is called the **relevant range.**
   e. Activity below or above this range may require major adjustments in operations that would change the amounts of total fixed costs.

   > See textbook Exhibit 2-2

   f. Activity outside the relevant range could also affect the *variable cost per unit of activity*, caused by changing efficiencies at very low or very high levels of activity; for example, because of material purchase discounts.

6. Accountants usually assume that costs behave in a *linear* or *straight-line* manner.
   a. Some costs may be *nonlinear*, that is behave not as a straight line, and they may be affected simultaneously by *several different* activities; therefore, we cannot always classify them into perfectly variable and perfectly fixed categories.
   b. Usually, however, we associate a given variable cost with only one measure of activity, and we assume that relationship is *linear*. (It is possible to test this assumption with statistical techniques.)
   c. As mentioned above, we also assume that fixed costs behave as a straight (horizontal) line within the relevant range.

> Before going on, be sure that you understand the distinctions between fixed and variable costs and that you understand the relationship between the relevant range and fixed and variable cost behavior.

B. **Cost-volume-profit analysis** facilitates management planning decisions by quantifying the effects on net income of (1) alternative activity levels and (2) combinations of product selling prices, variable costs per unit of activity, plus total fixed costs per period. This approach is often called **break-even analysis,** although the more appropriate term is *cost-volume-profit analysis,* often abbreviated as **CVP analysis.**

1. The most common CVP approach considers sales activity as the primary cost driver. We will assume that sales activity is the appropriate cost driver. Chapter 3 considers other cost drivers.

2. The **break-even point** is that level of activity (e.g., level of sales activity) where total costs equal total revenues. At this point there is zero net income.

3. The **margin of safety** is the difference between the planned level of sales activity and the breakeven sales activity.

4. **Contribution margin** is the excess of sales over variable costs, and it can be expressed as total dollars, dollars per product unit, percentage of sales, or ratio to sales.

5. *Example*: selling price $5, variable cost per unit $2, total fixed costs $600 per month.

6. **Contribution-margin technique** for computing *breakeven point* in terms of sales activity:
   a. Formula: **Break-even point in units = Fixed expenses ÷ Contribution margin per unit**

   Example: Break-even point in terms of sales units: divide total fixed expenses by contribution margin per unit:
   Contribution margin per unit is $5 - $2 = $3.
   $600 ÷ $3/unit = 200 units

   Prove this answer by filling the blanks:
   Sales: 200 units x $__5__ per unit $__1000__
   Less: Variable costs 200 units x $__2__ per unit   __(400)__
         Fixed costs per month $__600__ per month   __(600)__
   Net income $____0__

Introduction to Cost Behavior and Cost-Volume Relationships 17

b. **Formula: Break-even point in total dollar sale = Fixed expenses ÷ Contribution-margin ratio** or percentage of sales:
   Example: Contribution-margin ratio is $3 ÷ $5 = .6 = 60%.
   $600 ÷ .60 = <u>$1,000</u>
   Prove this answer by filling these blanks:
   Contribution margin $1,000 x __.60%__ $ __600__
   Less fixed costs per month $_600_ per month   __(600)__
   Net income $_____0

3. The **equation technique** of determining the break-even point is based on the fundamental relationships among the principal elements of the income statement:
   a. Sales   xxx
      Less:
         Variable expenses   xxx
         Fixed expenses   xxx
            Total expenses   xxx
         Net income   xxx
   b. The equation form of this income statement is:
   Sales - Variable costs - Fixed costs = Net income
      Example: selling price $5, variable cost per unit $2, total fixed costs $600, break-even sales units N, net income zero:
      $5N - $2N - $600 = 0
      $3N - $600 = 0
      $3N = $600
      N = $600 ÷ $3
      N = <u>200 units</u>
   c. The break-even point in total dollar *sales* for this example is 200 units x $5 = $1,000.

4. The contribution margin techniques and the equation technique are equivalent. Use whichever technique you wish. Note that the contribution-margin technique is merely the final step of the equation technique.
   a. Note that sometimes you only have enough data to use the contribution margin ratio approach.
   b. This happens most often when analyzing competitors' profitability.

5. Either method can be used, for example, to compute the sales necessary to attain a certain **target net income,** for example $300:
   a. Contribution margin technique (sales units):
      Target sales units= (Fixed expenses + Target net income) ÷ Contribution margin per unit
      Target sales units= ($600 + $300) ÷ $3/unit
      Target sales units= $900 ÷ $3/unit = <u>300 units</u>
   b. Contribution margin technique (sales dollars):
      Target sales dollars= (Fixed expenses + Target net income) ÷ Contribution margin ratio
      Target sales dollars= ($600 + $300) ÷ .60
      Target sales dollars= $900 ÷ .60 = <u>$1,500</u>

c. Equation technique (sales units and sales dollars):
$5N - $2N - $600 = $300
$3N = $300 + $600
$3N = $900
N = $900 ÷ $3 = <u>300 units</u>
Target sales dollars = $5/unit × 300 units = <u>$1,500</u>

7. The **graphical technique** is useful in portraying the concept of CVP analysis and the relationships among costs, volume, and profit.

> See textbook Exhibits 2-3 and 2-4

a. This technique can effectively communicate profit potentials over a wide range of sales activity.
b. When operating budgets are being considered, CVP graphs can improve management's understanding of budget relationships and effects.

> Before going on, be sure that you can express the same CVP model graphically, and in both contribution margin and equation formats.

C. Cost-volume-profit analysis helps managers identify critical levels of product sales, selling prices, variable costs per unit, and fixed costs per period.

1. However, it is often necessary in practice to make *trade-offs* (strike a balance) among the elements. For example, advanced technologies usually decrease variable costs per unit at higher fixed costs per period.

2. *Computer spreadsheet software* is widely used in planning activities to analyze trade-offs between different decisions about the elements of CVP relationships. Spreadsheet software eliminates mathematical errors and allows the decision maker to vary each CVP element systematically and observe the effects on, for example, breakeven or target sales. Spreadsheet software is an indispensible management tool.

> See textbook Exhibit 2-5

3. **Operating leverage** is the ratio of fixed costs to variable costs and is a measure of the riskiness of operations.
a. Companies with high operating leverage (large fixed costs relative to variable costs) are *riskier* than companies with low operating leverage (relatively low fixed costs). Small changes in sales activity cause large effects in the net income of high operating leverage companies, whereas small changes in sales activity do not affect low operating leverage companies as much.

> See textbook Exhibit 2-6

b. High operating leverage means low variable costs and high contribution margins. Even small increases in sales cause large increases in net income because contribution margins per unit are high. On the other hand, small decreases in sales have the opposite (adverse) effect.

c. In contrast, low operating leverage means high variable costs and low contribution margins. Small increases or decreases in sales activity do not affect net income very much because contribution margins per unit are small.

D. Do not confuse contribution margin with gross margin.
1. Recall *contribution margin* is the excess of sales over *total variable costs*, including both variable cost of goods sold and variable operating expenses, if any.
2. **Gross margin (or gross profit)** is the excess of sales over *total cost of goods sold*, including both variable cost of goods sold and fixed cost of goods sold, if any.

> Can you explain the concept of operating leverage, and do you know the distinction between contribution margin and gross margin?

E. (Appendix 2A) The *expected* **sales mix** is the relative proportions of products that a company expects to sell. The *actual* sales mix may vary from the planned mix.
1. CVP models can be modified to reflect sales mix assumptions.
    a. The simplest approach is to express each product as a multiple of the one product with the *least* unit sales.
    Example. Assume the Alphabet company expects that 2/3 of its unit sales will be Betas (B) and 1/3 of its unit sales will be Alphas (A); that is, a ratio of 3 Betas to 1 Alpha.
    The sales mix assumption can be expressed as B = 3A
    Substitute the value "3A" into the CVP equation for each occurrence of "B" and solve for the break-even or target level of A unit sales.
    b. The break-even or target level of B sales is three times that of A.
2. This analysis does not find the level of sales that will maximize profits. Another technique called linear programming can accomplish this analysis (see Chapter 17).

> Can you express the product mix assumption as an equation?

F. (Appendix 2B) When the organization pays taxes on its income, the amount of before-tax sales must be high enough to leave target profits after paying taxes.
1. Ordinarily, break-even analysis is not affected by taxes, because income is zero at breakeven.
2. In order to pay taxes on positive income, target income *before taxes* must be computed and entered into the CVP model.
    Example. Assume a tax rate of 30% and a target after-tax income of $210. What must the level of before-tax income be?

Net income before tax - taxes = Net income after tax
Net income before tax - (tax rate) x (Net income before tax) = Net income after tax
Net income before tax x (1 - tax rate) = Net income after tax
Net income before tax = Net income after tax ÷ (1 - tax rate)
Net income before tax = $210 ÷ (1 - .30)

$$= \underline{\$300}$$

$300 would be the target income used in the CVP model, not $210.

> Be sure that you can express an after-tax profit target in its before-tax equivalent before going on.

PRACTICE TEST QUESTIONS AND PROBLEMS WITH SOLUTIONS

True or False Statements

Determine whether each of the following statements is True (T) or False (F) and enter your answer, T or F, in the space provided.

__T__ 1. Cost driver activities refer to the levels of activities that cause total costs to vary.

__T__ 2. Over the relevant range of activity, variable costs stay the same per unit of activity.

__F__ 3. Accountants use fixed and variable cost relationships that are valid over all levels of cost driver activity. (RELEVANT RANGE ONLY)

__F__ 4. The break-even point can be determined simply by measuring the fixed and variable expenses in a given income statement and finding their total.

__F__ 5. Over the relevant range of activity, fixed costs per unit of activity stay the same. (FIXED COST REMAIN SAME → F/C PER UNIT VARY)

__T__ 6. In the very short run, all costs may be fixed.

__F__ 7. The excess of planned sales units over breakeven sales units is the gross margin. MARGIN OF SAFETY.

__T__ 8. Contribution margin, marginal income, and incremental income are synonymous terms.

__F__ 9. The contribution margin technique is valid for only some applications of CVP analysis, and the equation technique is valid for others.

__F__ 10. The number of product units that must be sold to earn a specified amount of net income can be computed by dividing the sum of fixed expenses and target net income by the unit contribution margin ratio.

__T__ 11. As sales exceed the break-even point, a small contribution-margin ratio would result in less additional profit than would a large contribution-margin ratio.

__F__ 12. Unfortunately, most computer spreadsheet software is too cumbersome to use for analyzing tradeoffs among elements of CVP models.

__F__ 13. A firm with high operating leverage enjoys more stable income than a firm with low operating leverage.

__T__ 14. Every different sales mix assumption can lead to a different break-even point.

__F__ 15. If the tax rate is 40%, in order to earn a target, after-tax income of $2.4 million, a company would have to attain total sales of $6 million.

6(.40) = 2.4M TAX ⇒ 6 - 2.4 = $3.6M

= 2.4 (1 - .40)
= $4M

Multiple Choice Questions

For the following multiple-choice questions, select the best answer(s) and enter identification letters in the spaces provided:

__D__ 1. Costs that tend to vary inversely with changes in activity level are: (a) total variable costs, (b) variable costs per unit, (c) total fixed costs, (d) fixed costs per unit.

__D__ 2. Total fixed costs are $60,000 when 20,000 product units are produced. When 30,000 units are produced, fixed costs would likely be: (a) $90,000 in total, (b) $3.00 per unit, (c) $40,000 in total, (d) $2.00 per unit.

__A__ 3. Total variable costs are $100,000 when 20,000 product units are produced. When 25,000 units are produced, variable costs would likely be: (a) $5 per unit, (b) $100,000 in total, (c) $4 per unit, (d) $105,000 in total.

$\frac{8-5}{8}$

__C__ 4. See the preceding test item. If 25,000 units are sold for $8 each, the contribution margin would be: (a) $5.00 per unit, (b) $100,000, (c) 37.5%, (d) 62.5%.

__A,D__ 5. When manufacturing volume decreases within the relevant range, fixed costs will be: (a) more per product unit, (b) the same per product unit, (c) less per product unit, (d) constant overall.

__C__ 6. Which is not true? We usually assume that a given variable cost: (a) is associated with only one activity level, (b) has a linear relationship with activity, (c) is constant per unit over all ranges of activity, (d) changes in direct proportion with activity.

FC ÷ CM
= 2,200 ÷ 2
(= 1100)

__D__ 7. Monthly production of a company consists of 2,000 units sold at $5.00 per unit. Total costs are $2,200 fixed and $6,000 variable. The break-even point per month is: (a) 440 units, (b) 733 units, (c) $10,000, (d) 1,100 units.   V=3 F=2

$\frac{20-8}{20}$ = .60

__C__ 8. Monthly sales of a company are $20,000 with total costs of $6,000 fixed and $8,000 variable. The break-even point per month is total sales of: (a) $14,000, (b) $15,000, (c) $10,000, (d) $20,000. $6,000 ÷ .60 = $10,000

FC ÷ CM
CM = 24-16
= 8

48,000/8

__B__ 9. A company produces a product for sale at $24 per unit. Costs are $48,000 per month for total fixed costs and $16 for variable costs per unit. The number of units to be produced and sold per month to break-even would be: (a) 7,500, (b) 6,000, (c) 3,750, (d) 3,000.

__A__ 10. Consider the facts of the previous test item. Sales units per month to obtain a profit of $12,000 per month before tax would be: (a) 7,500, (b) 6,000, (c) 3,750, (d) 5,000.   (48+12) ÷ 8 =

__A__ 11. If sales remain constant but the contribution margin ratio increased by 25%, total contribution would: (a) increase by the same percentage, (b) decrease by the same percentage, (c) be unaffected, (d) the answer depends on the level of fixed costs.

__D__ 12. Which of these is not true? The break-even point would be decreased by: (a) a decrease in fixed costs, (b) an increase in the contribution-margin ratio, (c) a decrease in the ratio of variable costs to sales, (d) a decrease in sales price.

Results in smaller CM.

__B__ 13. Gross margin is: (a) sales minus all variable costs, (b) sales minus cost of goods sold, including both variable and fixed elements, (c) sales minus breakeven sales, (d) sales minus cost of goods sold, excluding the fixed element.

__B__ 14. (Appendix 2A) A company produces and sells two products at contribution margins of $2 for X and $5 for Y. Fixed costs are $10,500. If the planned mix is five units of X for each unit of Y, the break-even units of Y would be: (a) 3,500, (b) 700, (c) 1,500, (d) 3,000. *2X + 5Y = 10,500*

__D__ 15. (Appendix 2B) A company produces a product for sale at $24 per unit. Costs are $48,000 for total fixed costs and $16.00 for variable costs per unit. The number of units to be produced and sold to obtain a $4,800 profit after income taxes of 60% would be: (a) 3,000, (b) 3,750, (c) 6,000, (d) 7,500. *P = 24; FC = $48,000; V = 16; CM = 8*

(4,800)(1 − .60) = 12K
8N = 48K + 12K = 60K = 7,500

Completion

Complete each of the following statements:

1. Whether a given cost is really fixed or variable depends heavily on: __relevant range__
   __length of planning period__
   __specific decision situation.__

2. High operating leverage means that __fixed costs__ are relatively __high__ compared to __variable__.

3. As production volume decreases, __fixed__ costs become larger on a per-unit basis.

4. The typical break-even graph shows a __linear__ type of behavior for costs and revenues over the relevant range.

5. A decrease in total fixed costs in a given case would cause the break-even point to __decrease__.

6. The sales in excess of break-even necessary to meet a before-tax profit target can be found by dividing __target income__ by __CM per unit__.

7. Break-even sales dollars can be found by __dividing__ __fixed costs__ by __CM ratio__.

8. The __CM margin__ technique and the __equation__ technique are equivalent methods of modeling __CVP__ relationships.

9. The __relevant range__ defines the limits of valid cost and revenue behavior relationships.

10. Different types of costs may have different __cost drivers__ other than sales activity levels.

Problems

1. This is a relatively simple review exercise that differentiates the behaviors of fixed and variable costs. All of the data pertain to the monthly production and sales of Como Company. Fill the blanks, assuming that all costs and expenses are divided into strictly fixed and strictly variable elements.

Sales Activity	Total Fixed Costs	Total Variable Costs	Fixed Costs per Unit	Variable Costs per Unit
5,000	$180,000	$120,000	$ 36 (a)	$ 24 (b)
6,000	$180,000 (c)	$144,000 (d)	$ 30 (e)	$ 24 (f)
4,000	$180,000 (g)	$ 96,000 (h)	$ 45 (i)	$ 24 (j)

2. Using the data given below, construct a cost-volume-profit graph in the format of the textbook Exhibit 2-3:

   Sales: $10 per unit

   Variable expenses: $6 per unit

   Fixed expenses: $2,000 per week

CM = 10 − 6 = 4

FC/CM = B/E

2000/4 = 500

CM RATIO = (10−6)/10 = .4

= $2000/.4 = $5,000

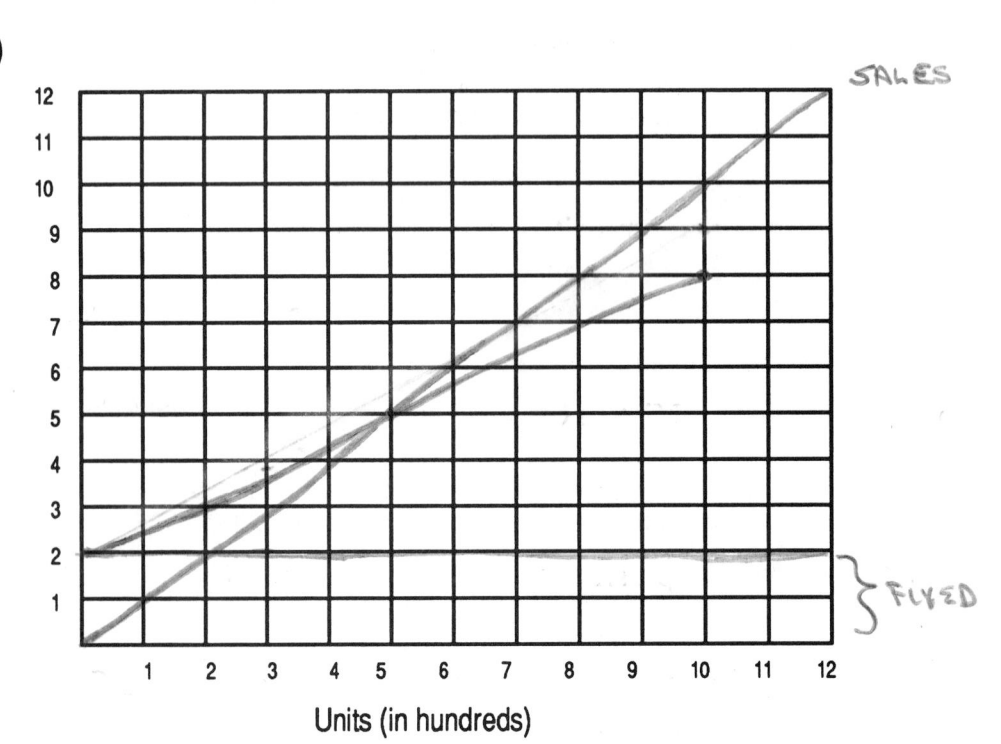

Dollars (in thousands)

What is the weekly break-even point?

(a) In units: 500 units

(b) In total sales dollars: $ 5,000

24 Chapter 2

3. A good practice problem. Given for one of the products of Juarez Co:

Sales price per product unit	$50
Variable expenses per product unit	$35
Total fixed expenses per month	$27,000

a. Contribution margin per product unit $ __15__ $50 - 35 = CM/UNIT

b. Break-even sales in units per month   __1800__ units   FC/CM = 27,000/15

c. Sales in units that will produce a net income of $9,000 per month   __2400__ units   (27+9)1000/15 =

d. Sales in units that will produce a net income of 20% of sales per month   _____ units   (.20)50N = 10N

e. Net income if 2,500 product units are sold per month $ __10,500__   37,500 - 27,000 = 10,500

f. The break-even sales in units if variable expenses are decreased by $3 per unit and if total fixed expenses are increased by $9,000 per month   __2000__ units

CM = 50 - 32 = 18/UNIT

(27+9)1000 / 18 = 2000

g. If the company desires a net income of $15,000 on a sales volume of 5,000 units per month, what must the unit selling price be, assuming no changes in the $35 variable expenses per unit or the $27,000 total fixed expenses? $ __$43.40__

NI = 15,000

5000(P-35) - 27,000 = 15K
P = $43.40

4. Another good practice problem.

Monthly data given for Minturn Corporation:

Sales	$50,000
Total fixed expenses	$12,000
Total variable expenses	$35,000

Find:

a. Variable-cost ratio   __70__ %   VC/SALES = 35/50 = .70

b. Contribution-margin ratio   __30__ %   (Sales-VC)/SALES = 15/50 = .30

c. Break-even sales dollars $ __40,000__   FC/CM% = 12,000/.30 = 40,000

Introduction to Cost Behavior and Cost-Volume Relationships 25

$FC + NI / CM\% = (12+9)000 / .30$
$= 70,000$

d. Sales that would produce a net income of $9,000, assuming no change in the variable-cost ratio or the total fixed expenses

$ 70,000

$FC = 9,000$
$VC = 35,000$
$SALES = 50K \times .80$
$= 40K$

e. Break-even sales if total fixed expenses are reduced by $3,000 and if selling prices are reduced by 20% per product unit, assuming no change in variable cost per product unit

$ 72,000

$CM\% = \frac{40-35}{40} = \frac{5}{40} = 12.5\%$ $9000/12.5 = 72,000$

5. (Appendix 2A) Summa Products, Inc. produces and sells two products as follows:

	Magna	Laude
Selling prices per unit...	$50	$36
Variable costs per unit...	$40	$30

Total fixed costs are $20,160 per week.   q/M   10   6

Compute the break-even point in terms of units per week for each of these planned mixes:

	Units of Magna	Units of Laude
a. Three Magnas for each Laude	_____units	_____units
b. Three Laudes for each Magna	_____units	_____units

6. (Appendix 2B) Monthly data given for Peripheral Storage, Inc.:

$P = (3,600)(1-.40)$
$= 6,000$

Product selling price per unit	$20	CM = 6/UNIT
Variable expenses per unit	$14	
Fixed expenses	$12,000	
Target profit *after* taxes	$3,600	
Income tax rate	40%	
Required unit sales?	3000	

$6000 + 12,000 / 6 = 3,000$
$NI + FC / CM = UNITS\ FOR\ B/E$

CHAPTER 2 SOLUTIONS TO PRACTICE TEST QUESTIONS AND PROBLEMS

True or False Statements

1. True Fluctuations in cost driver activity cause variable costs, which are components of total costs, to vary.

2. True The relevant range is the range of activity over which variable costs per unit are constant.

3. False — These fixed and variable cost relationships are valid only within the relevant range.

4. False — This is an incomplete and incorrect approach to CVP analysis. Find the breakeven point by dividing total fixed costs by the contribution margin per unit or by the contribution margin ratio.

5. False — Fixed costs in total stay the same over the relevant range, but fixed costs per unit vary in proportion to activity level.

6. True — In the short run, one may not be able to vary costs at all; conversely, in the long run, all costs may be variable.

7. False — The margin of safety is the excess of breakeven sales over breakeven sales. Gross margin is sales less total cost of goods sold.

8. True — These terms all refer to the amount additional income earned by selling additional units of product or service.

9. False — Any of the CVP techniques may be used. One method may be preferred because of user preference or because of specific communication desires, but if one of the techniques is valid, they all are.

10. False — This operation yields the target sales in dollars, not units. Dividing by unit contribution margin yields target sales in units (which can be multiplied by sales price to get sales dollars).

11. True — Additional profit beyond breakeven depends on the magnitude of the contribution margin per unit and the additional units sold.

12. False — This sort of analysis appears to be what spreadsheet software was designed to do.

13. False — High operating leverage means high fixed costs relative to variable costs (relatively high contribution margins). Small changes sales activity (either way) can cause wide swings in profitability.

14. True — This is the difficulty of planning for multiple products -- the sales mix assumption is critical to good planning. Even if total unit sales are as predicted, profits may depart from plans if the sales mix shifted.

15. False — Target sales are $4 million = $2.4 million ÷ (1 - .40).

Multiple Choice Questions

1. d — As activity level increases, fixed costs support more activity, and fixed costs per unit decrease. Variable costs per unit and total fixed costs are constant, and total variable costs vary *directly* with activity.

2. d — Assuming we are within the relevant range, total fixed costs should remain at $60,000. Fixed costs per unit would be $60,000 ÷ 30,000 units = $2 per unit.

3. a — Again assuming we are within the relevant range, variable costs per unit should remain unchanged at $100,000 ÷ 20,000 = $5 per unit. Variable costs in total should increase to $5 x 25,000 = $125,000.

4. c — The contribution margin ratio would be .375 = $(8 - 5) ÷ $8. Contribution margin per unit is $3 and total contribution margin is $3 x 25,000 = 75,000.

Introduction to Cost Behavior and Cost-Volume Relationships 27

5. a,d   As volume decreases, fixed costs support less activity, and costs per unit increase. Within the relevant range, total fixed costs remain constant, however.

6. c   We assume that the variable cost per unit is constant within the relevant range, not over all ranges of activity.

7. d   Variable cost per unit is $6,000 ÷ 2,000 = $3 per unit. Unit contribution margin is $5 - $3 = $2 per unit. Dividing fixed costs by the contribution margin per unit yields the breakeven sales activity in units: $2,200 ÷ $2/unit = 1,100 units.

8. c   The contribution margin ratio is $(20,000 - 8,000) ÷ $20,000 = .60. Dividing the fixed costs by the contribution margin ratio yields breakeven sales in dollars: $6,000 ÷ .60 = $10,000.

9. b   Break-even units are: $48,000 ÷ $(24 - 16) = 6,000 units

10. a   Sales in excess of break-even sales are required to attain the profit target. Total target sales are: $(48,000 + 12,000) ÷ $8 = 7,500. Alternatively, sales *over* break-even are: $12,000 ÷ $8 = 1,500 units (added to break-even sales of 6,000 = 7,500 units).

11. a   This is easiest to show by example. Let sales = $10,000 and variable costs = $6,000. The total contribution margin (CM) = $4,000 and the CM ratio = $(10,000 - 6,000) ÷ 10,000 = 40%. Increasing the CM ratio by 25% yields a CM ratio of 50%. this would raise the total CM to .50 x $10,000 = $5,000, which is 25% higher than before. Fixed costs are irrelevant to CM; fixed costs affect the percentage increase in net income, however.

12. d   Decreasing the sales price would raise the break-even point since the contribution margin per unit would be lower, and more units would have to be sold to cover the fixed costs. Each of the other events would lower the breakeven point.

13. b   Gross margin is sales less total cost of goods sold. (a) and (d) are the contribution margin, and (c) is the margin of safety.

14. b   Using the equation technique: $2X + $5Y - $10,500 = 0 (break-even profits)

   The product mix assumption is: X = 5Y (in units)
   Substituting 5Y for X yields: $2(5Y) + $5Y - $10,500 = 0
   $10Y + $5Y = 10,500
   $15Y = $10,500
   Y = 700 units
   For extra practice, find break-even units of X and prove that these are the break-even sales units (e.g., show that profits are zero).

15. d   First, find the before-tax profit target: $4,800 ÷ (1 - .60) = $12,000
   Using the equation technique:
   $(24 - 16)N - $48,000 = $12,000
   $8N = $12,000 + $48,000
   $8N = $60,000
   N = 7,500 units
   For extra practice, prove that this level of sales units will generate profit of $4800 after tax.

Completion

1. the relevant range, length of planning period, specific decision situation
2. fixed costs, high, variable costs
3. fixed
4. a linear (or straight-line)
5. decrease
6. the target profit, the contribution margin per unit
7. dividing, fixed costs, the contribution margin ratio
8. contribution margin, equation, CVP
9. relevant range
10. cost drivers

Problems

1. Como Company
   a. $180,000÷5,000 = $36
   b. $120,000÷5,000 = $24
   c. 180,000, constant in total within the relevant range
   d. 6,000 x $24 = $144,000
   e. 180,000÷6,000 = $30
   f. $24, constant per unit within the relevant range
   g. 180,000, constant in total within the relevant range
   h. 4,000 x $24 = $96,000
   i. 180,000÷4,000 = $45
   j. $24, constant per unit within the relevant range

Introduction to Cost Behavior and Cost-Volume Relationships 29

2.

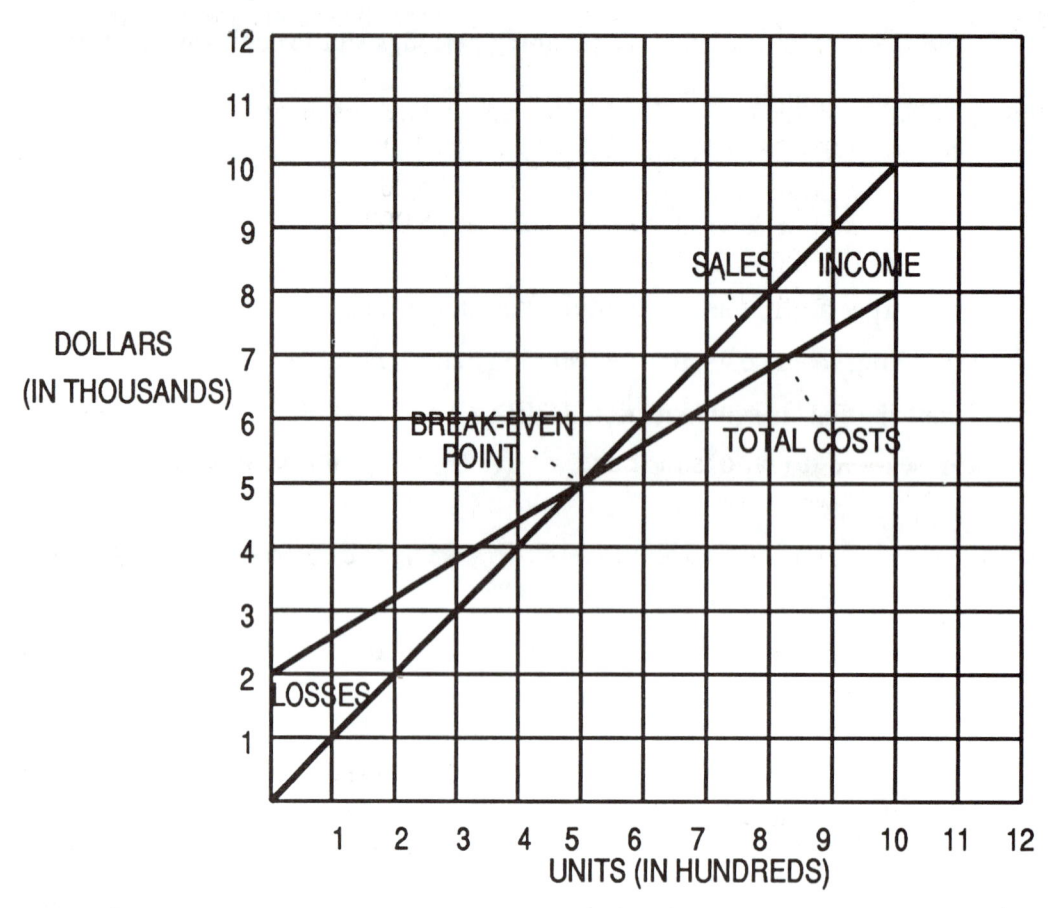

Break-even point can also be computed: fixed expenses divided by contribution margin per unit:
$2,000 ÷ ($10 - $6) = $2,000 ÷ $4 = 500 units, or, in dollars: 500 x $10 = $5,000.

3. Juarez Co.

a. Unit contribution margin is unit selling price less unit variable expenses: 50 - 35 = $15.

b. Break-even sales in units is total fixed expenses divided by unit contribution margin:
27,000 ÷ 15 = 1,800 units.

c. Unit sales to produce a target net income would be the sum of the total fixed expenses and the target net income divided by the unit contribution margin:
(27,000 + 9,000) ÷ 15 = 2,400 units.

d. Using the equation approach:
target profits = .20 x total sales = .20 x $50N = $10N
$(50 - 35)N - $27,000 = $10N
$15N - $10N = $27,000
$5N = $27,000
N = 5,400 units

e. Each unit would contribute $15 toward total fixed expenses. Therefore net income would be: (15 x 2,500) - 27,000 = 37,500 - 27,000 = $10,500.

30 Chapter 2

f. The new unit contribution margin would be: 50 (35 - 3) $18 per unit. The new total fixed expenses would be: 27,000 + 9,000 = $36,000. Therefore the new break-even sales in units would be: 36,000 ÷ 18 = 2,000 units.

g. Using the equation technique: Let P = the unknown sales price
$(P - 35) x 5,000 - $27,000 = $15,000
5,000P -$35x5,000 -$27,000 = $15,000
5,000P = $15,000 + 27,000 + $175,000
5,000P = $217,000
P = $43.40

4. Minturn Corporation:

a. Variable-cost ratio is total variable expenses divided by sales: 35,000 ÷ 50,000 = 70%.

b. Contribution-margin ratio is the complement of the variable cost ratio:
100% - 70% = 30%; or (50,000 - 35,000) ÷ 50,000 = 15,000 ÷ 50,000 = 30%

c. Break-even sales are total fixed expenses divided by the contribution-margin ratio:
12,000 ÷ 30% = $40,000.

d. Divide the sum of the fixed expenses and the desired net income (target net income) by the contribution-margin ratio:
(12,000 + 9,000) ÷, 30% = 21,000 --. .30 = $70,000.

e. The new total fixed expenses would be: 12,000 - 3,000 = $9,000. The new variable cost ratio (to total dollar sales) would be:
35,000 ÷ (50,000 - 20% of 50,000) = 35,000 ÷ 40,000   7/8, or 87.5%.

Therefore the new contribution-margin ratio would be 1/8, or 12.5%. The new break-even sales would then be the new total fixed expenses divided by the new contribution-margin ratio:

9,000 ÷ 1/8 = 9,000 x 8 = $72,000.

5. Summa Products, Inc.

Contribution margins are $50-$40 = $10 for Magna and $36 - $30 = $6 for Laude.

Using the equation approach 10M + 6L - 20,160 = 0 (break-even profits)
a. the product mix assumption is: M = 3L
10(3L) + 6L = 20,160
30L + 6L = 20,160
36L = 20,160
L = 560 units
M = 3L = 3(560) = 1,680 units
b. the product mix assumption is: L = 3M
10M + 6(3M) = 20,160
10M + 18M = 20,160
28M = 20,160
M = 720 units
L = 3M = 3(720) = 2,160 units

6. Peripheral Storage, Inc.

Required profit before tax = $3,600 ÷ (1 - .40) = $6,000
Using the equation technique:
$(20 - 14)N - $12,000 = $6,000
$6N = $6,000 + $12,000
N = $18,000 ÷ $6 = 3,000 units
Proof:

Sales: $20 x 3,000	$60,000
Less expenses:	
Variable $14 x 3,000	42,000
Fixed	12,000
Income before tax	$ 6,000
Taxes @ 40%	2,400
Income after tax	$ 3,600

CHAPTER 3

Variations of Cost Behavior

MAIN FOCUS AND OBJECTIVES

Previously, we identified two mutually exclusive patterns of cost behavior - strictly fixed and strictly variable. Now we introduce some variations of these cost behaviors. The objective of this chapter is to expand your understanding of cost behavior and introduce you to methods for measuring cost behavior. Important concepts covered in this chapter are:

- Step and mixed cost behavior
- Management influence on cost behavior
- Mathematical cost functions
- Activity analysis and measuring cost functions
- Engineering, account analysis, high-low, visual fit, and regression analysis methods of measuring cost functions

---

REVIEW OF KEY CONCEPTS

A. Understanding how cost drivers affect cost behavior is fundamental to planning and controlling costs. Some costs have multiple cost drivers, but in practice it is more common to use a single cost driver for any cost. Note that different costs may have different (single) cost drivers. The major types of cost functions in addition to fixed and variable costs, which have already been defined, are:

1. **Step-costs are costs with abrupt breaks in the pattern of total cost as activity volume shifts from one range to another.**
   a. Sometimes the breaks are small enough that the step cost can be approximated by a variable cost with little error.
   b. A step cost is just a fixed cost with multiple relevant ranges -- switching to a higher relevant range causes a step increase in fixed costs.

   | See textbook Exhibit 3-2 |

2. **Mixed costs are a combination of variable and fixed costs.**
   a. Examples of mixed costs include repairs, power, and the rental of a truck at a fixed monthly rate plus a mileage rate.

        b.   A mixed cost is just a variable cost on top of a fixed cost.

> See textbook Exhibit 3-3

> Before you go on to the next section, be sure that you understand how step and mixed costs behave with respect to cost driver activity.

B. Management influence on cost behavior.

1. Management decisions about *product and service attributes* such as quality, performance options, colors, finishes, and so on have a great influence on cost. Planning for costs must account for these cost effects.

2. **Capacity costs** originate from fixed outlays for assets, people, and programs. These outlays measure a company's cost of providing a particular capacity for such activities as production, sales, administration, and research.

3. **Committed fixed costs** are incurred because of a company's basic organization and the ownership of such long-term assets as land, buildings, machinery, and equipment.
    a. Examples are certain administrative salaries, insurance, property taxes, rent, depreciation, and long-term lease payments.
    b. Committed fixed costs cannot be decreased without changing contractual agreements and/or jeopardizing a company's ability to meet its long-range goals.
    c. Thus, capital expenditures, which lay the foundation for many fixed costs, must be planned very carefully (covered in Chapters 11 and 12).

4. **Discretionary fixed costs**, also called *managed* or *programmed costs*, arise from periodic budget appropriation decisions to implement top management policies.
    a. Examples include the costs of advertising, sales promotion, employee training programs, and research and development.
    b. Discretionary fixed costs usually do not depend directly on the volume of activity but are determined in advance by management for the budget period.
    c. In contrast to committed fixed costs, discretionary fixed costs could be drastically reduced if necessary in the short-run, but this may affect the ability of the organization to meet its long run goals.

5. Decisions about the *technology* used for manufacturing, customer service, and information systems have dramatic effects on cost behavior. Usually, improved technology trades off lower variable costs for higher fixed costs. Thus, decisions about capacity are critical to technolgy decisions.

6. *Cost control incentives* should affect decisions that managers, engineers, product designers, and sales personnel make about products and services. Incentives should be designed to promote both quality and cost control -- this is not an easy task. (Chapter 9 discusses this topic in more detail.)

> Before going on, can you explain how management decisions can affect product and service costs?

C. Measuring cost behavior is the first step in predicting or planning costs.
1. **A cost function** is a mathematical representation of cost behavior.
   a. Simple, linear cost behavior can be represented by the following equation:
   $$Y = F + VX$$
   b. Y is the *cost*; for example, power cost.
   c. X is the *cost driver*; for example, machine-hours.
   d. F is the periodic *fixed cost* (the intercept or value of Y when X is zero).
   e. V is the variable cost per unit of cost driver activity (the slope of the line, the amount of increase in Y for each unit of increase in X.
2. Measuring cost behavior is quantifying the relationship of Y to X by giving values to F and V.
3. Two principal criteria are used for accepting and using a particular cost function:
   a. **Economic plausibility.** The relationship must seem reasonable -- is there a believable cause and effect relationship between the cost and the proposed cost driver?
   b. **Reliability.** Reliability can be measured with "goodness of fit" -- how well does the cost function predict actual costs?
   c. Note that the cost-benefit criterion also applies -- do not spend more time, effort, and money measuring cost behavior than the organization will benefit through improved decision-making. But also note that some firms are spending considerable resources improving their measures of cost behavior because of intense competition.
4. Many organizations use *activity analysis* to choose plausible and reliable cost drivers.
   a. **Activity analysis** finds the most appropriate cost driver for each cost by looking for the underlying activities in the organization that cause costs.
   b. Costs that are caused by single, volume-related cost driver are the easiest to measure because the association of cost and cost driver are observable.
   c. In contrast, costs that are related to multiple, non-volume cost drivers can be difficult to measure because the association may not be readily observable.
   d. In practice many firms have used a single volume-related cost driver (e.g., units produced or direct labor hours) for all their costs. Because of increasing competition and changing technology, this practice has led to many incorrect cost predictions.
   e. Global competition and rapidly changing technology are two of the reasons why activity analysis is currently a vital management accounting issue.

> Do you know the meaning of the term "cost function", and can you explain each of its elements? Why should cost functions be plausible and reliable? Could you explain why activity analysis is important?

D. Cost analysts have developed feasible methods for measuring cost functions by making trade-offs between accuracy, cost, and timeliness.

1. **Engineering analysis** measures what costs *should be* based on technical plans, prior experience, and product or service prototypes.
   a. This method is widely used, but is costly and not timely.
   b. It is especially valuable for predicting the costs of new products or services.

2. **Account analysis** requires only limited past data to analyze what costs *have been*.
   a. This method is quick and easy to use, but the cost measures may not be valid because only limited data are used.

   > See the textbook example

3. The **high-low** method is a simple way to measure a cost function between two past levels of cost and cost driver activity. It also may be unreliable, however, because the choice of the two points is arbitrary and ignores other cost data.
   a. First choose a high and a low level of activity -- they should be representative of operations and not from unusual time periods.
   b. Measure the variable cost per unit as the change in cost divided by the change in activity.
   c. At either the high or the low point, the fixed cost measure is total cost less total variable cost.

   Example: Measure the power cost function using machine hours as the appropriate cost driver.

Month	Power cost	Machine hours
High: July	$12,000	2,000
Low: November	7,000	1,000
Difference	$5,000	1,000

   V = Change in cost ÷ Change in machine hours = $5,000 ÷ 1,000
   V = $5/machine hour
   F = $12,000 - $5 x 2,000 = $2,000 per month (at the high point)
   F = $7,000 - $5 x 1,000 = $2,000 per month (at the low point)
   The cost function is: Y = $2,000 per month + $5 X

   [handwritten: V = CHANGE Δ between high & low!]

   > See textbook Exhibit 3-4

4. The visual fit method fits a line through cost and cost driver levels plotted on a graph.
   a. This method is not used in practice, but it is a good introduction to what least squares regression accomplishes with statistics.
   b. The intent is to place a line through the data that captures the general tendency of total cost to vary directly with cost driver activity.
   c. The visual-fit method uses all data points instead of only the two used by the high-low method.

   > See textbook Exhibit 3-5

5. The **least-squares method** is a mathematical approach that uses all available data in a more objective way than the visual-fit method.

- a. All regression analysis in practice is done using a computer. If not for computers, very little regression would be performed in practice; there are too many calculations necessary.
- b. This method also provides statistics to show how well the regression line fits the data. For example R^2 measures how much of the fluctuation of a cost is explained by changes in cost driver activity. It is a common statistical measure of reliability or goodness of fit.

> See textbook Exhibit 3-6

- c. Regression requires considerable past data and a fair amount of statistical knowledge to interpret the results.

7. In summary, some form of engineering analysis is the most commonly used method for measuring cost functions, though regression analysis is gaining usage as more cost analysts become familiar with it and as accounting systems track costs and cost drivers more consistently.

> Before leaving this section be sure that you can describe the strengths and weaknesses of the different methods for measuring cost behavior. Do you understand the numerical example of the high-low method?

E. (Appendix 3) Regression analysis is nearly effortless on the computer. It is dangerous for that reason, though. Without statistical training you may not be able to interpret the regression results properly. If you are serious about cost analysis, you should take at least an introductory regression class and learn to use statistical software. A full treatment of statistical cost analysis obviously is beyond the scope of this text and study guide.

1. Computer software is very powerful.
   - a. Everyone should know how to use spreadsheets, but their statistical output is very limited.
   - b. Serious statistical analysis is easiest with serious statistical software; many good statistical software packages are available at most schools and large companies.
   - c. The effects of multiple cost drivers can be assessed with regression analysis.

2. Entering data without error is a critical first step.
   - a. Be sure that the cost and cost driver data are from the same time periods and that there are not recording errors.
   - b. Often accounting systems have not recorded cost or cost driver data in the way you would like. Resist the temptation to "fudge" the data to make it fit your desired analysis.
   - c. If you cannot get valid data, then you should not be using regression analysis. Use one of the other techniques until better data are available.

3. Plotting the cost data against each cost driver is a good idea because the graph will indicate obvious linear relationships and may highlight data errors.

4. Interpreting regression output requires statistical training, but some of the output is interpretable by novices:

a. The most important items to look for are the intercept or constant (F, fixed cost) and the X-coefficient(s) [V, variable cost(s)]. Use these to construct your cost function.
b. Low values of R^2 (which ranges from 0 to 1) indicate that the cost driver does not explain cost behavior. High values of R^2 obtained with plausible cost drivers is the desired outcome.

PRACTICE TEST QUESTIONS AND PROBLEMS WITH SOLUTIONS

True or False Statements

Determine whether each of the following statements is true-false (T of F), and enter T or F in the space provided:

__F__ 1. Explanation of accounting cost behavior requires only one cost driver.

_____ 2. Costs that vary with respect to cost drivers vary linearly.

_____ 3. Step cost and mixed costs are fundamentally different from fixed and variable costs.

_____ 4. Capacity decisions result in fixed costs that are more difficult to change than most other fixed costs.

_____ 5. Committed costs often involve legal, contractual payment obligations.

_____ 6. Discretionary fixed costs stem from periodic appropriation decisions that directly reflect top management policies. Therefore, these costs cannot be changed easily.

_____ 7. A useful cost function must be either plausible or reliable.

_____ 8. Analysis of the activities that drive costs is essential in all organizations.

_____ 9. Engineering analysis can only be used to measure what costs should be in manufacturing companies where engineering plans are available.

__T__ 10. Account analysis is the most objective cost measurement method because it relies on the accounting system for data.

__T__ 11. The high-low method can be unreliable because the choice of data points is arbitrary.

__T__ 12. Because it is the most objective method, regression analysis should be used to measure nearly all cost functions.

__T__ 13. Using activity analysis to select cost drivers results in appropriate cost functions.

__F__ 14. (Appendix 3) Spreadsheet software is most appropriate for statistically measuring cost functions.

__F__ 15. (Appendix 3) Because regression analysis is so easy on spreadsheet software, even novices should use it to measure cost functions.

Multiple Choice Questions

For each of the following multiple choice questions, select the best answer(s) and enter their identification letters in the space provided.

____ 1. Examples of committed fixed costs could include: (a) direct labor wages, (b) bond interest expense, (c) building depreciation, (d) management training costs.

____ 2. Examples of step-function costs could include: (a) salaries of billing clerks, (b) equipment rentals, (c) direct materials used, (d) research and development costs.

____ 3. Examples of discretionary fixed costs could include: (a) sales commissions, (b) fire insurance on factory building, (c) salaries of payroll clerks, (d) annual factory picnic and holiday party.

____ 4. Examples of strictly variable costs could include: (a) plant manager's salary, (b) wages of maintenance personnel, (c) heating and air conditioning costs, (d) office supplies.

____ 5. Cost prediction methods that use all relevant data points include: (a) least-squares method, (b) visual-fit method, (c) account analysis, (d) high-low method.

____ 6. In contrast to discretionary fixed costs, committed fixed costs are: (a) more difficult to measure and evaluate in terms of their outputs, (b) less easily influenced by management on a short-term basis, (c) both of these, (d) neither of these.

____ 7. Costs that are most likely to behave as variable costs are: (a) advertising, (b) direct labor, (c) research and development, (d) direct materials.

__B__ 8. The budgeted annual cost of operating a post-office truck is $4,400 plus $.20 per mile. In 19X2 the truck was to be driven 24,000 miles uniformly to deliver various mail items throughout the year. Two employees are needed for each truck. If these data were reflected in a linear equation to represent the cost function, the cost driver would be: (a) number of letters and packages delivered, (b) miles driven, (c) weight of mail delivered, (d) number of postal employees per truck.

__D__ 9. See the preceding test item. The total variable cost of operating a truck is (a) $.20 per mile, (b) $9,200 per year, (c) $24,000 per year, (d) $400 per month.   .20(24,000)

__B,C,D__ 10. See test item 8 above. The total cost of operating a truck would be (a) $24,000 per year, (b) $9,200 per year, (c) $.38 per mile, (d) $177 per week.   = 4800/12 = 400

__B__ 11. The monthly building maintenance cost of a company was $43,000 when machine hours were 2,000 and $38,500 when machine hours were 1,700. If machine hours is the appropriate cost driver for maintenance cost, the variable-cost per machine hour was: (a) $22.65, (b) $15.00, (c) $22.03, (d) $21.50.

__A__ 12. See the preceding test item. The indicated fixed cost per month was: (a) $13,000, (b) $23,000, (c) $0, (d) $4,500.

$$\frac{43,000 - 38,500}{2000 - 1,700} = 15$$

Completion

Complete each of the following statements by filling in the blanks:

FC = 43,000 − 15(2000)
   = 43,000 − 30,000
   = 13K

1. Measuring cost behavior is _____ and _____ how activities affect levels of costs.

2. Linear cost behavior is when a cost changes _____ with _____.

3. The two major types of cost behavior are _____ and _____ costs.

4. Variable costs that may fluctuate with sales merely because management has allocated in advance certain proportions of dollar sales are really _____ costs.

5. Mixed costs are a combination of _____ and _____.

6. Step costs can be treated as _____ costs when the _____ shifts.

7. Changing committed fixed costs can _____ and can _____ long run goals.

8. The slope and intercept of a straight line correspond to the _____ and _____ of a cost function.

9. _____ and _____ are two essential features of cost functions.

10. One danger of regression analysis is that by the time _____ are collected the _____ may be _____.

11. The _____ method requires statistical _____.

12. The high-low method may be unreliable because it _____.

Problems

1. Solari Instruments, Inc. uses a cost function for predicting the annual cost of operating its delivery trucks: Y = $28,000 + $.20 X. Identify or determine the symbol or amount that represents each of the following ideas or amounts:

   (a) The cost to be explained   Y

   (b) The cost driver   X

   (c) The slope of the regression line $ .20

   (d) The total cost if X is 200,000 $ 68,000

   (e) The mathematical value of the cost when the cost driver is zero $ 28,000

(f) Is (e) the expected cost at zero activity? Why or why not?

   Outside the relevant range of cost driver.

40 Chapter 3

2. Given for a mixed materials support cost of Spicer Company that accountants believe varies directly with direct labor (DL) hours:

Volume of activity in direct labor-hours per month	June	July	August	September	October
	50,000	60,000	70,000	80,000	90,000
Total cost per month	$14,000	$16,900	$18,000	$21,000	$22,800

a. Using the high-low method, compute the variable overhead cost per direct labor-hour.

HI - OCT   90,000 $22,800
LO - JUNE 50,000 $14,000

$$\frac{\Delta \text{COST}}{\Delta \text{LABOR}} = \frac{8,800}{40,000} = \$.22/\text{HR}$$

b. Compute the indicated fixed cost per month.

FC = 22,800 - (90,000)(.22)
   = 22,800 - 19,800
   = 3,000 / MO.

c. Express the cost behavior as a cost function:

Y = 3,000 + .22 (DL)

3. Consider the facts in problem 2 above. Activity analysis reveals that in fact materials support costs vary directly with the weight of material shipped, not direct labor hours.

 a. Discuss why managers may have looked for other cost drivers.

 b. How might activity analysis have discovered the relationship between materials support cost and weight of materials moved?

 c. Materials support cost expressed as function of weight of materials moved is:
    Y = $1,000/month + $.17xWeight of material moved in kilograms
    Compare and comment on predicted materials support costs using each cost driver for the following months:

	November	December	January	
Direct labor hours	50,000	70,000	90,000	Y = 3,000 + .22(DL)
Predicted cost	14,000	18,400	22,800	
Weight moved, kg	90,000	100,000	80,000	Y = 1000 + .17 (Kg)
Predicted cost	16,300	18,000	14,600	

Difference

 d. Actual material support costs in November, January, and December were: $16,000, $18,200, and $15,000, respectively. Which cost function is more reliable? Why?

* ABSOLUTE VALUE

DL	PRED	ACT	VAR*		KG	PRED	ACT	VAR
	14	16	2K			16.3	16.	.3
	18.4	18.2	.2K			18.	18.2	.2
	22.8	15.	5.8K			14.6	15	.4

AUG $2,667

$300

Variations of Cost Behavior 41

CHAPTER 3 SOLUTIONS TO PRACTICE TEST QUESTIONS AND PROBLEMS

True or False Statements

1. False — Accountants often assume that this is true, but it probably never is true. The costs of finding and using "true" cost behavior which might involve multiple cost drivers, however, may exceed the benefits. Thus, single cost drivers are most common in accounting cost functions.

2. False — Again, we often assume that variable cost behavior is linear, but it may not be. Economic theory, for example, predicts that variable or marginal costs are not linear. Within the relevant range, however, a linear cost function may be an acceptable approximation.

3. False — Step costs are a combination of fixed and variable costs. Step costs are fixed costs that shift as activity shifts from one relevant range to another.

4. True — Capacity costs generally result from long-term planning that sets fixed costs for long periods of time.

5. True — Committed costs do not have to be the result of legal obligations, though. Such costs as depreciation and research costs may be set by organizations that have made firm committments to capacity or research activity as part of long run strategy.

6. False — The first part of this statement is true, but what distinguished discretionary costs from committed is the relative ease with which they may be changed. Discretionary fixed costs can be changed relatively easily.

7. False — Useful cost functions must be *both* plausible and reliable.

8. False — Though all organizations might benefit from activity analysis, cost-benefit considerations may reveal that the benefits are less than the costs. Favorable cost-benefit tradeoffs from activity analysis are most likely when technological change is rapid and when the organization is in a highly competitive environment.

9. False — Engineering analysis can be appropriate in any organization where inputs can be related to outputs.

10. False — Account analysis typically relies on very few data points, which may not be representative of typical operations. Thus, the cost function that results may not be reliable.

11. True — The high-low method uses only two data points which are arbitrarily chosen to represent high and low levels of activity. Other data are ignored.

12. False — Regression analysis is the most objective method when sufficient relevant data are available and when the analyst understands the limitations of regression. Otherwise, another method may be more appropriate.

13. True — This *should* result, but of course an analyst can do a poor job of screening cost drivers for plausibility and reliability and select inappropriate cost drivers.

14. False — Spreadsheet software is good for "quick and dirty" cost analysis, but more specialized statistical software is generally more appropriate.

15. False — It is easy to use, but novices should not use regression analysis until they understand the limitations of the technique.

Multiple Choice Questions

1. b, c — Both of these are more typical committed fixed costs. Direct labor wages may be relatively fixed in some countries and in some companies that have permanent employment policies, however.

2. a, b — These two costs typically come in "chunks" as activity such as billing increases by a relatively large amount. Direct materials cost is typically variable. Research and development costs are typically discretionary fixed.

3. c, d — Sales commissions are typically variable costs. Fire insurance may be committed if, for example, a mortgage-holder requires insurance on the property.

4. c, d — A manager's salary is usually fixed. Likewise, maintenance personnel costs may be incurred as part of a preventive maintenance program. This may have an element of variable cost in it, however, so it would be a mixed cost. Heating and air conditioning costs are at least partially variable with respect to ambient temperatures (i.e., degree-days). Office supplies are probably variable with respect to staffing levels and office activity.

5. a, b — The other methods use only a few data points. It may be, though, that account analysis after the first time period of experience with a product or service uses the only relevant data point -- last period's.

6. b — The effects of discretionary and committed fixed costs are equally difficult to evaluate. Committed fixed costs are less easily changed in the short run.

7. d — Advertising and research and development may be planned as if they were variable (e.g., as a percentage of sales), but they really are discretionary fixed costs. Direct labor may be "sticky," that is, due to policy not very responsive to changes in activity. Usage of direct materials is usually directly variable with regard to measures of productive activity.

8. b — According to the problem, miles driven is the primary cost driver. Each of the others, however, could affect postal operating costs and are potential cost drivers. Activity analysis would determine if any of them is a cost driver.

9. d — Total annual variable cost is predicted to be $.20 × 24,000 miles = $4,800. This is $400 on a monthly basis if mileage is uniform over the year.

10. b, c, d — Total annual operating cost at 24,000 miles is $4,400 + $4,800 = $9,200. Total cost per mile at 24,000 miles is $9,200 ÷ 24,000 = $.38/mile. Total cost per week at 24,000 miles is $9,200 ÷ 52 = $177.

11. b — V = ($43,000 - $38,500) ÷ (2,000 - 1,700) = $15/machine hour

12. a — F = $43,000 - $15 × 2,000 = $13,000

Completion

1. understanding, quantifying
2. proportionately, cost driver activity
3. variable, fixed
4. discretionary fixed costs
5. variable, fixed costs
6. fixed costs, relevant range
7. be difficult, prevent attaining
8. variable cost per unit, fixed cost per period
9. plausibility, reliability
10. sufficient data, data, obsolete
11. regression, sophistication or knowledge
12. uses only two data points

Problems

1. (a) Y; (b) X; (c) $.20, (d) $28,000 + $.20 x 200,000 = $68,000; (e) $28,000; (f) No, because a cost driver level of 0 is probably outside the relevant range for which the fixed cost measure is valid.

2. June and October are the low and high months for cost driver activity. They seem representative.

    a. V = ($22,800 - $14,000) ÷ (90,000 - 50,000) = $8,800 ÷ 40,000 = $.22/ DL hour

    b. F = $22,800 - $.22 x 90,000 = $3,000 per month, also

    F = $14,000 - $.22 x 50,000 = $3,000 per month

    c. Y = $3,000 per month + $.22 x DL hours

3. a. Managers may have found that actual costs did not correspond to predicted costs using DL hours as the cost driver. The errors may have been sufficiently large to adversely affect decision making, prompting the application of activity analysis.

    b. Activity analysis can be based on direct observation of costs and activities, interviews with relevant personnel, and statistical analysis of past data. These efforts may have found that weight of materials moved explained past materials support costs better than other possible cost drivers and, more importantly, is expected to predict future materials support costs well.

c.

	November	December	January
Direct labor hours	50,000	70,000	90,000
	$3,000 + $.22(50,000)	$3,000 + $.22(70,000)	$3,000 + $.22(90,000)
Predicted cost	= $14,000	= $18,400	= $20,800
Weight moved, kg	90,000	100,000	80,000
	$1,000 + $.17(90,000)	$1,000 + $.17(100,000)	$1,000 + $.17(80,000)
Predicted cost	= $16,300	= $18,000	= $14,600
Difference (new compared to old)	$2,300 more	$400 less	$6,200 less

The two cost drivers do not seem to be positively correlated (as one goes up, the other goes up, too), so they are probably quite different measures of activity. If weight of materials is the more appropriate cost driver, then using DL hours results in inaccurate cost predictions.

d. Computing variances of actual from predicted costs using each cost driver gives each cost driver a goodness of fit "score."

Direct labor hours prediction	Actual costs	Variance*
$14,000	$16,000	$2,000
18,400	18,200	200
20,800	15,000	5,800
Average error		$2,667

Material moved prediction	Actual costs	Variance*
$16,300	$16,000	$300
18,000	18,200	200
14,600	15,000	400
Average error		$300

(*all expressed as positive numbers since an error is undesirable regardless of its direction)

Based on this limited data the weight of material moved is obviously the superior cost driver. the average error for the direct labor hours predictions is nearly 9 times as large. As long as it is relatively easy to monitor weight of materials moved each month, it should be the cost driver used for materials support cost. Many firms have found that direct labor hours is not a reliable cost driver for most support costs.

CHAPTER 4

Introduction to Cost Systems

MAIN FOCUS AND OBJECTIVES

The focus of this chapter is on how costs are classified, accumulated, and assigned to products, services, and periods. A key concept to learn from this chapter is that though classifications of costs are somewhat arbitrary, the goal of managerial cost systems is to identify and measure all the costs of activities and products and services that generate revenue. Major learning objectives include:

- Definition of important terms (cost, cost objective, cost accumulation, cost allocation)
- Distinction between direct and indirect costs
- Distinction between major categories of manufacturing costs
- Benefits of activity-based costing systems
- Reduction of non-value-added activities
- Distinction between product and period costs
- Differences between financial statements of merchandisers and manufacturers
- Construction of income statements using the contribution and the absorption approaches

---

REVIEW OF KEY CONCEPTS

A. Understanding cost systems requires first understanding some basic cost terms and relationships:

1. **Cost** is the monetary measurement of an exchange of resources for a particular purpose, for example, the dollars paid for printing presses or for typesetting labor by a newspaper publisher. Cost is a measure of the acquisition value of something -- e.g., what you paid for it. This number is not always obvious for many items.

2. **Cost objective** (or cost *object*) is any activity for which decision-makers need a separate measurement of costs, for example, the cost of operating the credit department or the cost of manufacturing pocket calculators.

3. A **cost accounting system** combines cost behavior and decision making information needs to measure the costs of cost objects. In many organizations, however, the cost accounting system must serve both decision-making needs and financial reporting requirements. Note that these may not be compatible, and some firms have multiple cost accounting systems -- one for financial reporting and one for decision making. (See the discussion of activity-based costing and cost management systems below.) Any cost accounting system has two main elements:
   a. The **accumulation** of initial costs by such natural classes as material or labor.
   b. The **allocation** (also called cost *assignment* or *attribution*) of these costs to cost objectives; for example, to evaluate the performance of organizational departments or to measure the costs of outputs (end products and services produced for customers).

   > See textbook Exhibit 4-1

4. The terms **direct costs** and **indirect costs** refer to cost relationships to a particular cost objective.
   a. Essentially, the distinction between direct and indirect costs depends on the *economic feasibility of their traceability to the cost object.*
   b. **Direct costs** can be identified specifically with a given cost object.
   c. **Indirect costs** cannot be identified specifically with a given cost object and are regarded as costs of overall operations.
   d. Some costs can be identified as direct costs at a relatively high level in an organization, but are indirect costs at lower levels because the cost cannot be more more specifically identified to basic activities.
   For example, although a foreman's salary may be direct to the Painting Department that she supervises, it would be indirect to the individual products painted by her department.
   e. A major goal of improved cost accounting systems (see activity-based costing below) is to more accurately and thoroughly assign costs to basic activities, products, and services. In concept, most costs could be classified as direct costs at the product level if we understood cost behavior better and if we knew the appropriate cost drivers for each cost. Of course, we must consider the cost-benefit rule.

   > Before going on, be sure that you understand the real, economic reason for the distinction between direct and indirect costs.

B. When products or services are the cost objective, the three major categories of costs are:
   1. **Direct material cost** is the acquisition cost of materials that are physically identifiable as part of the product and can be traced to the product in an economically feasible way. For example, fabrics, wood, and hardware can be traced to a line of chairs made by a furniture manufacturing company, but it may not be worthwhile to trace glue and fasteners directly to chairs.
   2. **Direct labor cost** is the wages of labor that can be identified specifically and exclusively with the product in an economically feasible way. For example,

wages of furniture makers can be traced to a line of chairs, but it may not be feasible to directly trace top management salary costs to chairs.

3. **Overhead cost** includes all costs other than direct material and direct labor that are associated with operations. For example, most companies do not try to trace cleaning supplies consumed, custodial labor used, power costs, and depreciation of facilities directly to products or services.
   a. These are **indirect** costs in relation to the products manufactured or services provided.
   b. Other terms used for *overhead* are **burden, manufacturing overhead, manufacturing expenses,** and **indirect costs.**
   c. **Variable overhead** includes supplies, most indirect labor, and other costs that can be shown to vary with some relevant production activity.
   d. **Fixed overhead** usually includes supervisory salaries, property taxes, rent, insurance, depreciation, and other support costs that have no discernable (short-run) relationship with any production activities.

> See textbook Exhibit 4-2

4. In many modern factories, direct labor cost is so small compared to other manufacturing costs, that firms treat direct labor cost as another overhead item and do not trace it directly to products.
   a. This is an application of the cost-benefit rule -- tracing direct labor to products would cost more than it is worth.
   b. These companies usually maintain two major cost categories: **direct material cost** and **conversion cost**, which is direct labor plus overhead.
   c. A few companies maintain two other major cost categories: **prime cost**, which is **direct material and direct labor**, and overhead cost.

5. Tracing direct costs in service organizations is more difficult than in manufacturing organizations, but the issues are the same.
   a. As discussed in Chapter 2 the output of service organizations is less observable and more labor-intensive, making tracing more difficult.
   b. Note that many professional lawyers, accountants, and management consultants record their client-activities to the minute so that costs of their time can be traced directly to services provided to clients.

> Can you explain the difference between direct materials, direct labor, and overhead costs? Why do some firms treat direct labor as an overhead cost item? Is there a fundamental difference between classifying costs in service organization and a manufacturing firm?

C. Changes in global competition and manufacturing and information technologies are changing the way cost systems are designed.

1. **Activity-based costing** (ABC) applies activity analysis (see Chapter 3) to determine appropriate cost drivers for each important activity.
   a. Costs are accumulated for these activities (which are one level of cost objects).
   b. Costs of activities are then assigned to products and services according to their usage of basic activities. See the figure below:

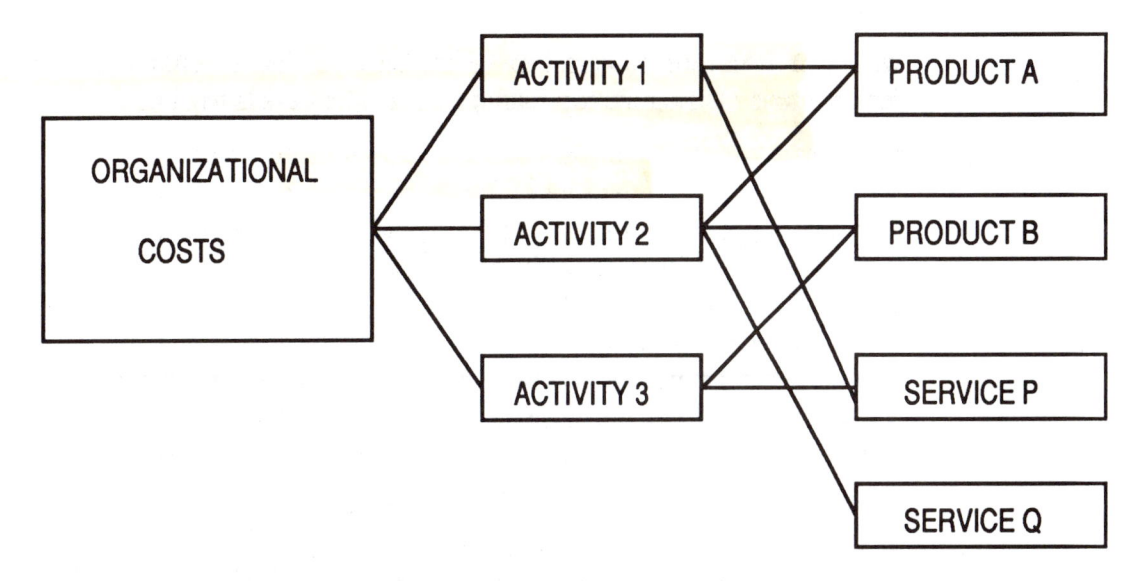

```
                    ┌──────────┐         ┌──────────┐
                 ┌─►│ACTIVITY 1│────────►│PRODUCT A │
                 │  └──────────┘ ╲    ╱  └──────────┘
┌──────────────┐ │                ╲  ╱
│ORGANIZATIONAL│ │  ┌──────────┐   ╲╱   ┌──────────┐
│              │─┼─►│ACTIVITY 2│───╳────►│PRODUCT B │
│    COSTS     │ │  └──────────┘  ╱ ╲   └──────────┘
└──────────────┘ │                ╲  ╲
                 │  ┌──────────┐ ╱    ╲ ┌──────────┐
                 └─►│ACTIVITY 3│─────── ►│SERVICE P │
                    └──────────┘        └──────────┘
                                        ┌──────────┐
                                        │SERVICE Q │
                                        └──────────┘
```

(Note that not all activities support all products and services in this example

- c. As a result of understanding cost behavior and appropriate cost drivers, ABC systems trace most costs to products and services by focusing on basic activities rather than traditional cost categories. If the activity analysis is correct, ABC product and service costs are more accurate than traditional costs.
- d. Many firms are currently experimenting with developing ABC systems, and they may be common practice in several years. See R. Cooper and R. Kaplan, *The Design of Cost Management Systems: Text, Cases, and Readings*, Prentice-Hall, 1992 for a basic treatment of ABC systems.
- e. As mentioned in Chapter 3, organizations with rapidly changing technology and strong competitors are most likely to benefit from ABC systems.

2. Cost accounting systems that are designed primarily to aid management decision making (rather than financial reporting) are called **cost management systems**.
   - a. Cost management systems rely heavily on activity analysis and ABC (above).
   - b. As discussed in Chapter 1, management accounting serves decision makers best when cost management systems are parallel to the decision-making process.
   - c. Cost management systems must be consistent with the organization's strategy by providing planning and scorekeeping information relevant to the organization's goals and objectives (see Chapter 9 for detailed discussions).

3. Perhaps the greatest benefit of activity analysis is improved organizational efficiency through the identification of duplication of effort and *non-value added activities*.
   - a. Activity analysis will identify people and groups within an organization that are duplicating the effort of other functions -- are they both necessary?

- b. **Value-added activities** enhance the value of the product or service as seen by customers and clients; these activities are why people buy this product or service. These activities should be expanded or improved.
- c. In contrast, **non-value-added activities** do not enhance the value of the product to customers; the customer could care less about these activities. These activities should be eliminated if possible, and resources devoted to these activities should be redeployed to value-added activities.
- d. This is emerging as an important area of management accounting.

4. The importance of new cost management systems, activity analysis, and reduction of non-value-added activities is seen as firms adopt **Just-in-Time** methods and philosophy.
   - a. The focus of the JIT philosophy is elimination of waste.
   - b. Waste is eliminated by getting rid of non-value-added activities (such as holding inventories, transporting assemblies, and so on) and by maximizing quality (e.g., reducing defects and conforming products and services to customer requirements).
   - c. Cost management systems that are consistent with JIT approaches measure and report defective rates, production flow, and **cycle time**, which is the time from inception to completion of a product or service.
   - d. Short cycle times are possible only with good product and process design, minimum defects, and smooth production flow.

> Can you explain activity-based costing and the role of cost management systems? Do you sense that there is tension between decision-making needs of managers and financial reporting requirements?

D. Cost accounting systems serve the requirements of financial reporting by accumulating costs and assigning them either to *products* and *services* or to *reporting periods*. The primary financial reporting concern is that all costs incurred in a period are allocated to products or time periods.

> See textbook Exhibit 4-3

1. **Product costs** are costs identified with products produced or purchased for resale. These costs are charged against income (i.e., become *product expenses*) when the products are sold. Until products are sold, these costs remain as inventory (unless, for example, the products are obsolete).
   - a. Product costs for *financial reporting* include direct materials, direct labor, and manufacturing overhead.
   - b. For income tax reporting only, some sales and administrative costs also are classified as product costs.
   - c. Note the three stages of inventory flow for a manufacturing company: direct costs plus overhead $\Rightarrow$ work in process $\Rightarrow$ finished goods.
   - d. For managerial accounting, classification of product costs depends on traceability of costs.

2. **Period costs** are costs that are not assigned to products and are charged against the income of the period (i.e., become *period expenses*).

a. Period costs of manufacturing firms include most sales and administrative costs.
b. Note that merchandising and service firms treat all indirect costs as period costs -- service firms cannot not inventory their output.
c. Classification of period and product costs also depends on the income measurement method used (see the discussion on the contribution and absorption approaches below).

3. Cost accounting systems for financial reporting may not serve managerial decision making because:
a. Financial cost accounting assures that all costs of a period are accounted for and is not particularly concerned with how accurately they are assigned across different products and services.
b. Some major period costs may in fact be traceable to products and services but are not traced.
c. The primary reason is that the *financial reporting* cost-benefit comparison does not favor improved cost information.

4. According to their traceability, costs may be classified as direct or indirect costs *and* as product or period costs. This may be confusing:
a. Product costs include direct production costs and some allocation of indirect *production* costs.
b. Period costs include costs that are indirect to production, but may be direct to different cost objects such as departments. For example, sales costs may be regarded as indirect to products, but as direct to the marketing department, and are period costs for the company.

> Do you understand the potentially overlapping distinctions between direct/indirect and product/period costs for financial reporting? Do you also understand why there is not just one category of cost -- direct cost? (traditional practices and traceability of costs)

E. The financial statements of merchandisers and manufacturers differ because of the types of goods they sell.

1. Merchandising companies sell goods without changing their basic form.
a. Their balance sheets usually carry only one major type of inventory item, merchandise.
b. Their income statements report the cost of goods sold as the purchase cost of merchandise acquired and resold, including freight charges.

2. Manufacturing companies transform materials into other goods through the use of labor and factory facilities.
a. Their balance sheets usually report three major types of inventory: direct materials, work in process, and finished goods.
b. Their income statements show the manufacturing cost of goods produced and sold.

> Refer again to textbook Exhibit 4-3.
>
> Exhibit 4-4 is a more detailed income statement of a manufacturing company

Introduction to Cost Systems 51

4. The three types of manufacturing inventories are affected by movements of resources (transactions) among them:

Change	Direct materials	Work-in-process	Finished goods
Increase	Purchases of materials	Use of materials, labor, and overhead	Completion of products
Decrease	Use of materials	Completion of products	Sale of products

> See textbook Exhibit 4-5

F. If things weren't confusing enough, there are two important forms of the income statement:

1. **The absorption approach** is also called *absorption costing, full costing, traditional costing,* or *functional costing*.
   a. All manufacturing costs, *including fixed factory overhead*, are considered to be inventoriable or product costs that do not become expenses until sales take place.
   b. Note that the absorption approach makes a primary classification of costs according to *manufacturing versus non-manufacturing functions*, emphasizing the *gross profit margin* available to cover selling and administrative expenses.

   > See textbook Exhibit 4-8

2. **The contribution approach** is also called *variable costing, direct costing,* or *marginal costing*.
   a. Only variable manufacturing costs *(excluding fixed factory overhead)* are considered to be inventoriable or product costs.
   b. Note that the contribution approach makes a primary classification of costs into *variable versus fixed costs*, emphasizing the *contribution margin* available to cover the fixed costs.

   > See textbook Exhibit 4-9

3. To summarize the difference between these two models of the income statement, the primary classification of costs is:
   a. The absorption approach is classification of costs by management functions and is required by financial reporting.
   b. The contribution approach is classification of costs by cost behavior, parallels cost-volume-profit analysis, and is consistent with management planning and control.
   c. The contribution approach should be used for scorekeeping and attention-directing, but the absorption approach is often used internally because of the added cost of the additional contribution margin information.

> Do you feel comfortable with the different approaches to measuring net income? What are product and period costs under the absorption approach? ... under the contribution margin approach?

G. (Appendix 4) Manufacturing companies that account separately for labor costs maintain many classification of labor besides direct labor:
1. Indirect labor (including security, custodial services, rework, idle time, and overtime premiums)
2. Supervisory salaries
3. Payroll fringe costs (including insurance and pension costs)

PRACTICE TEST QUESTIONS AND PROBLEMS WITH SOLUTIONS

True or False Statements

Determine whether each of the following statements is True or False (T or F) and enter your answer in the space provided.

__T__ 1. A particular cost may be simultaneously both direct and indirect.

__F__ 2. If products are the cost objectives, examples of direct material cost would include fuel for machinery and abrasives for shaping products. *Indirect FOH*

__F__ 3. For product costing purposes, conversion cost is direct labor plus direct material cost. *= DIRECT LABOR + OH*

__T__ 4. Product costs of a floor covering manufacturer would include direct material cost and variable factory overhead.

__F__ 5. Period costs would usually include fire insurance on factory machinery and sales commissions. *INDIRECT PRODUCT / PERIOD*

__T__ 6. For financial reporting, indirect product costs are inventoried and eventually become expenses.

__F__ 7. Period costs would usually include depreciation of both factory equipment and sales equipment. *FACT DEP ⇒ PRODUCT COST*

__F__ 8. The purpose of activity-based costing is to provide more accurate product costs for financial reporting. *IMPROVE INTERNAL DECISION MAKING.*

__T__ 9. Fixed factory overhead should be treated as a period cost in the contribution approach to measuring income.

__T__ 10. A non-value-added activity could be eliminated without adversely affecting product quality. *(MAYBE.... YOU HOPE)*

__F__ 11. Unlike activity-based costing systems, cost management systems are focused on management decision-making needs. *ABC - MGMT DECISION TOOLS.*

__T__ 12. A fundamental difference in financially reported income for manufacturers and merchandisers is that manufacturers inventory some indirect costs, whereas merchandisers do not.

__F__ 13. One goal of JIT is to smooth the transfer of resources through the three stages of manufacturing inventories. *JIT ELIMINATES NEED FOR INV. ACCT'G STAGES.*

__T__ 14. Variable factory overhead is inventoriable in both the absorption approach and the contribution approach to measuring income.

Introduction to Cost Systems 53

__T__ 15.   (Appendix 4) Payroll fringe costs that are related to direct labor are classified conceptually as direct labor but are classified in most companies as factory overhead.

Multiple Choice Questions

For the following multiple-choice questions, select the best answer(s) and enter the identification letter(s) in the spaces provided:

__D__ 1.   The usual basis for distinguishing between direct and indirect product costs is the economic feasibility of their tracing to a given: (a) product unit, (b) time span, (c) manufacturing department, (d) cost objective.

__A/D__ 2.   When products are the cost objects, typically the three *major* categories of manufacturing costs are direct labor, direct materials, and: (a) indirect manufacturing costs, (b) indirect materials, (c) indirect labor, (d) manufacturing overhead costs.   SYNONOMOUS TERM.

__D__ 3.   If products are the cost objectives, examples of direct labor cost for a manufacturer of oil well drilling tools would include: (a) salary of the plant superintendent, (b) salary of the sales manager, (c) wages of a secretary in the plant office, (d) wages of a machinist in the plant.

__A,B,D__ 4.   If products are the cost objects, examples of factory overhead cost would typically include: (a) wages of an assembly worker, (b) salary of the plant manager, (c) sales distribution costs, (d) cleaning supplies.

__A/C__ 5.   If products are the cost objectives, the wages of factory janitors and maintenance personnel would usually be classified as: (a) factory overhead cost, (b) direct labor cost, (c) product cost, (d) period cost.

__B__ 6.   These amounts are included in the operating statement of a company: direct material costs $40,000, selling expenses $25,000, factory overhead $43,000, interest expense $6,000, direct labor $55,000, work-in-progress inventory $13,000. The conversion cost is: (a) $138,000, (b) $98,000, (c) $169,000, (d) $95,000, (e) $109,000.   CONV = DIR LABOR + FOH
= 55 + 43 = 98

__B__ 7.   These amounts appear in the *absorption* income statement of a company: depreciation of factory building $4,200, fire insurance on work in process $2,500, lubricants used in manufacturing operations $3,500, distribution costs $3,000. The total product costs included above are: (a) $6,000, (b) $10,200, (c) $13,200, (d) $6,500, (e) $7,200.   ALL FOH = 4.2 + 2.5 + 3.5
= 10.2

__D__ 8.   See the preceding test item. The total *period* costs included are: (a), $4,200, (b), $2,500, (c) $6,000 (d) $3,000.   PERIOD - NON MANUF. COSTS.

__D__ 9.   Given for Wye Co. (in thousands): sales $80, direct material $12, direct labor $22, selling and administrative expenses $15 (two-thirds fixed), factory overhead $24 (three-fourths fixed), inventories negligible. Compute amount of gross profit: (a) $7, (b) $28, (c) $35, (d) $22.   SALES - ALL PROD. COST

__C__ 10.   See the preceding test item. Compute amount of contribution margin: (a) $22, (b) $47, (c) $35, (d) 40.

CM = SALES - ALL VAR. COST
= 80 - 12 - 22 - 5 - 6
= 35

= 80 - 12 - 22 - 24
=

__D__ 11. The income statement of a manufacturing company included these amounts: selling expenses $40,000 (75% fixed), variable factory overhead $25,000, fixed factory overhead $45,000, direct labor $60,000, fixed general administrative expenses $35,000, direct materials used $50,000, inventories negligible. In the contribution margin income statement, total period costs would be: (a) $180,000, (b) $120,000, (c) $75,000, (d) $110,000.   TOT PER = ALL FIXED COSTS.
30 + 45 + 35 = 110

__C__ 12. See the preceding test item. In the absorption income statement, total period costs would be: (a) $120,000, (b) 80,000, (c) $75,000, (d) $95,000.   = ALL NON MANUF.
= 40 + 35 = 75

__C__ 13. (Appendix) A factory employee's wage is $12 per hour for straight time and $18 per hour for time over 40 hours per week. If the employee worked 47 hours in one week, the amount of direct labor cost would be: (a) $480, (b) $564, (c) $606, (d) $42.

Completion

Complete each of the following statements by filling in the blanks:

1. Minor materials that become a physical part of a manufactured product but are difficult to trace to specific product units are classified as __indirect or OH__.

2. Conversion cost is __direct labor__ plus __manufacturing OH__.

3. The three main categories of inventory for a manufacturing company are:

   __Direct Materials__

   __Work-in-process__

   __finished goods__

4. Activity based costing applies _____ and _____ to measure accurate _____.

5. (Appendix) Idle time and overtime premium are are classified as _____ labor costs.

6. Cost accounting systems _____ and _____ costs for both _____ and _____ needs.

7. What distinguishes a direct cost from an indirect cost is __traceability__.

8. What distinguishes a period cost from a product cost is __traceability__ and the __approach to net income__.

9. JIT manufacturing methods reduce cycle time by _____ and _____ and _____.

10. Classify each of these costs of Vogon Construction Company as a product cost or period cost, assuming use of the absorption approach (for simplicity, assume all projects are started and finished in a single period):

		Product cost	Period cost
Fire insurance on equipment building	a.	X	
Sales commissions	b.		X
Salary of company controller	c.		X

Introduction to Cost Systems 55

Concrete used on projects	d.	x	
Costs of a general management training program	e.		x
Property taxes on construction machinery	f.	x	
Freight on materials purchased	g.	x	
Supervisory salaries, materials storeroom	h.	x	
Power for maintenance equipment	i.	x	
Depreciation of sales office furniture	j.		x

11. For each of the transactions of Dent Metal Manufacturing Company, indicate the effect on the company's balance sheet items [increase (I), decrease (D), or no effect(N)].

Balance Sheet Items

Transaction	Direct Materials	Work in Process	Finished Goods	Retained Income
a. Purchased direct materials	I	N	N	N
b. Issued materials for use in production	D	I	N	N
c. Incurred direct labor cost	N	I	N	N
d. Incurred factory overhead cost	N	I	N	N
e. Completed the finished goods	N	D	I	N
f. Sold the goods (revenues)	N	N	D	I
g. Cost of the goods sold	N	N	D	D
h. Incurred selling expenses	N	N	N	D
i. Incurred general administrative expenses	N	N	N	D

Problems

1. The income statement of Zaphod Corporation included these items (in thousands):

Sales	$1,800
Selling expenses (all variable)	320
Direct labor cost	420
General administrative expenses (all fixed)	180
Direct materials used	340
Fixed factory overhead costs	220
Variable factory overhead costs	100
Interest expense (fixed)	40
All inventories	negligible

a. Assuming the absorption approach to income measurement is used, compute:

Prime cost	420 + 340 = 760	DIRECT LABOR + DIR. MTL
Conversion cost	420+220+100 = 740	DIRECT LABOR + FOH + V FOH
Total product costs	420+340+220+100 = 1080	DIR LAB + DIR MTL + FOH + VFOH
Gross margin	1800 - 1080 = 720	SALES - TOT PROD. COST
Total period costs	320+180+40 = 540	SELL'G EXP + GEN. ADMIN + INT
Net income	720 - 540 = 180	GROSS MARGIN - TOT PER. COST

b. Assuming the contribution approach to income measurement is used, compute:

Total variable costs	320+420+340+100	= $1,180
Total fixed costs	180+220+40	= $440
Contribution margin	1800 - 1180 = $620	: SALES - VC
Net income	620 - 440 = $180	: CM - FIX COSTS

2. Given for Krikkit Company's operations for the year ending December 31, 19X2:

Sales	$160,000
Direct material	25,000
Direct labor	32,000
Indirect manufacturing costs:	
Variable	$ 5,000
Fixed	25,000
Total	$30,000
Selling expenses:	
Variable	$16,000
Fixed	23,000
Total	$39,000
Administrative expenses:	
Variable	$ 2,000
Fixed	12,000
Total	$14,000

a. Prepare an income statement in the absorption form (omit statement heading).

SALES		160,000	160,000
LESS MANUFACTURE OF CGS.			
DIR. MTL.		25,000	
DIR LABOR		32,000	
INDIRECT. MANUF.		30,000	87,000
GROSS PROFIT			73,000
LESS NON-MANUF			
SELLING EXP.		39,000	
ADMIN. "		14,000	53,000
OPER. INCOME			20,000

b. Prepare an income statement in the contribution form (omit heading).

SALES:			160,000
LESS VARIABLE EXP.			
DIR. MTL.	25,000		
DIR LABOR	32,000		
VAR. IND. MANUF.	5,000		
TOT VAR. MANUF	$62,000		
VAR. SELLING	16,000		
VAR. ADMIN	2,000	TOT. VAR.	80,000
CONT. MARGIN			80,000
LESS FIXED EXPENSES			
MANUF.	$25,000		
SELL'G	23,000		
ADMIN	12,000		
TOTAL FIXED			60,000
OPER. INCOME			20,000.

CHAPTER 4 SOLUTIONS TO PRACTICE TEST QUESTIONS AND PROBLEMS

True or False Statements

1. True — Whether a cost is indirect or direct may depend on the referenced cost object. For example, supervisory salaries are direct to a department but are probably indirect to products made in the department.

2. False — These items are probably difficult to trace to products, so they would be classified as indirect product costs -- overhead.

3. False — Conversion cost is direct labor plus overhead cost. Prime cost is direct material plus direct labor cost.

4. True — These are identifiable product costs. Variable overhead would be an indirect product cost, however.

5. False — Insurance on factory machinery would be classified as an indirect product cost. Sales commissions, however, are period costs.

6. True — Both direct and indirect product costs are inventoried and expensed when items are sold.

7. False — Depreciation of factory equipment is a product cost. Depreciation of sales equipment is a period cost, however.

8. False — The primary purpose of ABC is to improve internal decision-making. May not affect the "bottom-line" numbers reported since many effects will be across products and services. That is, total costs are the same, but how they are assigned to products and services may vary significantly.

9. True — All fixed costs are treated as period costs in the contribution margin approach. Some proponents of ABC think it is incorrect not to allocate fixed product costs to products, so ABC is not necessarily consistent with the contribution approach.

10. True — Maybe. If processes and services are redesigned so that the non-value-added activities are not necessary, then product quality will probably be improved. For example, redesigning a product and process so that defects are unlikely reduces if not eliminates the need for quality control testing, which itself does not add value. Just dropping quality testing, however, would reduce overall product quality.

11. False — ABC is generally part of a cost management system that is focused on management decision making.

12. True — Manufacturers pass indirect product costs through inventory accounts, whereas merchandisers treat all indirect costs as period costs.

13. False — A goal of JIT is to *eliminate* the need for these inventory accounts and stages.

14. True — Fixed factory overhead, however, is not. Only in the absorption approach is fixed factory overhead inventoriable.

15. True — This is traditional practice, but the reasoning is that most work that happens to be done during overtime periods could have been done at some other time. Thus, overtime is a cost of all work in the period. This is not always true, however.

Multiple Choice Questions

1. d It may not be feasible (given current technology and cost-benefit considerations) to trace the cost of every resource to each product that uses the resource. The costs for which specific tracing is infeasible are called indirect costs; these costs are assigned to products using some allocation method.

2. a, d These terms are synonymous. Indirect materials and indirect labor are part of manufacturing overhead.

3. d Machinist wages should be directly traceable to products. The labor costs of the plant superintendant and secretary would be classified as indirect product costs. In most systems, the salary of the sales manager would be classified as a period cost.

4. a, b, d Most systems treat sales distribution costs as period costs. Some ABC systems, however, would trace distribution costs to products.

5. a, c Wages of factory employees are classified as factory overhead, which is a product cost.

6. b Conversion cost is direct labor plus factory overhead = $55,000 + $43,000 = $98,000. Prime cost is direct material plus direct labor = $40,000 + $55,000 = $95,000.

7. b Product costs include all factory overhead costs, which in part are: $4,200 + $2,500 + $3,500 = $10,200.

8. d Under absorption costing, non-manufacturing costs are period costs, which in part are: $3,000.

9. d Gross profit equals sales less all product costs = $(80 - 12 - 22 - 24) = $22.

10. c Contribution margin equals sales less all variable costs = $(80 - 12 - 22 - 5 - 6) = $35.

11. d In the contribution margin approach, total period costs equal all fixed costs = $(30 + 45 + 35) = $110,000.

12. c In the absorption approach, total period costs equall all non-manufacturing costs = $(40 + 35) = $75,000.

13. b In most systems, the amount of direct labor would be the total straight-time wages = $12 x 47 = $564. The overtime premium of ($18 - $12)x7 = $42 would be charged as indirect labor or overhead.

Completion

1. indirect materials or overhead

2. direct labor cost plus manufacturing overhead cost

3. direct materials, work-in-process, finished goods

4. cost behavior, activity analysis, product and service costs

5. indirect

6. accumulate, allocate, financial reporting, managerial decision making

7. traceability

8. traceability, approach to net income (absorption or contribution margin)

9. improving process flow, reducing defectives, eliminating non-value-added activities

10.

		Product cost	Period cost
Fire insurance on equipment building	a.	x	
Sales commissions	b.		x
Salary of company controller	c.		x
Concrete used on projects	d.	x	
Costs of a general management training program	e.		x
Property taxes on construction machinery	f.	x	
Freight on materials purchased	g.	x	
Supervisory salaries, materials storeroom	h.	x	
Power for maintenance equipment	i.	x	
Depreciation of sales office furniture	j.		x

11.

Balance Sheet Items

Transaction	Direct Materials	Work in Process	Finished Goods	Retained Income
a. Purchased direct materials	I	N	N	N
b. Issued materials for use in production	D	I	N	N
c. Incurred direct labor cost	N	I	N	N
d. Incurred factory overhead cost	N	I	N	N
e. Completed the finished goods	N	D	I	N
f. Sold the goods (revenues)	N	N	N	I
g. Cost of the goods sold	N	N	D	D
h. Incurred selling expenses	N	N	N	D
i. Incurred general administrative expenses	N	N	N	D

1. Zaphod Corporation:
    a. absorption approach:

Prime cost	420 + 340 = $760
Conversion cost	420 + 220 + 100 = $740
Total product costs	420 + 340 + 220 + 100 = $1,080
Gross margin	1,800 - 1,080 = $720
Total period costs	320 + 180 + 40 = $540
Net income	720 - 320 - 180 - 40 = $180, or 720 - 540 = $180

Introduction to Cost Systems 61

b. contribution approach:

Total variable costs	320 + 420 + 340 + 100 = $1,180
Total fixed costs	180 + 220 + 40 = $440
Contribution margin	1,800 - 1,180 = $620
Net income	620 - 440 = $180

(Note that net income is the same, regardless of the income approach. This is not always true -- when inventories are involved, income measures could differ. Complications are covered in Chapters 15 and 16.)

2. a.

Absorption Income Statement

Sales		$160,000
Less manufacturing cost of goods sold:		
Direct material....................	$25,000	
Direct labor........................	32,000	
Indirect manufacturing costs	30,000	87,000
Gross profit		$73,000
Less nonmanufacturing costs:		
Selling expenses	$39,000	
Administrative expenses	14,000	53,000
Operating income		$20,000

2.b.

Contribution Income Statement

Sales		$160,000
Less variable expenses:		
Direct material	$25,000	
Direct labor	32,000	
Variable indirect manufacturing costs	5,000	
Total variable manufacturing cost of goods sold	$62,000	
Variable selling expenses	16,000	
Variable administrative expenses	2,000	
Total variable expenses		$ 80,000
Contribution margin		$ 80,000
Less fixed expenses:		
Manufacturing	$25,000	
Selling	23,000	
Administrative	12,000	
Total fixed expenses		$ 60,000
Operating income		$ 20,000

CHAPTER 5

Relevant Information and Decision Making: Part One

MAIN FOCUS AND OBJECTIVES

This entire chapter is based upon a single critical step in decision-making-- *identifying and using relevant information*. Only the costs and revenues that are *expected in the future* and that *differ among alternative actions* are relevant costs and revenues for choosing among alternative courses of action. Each decision setting appears different, yet the relevant information is the same -- what costs and revenues will change as a result of choosing each alternative? Your learning objectives are to

- Discriminate between relevant and irrelevant information for making decisions
- Understand the main elements of the decision process
- Analyze accepting or rejecting special sales orders
- Understand the pitfalls of the unit-cost approach
- Analyze adding or deleting product lines
- Optimize use of scarce productive capacity
- Understand the factors affecting sales pricing decisions
- Compute a target sales price

REVIEW OF KEY CONCEPTS

A. The basis of management planning is selecting the best course of action from all the feasible alternatives.

　1. Each possible decision can have different future effects. For example, the choice of whether a firm should locate a new plant in Michigan or in Tennessee may have significant impacts on productivity, distribution costs, and profitability.

　2. Therefore, making decisions always involves making and anlayzing predictions about the future consequences of current alternative choices.

> See textbook Exhibit 5-1

3. **Relevant data for managerial decision making** are predicted costs and revenues associated with each of the feasible alternative actions.
   a. Though there is no harm in identifying *all* the costs and revenues of alternative choices, really the *relevant data* are the expected future costs and revenues that will *differ among alternatives*. As a simple example, if two products are being considered for future sale, and expected sales prices and quantities are equal, only predicted *costs* are relevant to choosing between them. Sales prices and quantities, since they are the same for both, are irrelevant to choosing between the products.
   b. The only valid role for historical data is in predicting future consequences. What happened in the past has passed. This seems obvious, but some managers are unwilling to let the past go, and they worry about abandoning costs that they have already spent but that are irrelevant to future courses of action. For example, it really does not matter if you spent $10,000 for a piece of equipment just a year ago if the best course of action is to replace it now. Its current disposal value is probably relevant, though.
   c. Decision makers and information systems trade-off accuracy and relevance. The best circumstance would be to have both accurate and relevant information -- that is the goal of activity-based costing, for example, discussed in Chapters 3 and 4.
   d. In general, it is better to have somewhat inaccurate but relevant data than to have accurate but irrelevant data. For example, activity-based costs that are not precise are *probably* more useful than costs from financial reports that account for all costs to the penny, but which use completely inappropriate cost drivers to do so.

> Can you define relevant information for managerial decision making? What is the role of past costs?

B. There are situations when *accepting special, reduced-price sales orders* is beneficial. A careful manager would consider several issues before agreeing to sell a product at lower than the customary price:

1. Is there excess productive capacity? If not, the special order would displace current activity at regular, full prices and you should probably reject the order.

2. Would the lower price of the special order adversely affect the current and future sales of the company?
   a. If other customers learn that you are willing to sell at reduced prices, everyone may expect discounted prices.
   b. Do you want to be a discount supplier?
   c. If not, and you fear that the special order will erode future prices, you should probably reject the order.

3. If there is excess capacity, *and* if future prices will not be adversely affected, what is the other relevant information for choosing whether to accept the special order?

a. In such a case, the average overall unit costs based on data from the absorption cost-based income statement would *not* serve as an appropriate basis for evaluating these orders.
b. Absorption costs contain some allocation of fixed costs that probably will not increase in the future as a result of the special order.
c. The only costs that usually would change in the future are the variable costs affected by accepting the special sales orders. These costs can be more clearly identified from the *contribution margin-based* income statement.

> See textbook Exhibit 5-2

d. Ordinarily fixed costs would not change as a result of the decision because with excess capacity no additional capacity (and related fixed costs) would be necessary. However, special orders might affect certain fixed costs, which would be relevant to the decision.

> See textbook Exhibit 5-3

4. Note in Exhibit 5-3 that there is a $100,000 advantage in accepting 100,000 units of a special order at a $13 selling price despite the fact that this is $2 less than the average absorption cost of ($12,000,000 + $3,000,000) ÷ 1,000,000 units = $15 per unit.

5. Thus, on the basis of a relevant-cost approach, it might be a good idea to use excess capacity and accept some special orders at selling prices *below* average unit costs that include all fixed and variable costs.

6. The important point is that such decisions should depend primarily on the revenues and costs expected to change.

7. You should beware of the misleading effects of *unitizing fixed costs* because this could create the false impression that these are variable costs.
a. Furthermore, *spreading* fixed costs over more units does not reduce the total amount of fixed cost.
b. This is why though one can omit some fixed costs from analyses because they do not differ across alternatives, it is safer to be sure that all costs, fixed and variable, are explicitly considered. If some fixed costs are the same across alternatives, fine, they will not affect the analysis, but including them may keep you from forgetting a fixed cost that does change.

8. Because many costs have multiple cost drivers, relevant costs of special orders may be caused by more than just the number of units in the special order.
a. For example, any differences in complexity (features, capabilities, etc.) could result in variable costs that are different than usual.
b. Product differences also may result in additional fixed or step costs (e.g., setup costs).

> Before going on to the next decision setting, are you sure that you understand what costs and revenues are relevant to analyzing special orders? What if capacity is limited? What if future sales will be affected by the special order?

C. Another important management decision deals with the *deletion* or *addition of products or departments*.
1. As with the special order decisions, consider effects on capacity first.
    a. If a product or department is added, is there currently sufficient capacity to accomodate it? If not, additional capacity costs will be necessary.
    b. If a product or department is dropped, what, if any, are the alternative uses of the freed-up capacity?
2. In addition to capacity costs, other relevant data are revenues and fixed and variable costs that will change as a result of adding or dropping products or departments.
    a. Of course, adding or dropping operations will add or drop the revenues of the specific product or department. In addition to these, determine whether the change will affect sales of other products or departments.
    b. **Avoidable costs,** (sometimes called *separable* costs) are those costs that will not continue by changing or deleting an ongoing operation. Conversely, adding a product or department adds those costs.
    c. **Unavoidable costs** are those costs that will continue even after dropping a product or department. These are *common* costs of facilities and services shared by several departments or product lines that come in large, indivisible "chunks."
3. The text demonstrates a useful way to analyze product/department additions/deletions. This method lists the changes in revenues and costs of each change and then adds or subtracts these changes from the total to obtain the net effect. You should study this method.

> Do you understand that the information relevant to adding or dropping products or departments is fundamentally the same as in the case of special orders? Future costs and revenues that will change as a result of each decision are relevant.

D. A basic management decision is *determining the best use of the capacity of a multiple-product or service facility*.
1. So far, we have not considered that productive capacity is limited. If capacity were unlimited, then any product or service with a positive contribution margin is a desirable use of capacity.
    a. Capacity is rarely if ever unconstrained, so managers must be careful to use capacity wisely.
    b. In general, there are multiple dimensions of capacity, each of which is limited. For example, machining capacity, computing capacity, limited skilled labor, limited capital, and so on.
    c. In this chapter we consider the situation of only a single capacity constraint. A method for considering multiple capacity constraints is in Chapter 17.
2. Since fixed costs and target profits must be covered, managers must choose products and services that generate the most contribution margin possible from limited capacity. This suggests a straightforward approach:
    a. Measure the contribution margin of each product or service.

- b. Divide each contribution margin by the amount of capacity needed to produce each unit of product. This is the *contribution margin per unit of limited or constrained capacity*. For example, if a product's unit contribution margin is $10 and each unit of product requires 2 hours of limited machining time, the contribution margin per unit of constrained capacity is $5 contribution per machine hour.
- c. Rank all products by their contribution per unit of constrained capacity.
- d. Choose the alternative products or services that offer the highest contribution margin per unit of limited capacity first. If you cannot sell all of the highest-ranked product that you could produce, work your way down the ranking until all the constrained capacity is budgeted.
- e. This is the mix alternative products or services that offers the highest total contribution margin from fully using limited capacity.
- f. One could begin by looking at the total contribution margins from producing only each of the alternative products, but this is more cumbersome, especially if there are sales limits.

3. Looking merely at product or service unit contribution margins is not sufficient.
- a. Product A may have a relatively high contribution margin and may look attractive, but it may consume too much capacity.
- b. The facility may be able to produce so many more of product B which has a lower unit contribution margin but uses much less capacity per unit of B that total contribution margin is greater making B.

4. This decision appears different from the first two, but consider:
- a. Capacity is constrained, and fixed costs will not change as a result of which products or services are selected.
- b. The revenues and costs that will change as a result of choosing alternative products are reflected in the contribution margins (per unit of constrained capacity or in total).
- c. Computing the contribution margin per unit of constrained capacity is an intuitive short-cut in this type of decision.

> Before going on to the next decision setting, can you explain the similarities among all of the three preceding decisions? What are the differences? Only the settings differ.

E. An extremely important management decision is *setting regular selling prices*. Basically, four major factors may influence pricing decisions: *market competition, legal restrictions, customers, and costs*.

1. The level of market competition may either:
   a. Dictate what the price of a product or service is. At the extreme, this is **perfect competition** where a firm can sell all of a product it wants at the market price.
   b. Allow a firm to affect price by choosing sales quantities. This is **imperfect competition** -- total sales depends on the price charged.
2. In economic theory, the firm chooses the sales level that maximizes profits.
   a. In *perfect competition*, the firm would sell products up to the point where the **marginal cost** (the incremental cost of producing one more unit of product) equals the market sales price. Cost does not determine price at all, but does determine how much product the firm should produce.
   b. In *imperfect competition*, managers produce up to the point where marginal cost is just equal to **marginal revenue**, the additional revenue earned from an additional sale. Thus, costs determine price indirectly by identifying how much product the firm should produce.

   > See textbook Exhibits 5-5 and 5-6

   c. In practice, however, marginal cost is difficult to observe, so managers use variable cost as an estimate.
   d. As we have seen, within the relevant range, a constant variable cost is a reasonable estimate of the incremental cost of producing additional units.

   > See textbook Exhibit 5-7

   e. Many of the concepts of economic theory are difficult to observe in practice. However, firms should be very aware of their competition's pricing practices, because customers shop around.
   f. Even when managers say that they set prices by adding a **markup** to their costs, they admit that these *markups are adjusted for market conditions*.
   g. Costs are important for pricing, but markets are more important.
   h. As we have seen above, costs are extremely important for the *production decision* -- given the price, should we produce this product? How much?
3. Pricing of goods is subject to certain U.S. and international laws that prohibit predatory and discriminatory pricing.
   a. **Predatory pricing** is designed to unfairly drive out competition. Courts have ruled that prices below variable cost are predatory.
   b. **Discriminatory pricing** is charging different prices to different customers for the same product or service. This practice is legally defensible only if the firm can demonstrate that differences in cost driver activity across customers lead to different costs.
   c. Thus, knowledge of cost behavior is not only good for planning and control, it is essential for the legal environment of business.
4. Knowledge of customers' requirements and willingness to pay are essential to competing in markets for products and services.
   a. **Target costing** is a relatively new product design approach that works backward from the market price to a target production cost of a product that meets both customer needs and offers a required return on sales. This

approach is common among Japanese firms, who argue that they are more market-oriented than most U.S. firms.

    b. *Target cost = Market price - required return on sales.*

    c. As in the theory of perfect competition, if the product cannot be produced at the target cost, the company either will redesign the product or production process or will drop the product.

5. Many U.S. managers compute their target prices on the basis of certain costs, called **cost-plus pricing** or **target pricing.**

    a. Essentially, this method adds a "markup" to some cost figure to obtain a selling price that will generate an adequate return on investment. Commonly used cost bases include:

    b. *Total variable costs:* variable manufacturing cost plus variable selling and administrative cost.

    c. *Absorption cost:* variable manufacturing cost plus fixed manufacturing cost.

    d. *Full cost:* (also called fully allocated or fully distributed cost): absorption cost plus total selling and administrative costs.

> See textbook Exhibits 5-8 and 5-9

    e. Many firms use absorption cost or full cost as the base for target prices because these costs indicate the levels of costs that must be recovered in the long run to remain in business.

    f. Regardless of the cost base used to set initial target prices, one can arrive at the same target price by using different percentage markups. Remember, in most cases these markups are adusted for market conditions anyway. If customers will not pay target prices, firms will adjust prices or costs (to allow price adjustments) or will not produce the product -- just as predicted by economic theory.

    g. Some industries though, set prices directly on costs. These are *rate-regulated industries* that governments have granted some form of monopoly (imperfect competition) power. Markups are generally prescribed by law or by regulation. Therefore, determining the cost base of these industries is very critical to both the firm and to regulators and the rate-paying public.

6. Regardless of the cost base used to set target prices the contribution margin approach to measuring income offers some advantages over the absorption costing approach:

    a. More detailed information is available regarding changing levels of variable and fixed costs at different levels of production.

> See textbook Exhibit 5-10

    b. The contribution approach provides insights that help management weigh the short-term benefits of cutting prices against possible long-term disadvantages of price cutting and undermining the price structure of an industry.

c. As in the other decision-making settings discussed in this chapter, the pricing decision should consider effects of capacity and what revenues and costs will change as a result of choosing alternative prices.
d. The only difference in this setting is the consideration of external regulation on pricing and the effects of competitors' prices and customers' actions on revenues.

> Before going on to the practice test, be sure that you understand the external influences on pricing (competitive and legal) and the role of costs in determining prices (theoretically and practically).

PRACTICE TEST QUESTIONS AND PROBLEMS WITH SOLUTIONS

True or False Statements

Determine whether each of the following statements is True (T) or False (F) and enter your answer in the space provided.

__T__ 1. Pueblo Corp. must choose between two alternative future actions. If a certain predicted variable cost per unit is the same for each action, that cost is not relevant to the decision.

__F__ 2. Past costs are never relevant to decisions about the future.

__T__ 3. When there is idle plant capacity and reduced-price special orders are received, the relevant-cost approach might indicate acceptance of orders at prices below the overall average unit cost.

__F__ 4. The relevant information approach to evaluating reduced-price special orders implies that future fixed costs are always irrelevant.

__F__ 5. The relevant data for pricing a special sales order that can be filled from idle plant capacity would include expected future unit costs of variable production costs and fixed production costs.

__T__ 6. Although one of a company's several product lines may consistently show a net loss, dropping this product line could decrease the company's total net income.

__F__ 7. Unavoidable costs are those costs that will change as a result of dropping a department or product line.

__F__ 8. In a multiple-product plant, the criterion for maximum profits for a given capacity is to choose the products with the greatest contribution-margin ratio or percentage.   CM/UNIT CONSTRAINED CAPACITY!

__F__ 9. Deciding which products to produce is a fundamentally different problem than choosing to accept a special order or to drop a product line.

__F__ 10. In perfect competition, firms can affect sales prices by setting marginal revenue equal to marginal cost.

__F__ 11. If firms can affect sales prices, they can charge any price they want and customers have no choice but to pay the prices.

__T__ 12. Target costing works backwards from sales price to determine acceptable product or service costs.

__F__ 13. One problem of cost-based pricing is that the resulting prices are inflexible to market conditions.

__T__ 14. Absorption costs are commonly used as bases for pricing because this base might prevent managers from accepting marginal orders.

__F__ 15. The relevant information approach to decision making means that every type of decision has unique information needs.

Multiple Choice Questions

For the following multiple-choice questions, select the best answer(s) and enter the identification letter(s) in the spaces provided:

__A,B,C,D__ 1. In imperfect competition, price is: (a) set by regulators, (b) set by market conditions, (c) set by equating marginal cost to marginal revenue, (d) set by marking up product cost.

__D__ 2. Each month Winn Co. makes 400 units of Product C at a $40 variable cost per unit and $1,200 of total fixed costs. If a special order for 50 units from a customer is accepted at a price of $42 and requiring a $100 special set-up cost, Winn Co. will have: (a) a $100 contribution, (b) a $2-per-unit contribution, (c) a $.88-per-unit contribution, (d) no financial incentive to accept. 2×50 −100 = 0

__D__ 3. Each month Lewis Co. manufactures 600 units of a certain product at a variable cost of $20 per unit. Total monthly fixed costs are $4,200. A special order is received for 100 units at a price of $27 per unit. Fixed costs would increase by $350 if the offer is accepted. Relevant to deciding to accept or reject this order is: (a) the old average fixed cost per unit: $4,200/600 = $7 per unit, (b) the new average fixed cost per unit: $4,550/700 = $6.50 per unit, (c) the difference between these unit costs: $7 - $6.50 = $.50, (d) the increase in fixed costs of $350.

__C__ 4. Jackson Company produces and sells 500 units of a product each month with total variable costs of $6,000 and total fixed costs of $6,000. Idle capacity would permit the acceptance of a special sales order for 100 units each month. The average unit cost per month of producing and selling the total output, if the special order is accepted, would be: (a) $12, (b) $18, (c) $22, (d) $24.

__D__ 5. See the preceding test item. Of the following prices, which is the lowest acceptable selling price? (a) $22, (b) $10, (c) $23, (d) $15.

__D__ 6. Spinetto Company has 6,000 hours of plant capacity available each month for making two products, A and B, each with a selling price of $50 per unit. Five units of A can be made in one hour at a total variable cost per unit of $41, or three units of B can be made in one hour at a total variable cost per unit of $29. The number of hours that should be used each month to make B is: (a) 6,000, (b) 3,000, (c) 2,000, (d) zero.

__C__ 7. Contribution margin for pricing is equal to sales revenue minus: (a) variable manufacturing expenses, (b) all manufacturing costs, (c) all variable expenses, (d) all fixed and variable expenses.

__A__ 8. Absorption cost for pricing is equal to: (a) total manufacturing cost, (b) manufacturing cost plus selling and administrative cost, (c) full cost, (d) fully allocated cost.

__A,c__ 9. The contribution approach to pricing makes a basic distinction between: (a) relevant and irrelevant costs, (b) past and future costs, (c) fixed and variable costs, (d) manufacturing and nonmanufacturing costs.

__C__ 10. "Cost-plus pricing" adds a "markup" to cost to reach a total that is: (a) profit, (b) return on investment, (c) selling price, (d) full cost.

__A__ 11. Each month, a company incurs for a certain product $60,000 of total manufacturing costs (half fixed, half variable) and $20,000 of non-manufacturing costs (half fixed and half variable). Its monthly sales are $100,000. The markup percentage on full cost to arrive at the existing (target) selling price is: (a) 25%, (b) 12.5%, (c) 20%, (d) 10%.

__B__ 12. See the preceding test item. The markup percentage on absorption cost to arrive at the existing (target) selling price is: (a) 33%, (b) 67%, (c) 40%, (d) 50%.

__B__ 13. See item 11 above. The markup percentage on total variable cost to arrive at the existing (target) selling price is: (a) 60%, (b) 150%, (c) 250%, (d) 40%.

__A__ 14. See item 11 above. The markup percentage on total variable manufacturing cost to arrive at the existing (target) selling price is: (a) 233%, (b) 30%, (c) 70%, (d) 333%.

Completion

Complete each of the following statements by filling in the blanks.

1. The costs that are relevant to managerial decision making include only the costs that _____ for each alternative course of action.

2. _____ costs are themselves _____ to _____ but may be relevant to the prediction of future costs.

3. When a multiple-product plant is being operated at capacity, the criterion for attaining maximum profits is the largest contribution _____.

4. The accountant's role in managerial decision making is _____.

5. The danger of using unit costs for decision making is that unit costs treat _____ costs as if they were _____.

6. As activity levels increase fixed cost in total _____ and fixed cost per unit _____.

7. The decision to accept a special order should consider _____, _____, additional _____ and additional _____.

8. The decision to drop a product line should consider use of _____, effects on _____ and additional _____ and _____.

72 Chapter 5

9. The pricing decision should consider _____ actions, _____ willingness to pay, and additional _____ and _____.

10. a. List the similarities of all the decisions considered in this chapter:

_____
_____
_____

b. List the differences among these decisions:

_____
_____
_____

Problems

1. The Real Time Products Company has a monthly plant capacity of 1,500 product units. Its predicted operations for the year are:

Sales (1,000 units)	$51,500
Manufacturing costs:	
Fixed	$18,000
Variable	$17 per unit
Selling and administrative expenses:	
Fixed	$4,500
Variable (sales commissions)	$3 per unit

If the company accepts a special order from a customer for 200 units at a selling price of $18 each, how would the total predicted net income for the month be affected, assuming no effect on regular sales at regular prices? No sales commissions would be required by the special order, but an extra delivery cost of $350 would be required. Indicate the amount and whether it is an increase or a decrease. Ignore income taxes. Complete the following two, equivalent analyses:

a.

Item	Company as a whole without special order	Special order	Company with special order
Sales	$51,500	200×18 = 3,600	$55,100
Less variable expenses			
Variable manufacturing	17×1000 = $17,000	200×17 = 3400	$20,400
Variable sales and admin	3×1000 = $3,000	N/A	3,000
Contribution margin	$31,500	$200	31,700
Less fixed expenses	18,000	N/A	18,000
Fixed manufacturing	4,500	N/A	4,500
Fixed Sales and admin	EXTRA DELIVERY	$350	$350
Net income	$9,000	$150	$8,850

b. Additional revenues: $3,600
    Additional variable costs: $3,400
    Additional fixed costs: $350
    Net effect of special order: ($150) Loss

2. The fast-food branch of Illegal Seafoods sells two items: (1) fish and chips and (2) seafood salad. The branch is considering dropping fish and chips and expanding its offering of seafood salad by 50%. Dropping fish and chips means that the branch will no longer need to lease a hot oil cooker at $100 a month. Other equipment costs will remain. Employment will remain constant. A condensed, budgeted monthly income statement with both products is below:

	Total	Fish and Chips	Seafood Salad
Sales	$6,000	$2,000	$4,000
Less expenses:			
Food materials	$1,500	$500	$1,000
Labor	1,600	800	800
Equipment	700	600	100
Total expenses	$3,800	1,900	1,900
Operating income	$2,200	$ 100	$2,100

What is the effect of dropping fish and chips? Are there other considerations?

	Current Total	Drop Fish and Chips	50% Increase Seafood Salad	Net Effect of Change
Sales	$6,000	(2000)	$2,000	6,000
Less expenses:				
Food materials	$1,500	(500)	(500)	1,500
Labor	1,600	(800)	(800)	1,600
Equipment	700	(100)		600
Total expenses	$3,800	(1,400)		
Operating income	$2,200	(600)	1700	2,300

3. Lighthouse Appliances has three product lines: Washers, Dryers, and Freezers. The company furnished the following data for its most recent year (in millions):

	Washers	Dryers	Freezers	Total
Sales	$90	$70	$30	$190
Avoidable fixed expenses	10	8	6	24
Unavoidable fixed expenses, allocated equally	10	10	10	30
Variable expenses	50	40	20	110
Net income (loss)	$20	$12	$(6)	$ 26

74 Chapter 5

a. Prepare a projected operating statement using the contribution approach. Assume that the Freezers product line will be discontinued with no effects on sales of the other product lines or on the total assets used by the company.

	Washers	Dryers	Total
Sales	$ 900	$ 700	$ 1,600
Less Exp.			
VARIABLE	500	400	900
C/M	400	300	700
LESS AVOIDABLE FIXED	100	80	180
PROFIT CONT TO FIXED COST	300	220	520
LESS UNAVOIDABLE FIXED			300
Net income			220

b. On the basis of the statement you have prepared, would you advise the elimination of the Freezers product line? Explain.

NO, NII dropped from $26M TO $22M.

4. John Storey Corporation has 4,500 hours of plant capacity per month available for manufacturing two products with the following characteristics:

	Bafflers	Hatches
Selling price per unit	$ 40.00	$ 50.00
Variable costs per unit	$ 30.00	$ 35.00
Units that can be manufactured in one hour (Bafflers or Hatches)	9 units	5 units

$B_{CM} = \$90 \quad H_{CM} = \$75$
$\$10 \times 9 = \quad \$15 \times 5 =$

Compute the number of its 4,500 available production hours that this company should allocate to the manufacture of each product: ALL BAFFLERS

5. CompuStor Electronics, Inc. produces a pocket calculator and presents the following summary of typical operations (in thousands):

	Total	Fixed	Variable
Manufacturing costs......	$ 840	$280	$560
Nonmanufacturing costs...	$ 560	$140	$420
Sales (100,000 units)	$1,470		

Compute the markup on cost that would arrive at the target selling price, using each of the following cost bases:

a. Absorption cost:

b.   Full cost:

c.   Variable manufacturing cost:

d.   Total variable cost:

CHAPTER 5 SOLUTIONS TO PRACTICE TEST QUESTIONS AND PROBLEMS

True or False Statements

1. True — Since that cost will not differ between the alternatives, it is irrelevant to the choice between the alternatives. There is no harm, though, including that cost as long as costs that differ are identified.

2. False — Though past costs cannot differ among future alternatives, past costs may help predict future costs.

3. True — Overall average cost may include some fixed costs that will not change as a result of accepting the special order. These costs are irrelevant to the decision. Therefore, an acceptable price may be lower than average cost, but higher than variable cost (plus any fixed costs that are affected).

4. False — Some fixed costs may change as a result of current decisions. These fixed costs would be relevant to decision making.

5. False — Only those costs that will vary as a result of taking a special order are relevant. Variable costs are relevant, but fixed costs per unit generally are not relevant since fixed costs in total are usually not affected.

6. True — The product line that shows a loss may generate a positive contribution toward covering common fixed costs. The relevant costs of the product line include variable costs and avoidable fixed costs, not common fixed costs.

7. False — Avoidable costs are the costs that will be saved if a product or department is dropped. Unavoidable costs will still be incurred after the product or department is dropped.

8. False — This computation is not sufficient to rank the profitability of products. The proper calculation is the contribution margin per unit of constrained capacity. Alternatively, one can compute the total contribution margin from different combinations of products, but this is cumbersome without computer support.

9. False — These decisions are fundamentally similar: consider effects of capacity and future revenues and costs that will change as effects of the alternative decisions.

10. False — In perfect competition, firms do not set prices. Market prices are set by market forces. Firms choose the quantity to produce by producing up to the point where marginal cost equals the market price (marginal revenue). In imperfect competition, firms simultaneously determine price and quantity sold by producing up to the point where marginal cost equals marginal revenue (the price that depends on the quantity sold).

11. False   Customers can always choose to not buy the product at all or to find a substitute at a better price. So firms might try to charge a very high price, but customers may not buy.

12. True   The sequence is: determine what customers will pay for a product with given characteristics and subtract the required return on sales (or profit margin or markup) to determine the target cost.

13. False   Prices that result from cost-based pricing can always be (and often are) adjusted for market conditions. Cost-based pricing is more of a guideline than a rigid rule.

14. True   If managers feel that they generally should generate sufficient contribution to cover fixed costs, then absorption cost or full cost-based target prices might reinforce that policy. Problems arise with special orders and other "one-time" projects where the temptation to utilize idle capacity might outweigh pricing guidelines.

15. False   Though each type of decision has some differences, they all need common information -- effects of capacity and future costs and revenues that will change.

Multiple Choice Questions

1. a, b, c, d   Each of these may be true. Regulators may influence prices of rate-regulated companies that the public has granted some monopoly power. Market conditions include prices of other, substitute goods to which customers may switch. Ideally, the firm will produce up to the point where marginal cost equals marginal revenue. Firms may not know what marginal revenue could be at different sales levels, so they may approximate marginal revenue by marking up product cost.

2. d   The total contribution of the special order is $(42 - 40) x 50 - $100 = 0. Thus, there is no obvious incentive to accepting the special order at that price.

3. d   Only the costs that will change are relevant. These include the variable costs and the $350 change in fixed costs.

4. c   The variable cost per unit is $6,000 ÷ 500 = $12. The average fixed cost per unit with the special order is $6,000 ÷ 600 = $10. The average cost is $12 + $10 = $22.

5. d   The lowest price, $10, is below variable cost, so it is not acceptable. The other costs exceed variable cost, but the $15 price is the lowest acceptable price.

6. d   The contribution margin per hour for A is $(50 - 41) x 5 = $45 per hour. The contribution margin per hour for B is $(50 - 29) x 3 = $63. Assuming the total output could be sold, only B should be produced. The total contribution from making all A is $(50 - 41)x 5 x 6,000 = $270,000, whereas fromB it is $(50 - 29) x 3 x 6,000 = $378,000.

7. c   The definition of contribution margin is unchanged from previous discussions.

8. a   Likewise, the definition of absorption cost is unchanged. Fully allocated cost would include selling and administrative cost.

9. a, c   The costs relevant to pricing using the contribution margin approach are variable costs.

10. c	Cost plus the markup equals price. The amount of the markup may be based on a required return on investment.
11. a	The total amount of the markup (in thousands) is $(100 - 60 - 20) = 20. As a percentage, the markup over full cost is $20/$80 = 25%.
12. b	The markup over absorption cost is $(100 - 60) = 40. As a percentage markup over absorption cost, the markup is $40/$60 = 67%.
13. b	The markup over variable cost is $(100 - 30 - 10) = 60. As a percentage markup over variable cost, the markup is $60/$40 = 150%
14. a	The markup over variable manufacturing cost is $(100 - 30) = 70. As a percentage markup over variable manufacturing cost, the markup is $70/$30 = 233%

Completion

1. will change or that will differ between
2. Past or historical, irrelevant, to decisions
3. margin per unit of constrained or limited capacity
4. to understand and communicate relevant information
5. fixed costs, variable costs
6. is unchanged within the relevant range, decreases
7. whether there is excess capacity, effects on current and future sales, revenues, costs
8. freed-up capacity, products or departments, revenues, costs
9. competitors', customers', revenues, costs
10. a. similarities include concerns for capacity, additional revenues, and additional costs

    b. differences include: special order: effects on future sales prices; drop/add product line: effects on sales of other products; optimal use of capacity: capacity constraints; pricing: competitors' actions, legal restrictions. (some of these rightly could be considered part of answer "a")

Problems

1. Real Time Products Company

a.

Item	Company as a whole without special order	Special order	Company with special order
Sales	$51,500	200 x $18.= $3,600	$55,100
Less variable expenses			
Variable manufacturing	1,000 x $17 = $17,000	200 x $17.= $3,400	$20,400
Variable sales and admin	1,000 x $3 = 3,000		3,000
Contribution margin	$31,500	$200	$31,700
Less fixed expenses			
Fixed manufacturing	$18,000		$18,000
Fixed Sales and admin	$ 4,500	350	4,850
Net income	$ 9,000	$(150)	$8,850

b. Additional revenues: 200 x $18.= $3,600
    Additional variable costs   200 x $17.= $3,400
    Additional fixed costs   350
    Net effect of special order $(150)

Since the special order reduces income by $150, the company has no financial incentive to accept the order.

2. Illegal Seafoods

	Current Total	Drop Fish and Chips	50% Increase Seafood Salad	Net Effect of Changes
Sales	$6,000	($2,000)	$2,000	$6,000
Less expenses:				
Food materials	$1,500	$(500)	$500	$1,500
Labor	1,600	(800)	800	1,600
Equipment	700	(100)		600
Total expenses	$3,800	(1,400)	$1,300	$3,700
Operating income	$2,200	$(600)	$700	$2,300

The effect is to increase income by $100 per month. Illegal Seafoods should be concerned that they may not have anticipated the effects of dropping fish and chips on the sales of seafood salads. People may come to the branch in groups, some of whom may want fish and chips. As a result the whole group may go elsewhere and increased seafood salad sales will not materialize as expected.

3. a

Lighthouse Appliances
Income Statement without Freezers

	Washers	Dryers	Total
Sales	$900	$700	$1,600
Less variable expenses	500	400	900
Contribution margin	$400	$300	$700
Less avoidable fixed expenses	100	80	180
Profit contribution to unavoidable costs	$300	$220	$520
Less unavoidable fixed expenses			300
Net income			$220

b. No, because the company's net income would be reduced from $260 million to $220 million without any reduction in the total assets used by the company.

4. ## John Storey Corporation

	Baffles	Hatches
Selling price per unit	$40.00	$50.00
Less variable costs per unit	30.00	35.00
Contribution margin per unit	$10.00	$15.00
Multiply by number of units that can be manufactured per hour	9	5
Contribution to profit and joint costs per hour of plant capacity	$90.00	$75.00

Conclusion: All 4,500 hours should be allocated to the manufacture of Bafflers because they would make the larger contribution per unit of limited capacity (hours of plant capacity).

5. CompuStor Electronics, Inc.

1. The markup over absorption cost is $(1,470 - 840) ÷ $840 = 75%

2. The markup over full cost is $(1,470 - 840 - 560) ÷ $(840 + 560) = 5%

3. The markup over variable manufacturing cost is $(1,470 - 560)÷$560 = 162.5%

4. The markup over total variable cost is $(1,470 - 560 - 420) ÷ $(560 + 420) = 50%

CHAPTER 6

Relevant Information and Special Decisions Part Two

MAIN FOCUS AND OBJECTIVES

This chapter extends the application of relevant-information analysis for decision making. Remember that relevant costs and revenues consist of: *estimated future costs and revenues that differ between alternative courses of action.* This chapter's learning objectives are to:

- Understand the concept of opportunity cost and its importance for decision making

- Analyze decisions to make or buy certain parts or products

- Use differential or opportunity cost approaches to determine whether to process joint products beyond split-off

- Determine relevant information for the decision to scrap or rework obsolete inventory

- Analyze whether to keep or replace old equipment

- Explain again how unit costs can be misleading

REVIEW OF KEY CONCEPTS

A. When managers choose an alternative course of action that prevents taking other alternatives as well, they should consider the *opportunity cost* of the exclusive decision.

1. Scarce resources are facts of life. You cannot pursue every profitable or worthwhile opportunity. By choosing only what appear to be the best opportunities, you are giving up the others.

2. **Opportunity cost** *is the highest contribution to profit that you must give up because selecting one alternative prevents you from also selecting another.*

3. Opportunity cost is as real a cost as the expected costs of raw materials for a proposed product.

a. You expect to pay out of pocket costs for materials, and you likewise expect to give up the contribution from the next-best project you are unable to pursue because resources are limited.

b. Opportunity costs, however, do not show up in accounting systems because opportunity costs are predicted costs, not the result of actual accounting transactions.

4. An example of opportunity cost is the current income a full-time college student gives up in order to attend school.

a. That foregone income is as real a cost to the student as the money paid for tuition, fees, and books.

b. On purely economic grounds, the student must expect that increased future income earned after college will more than offset the income foregone during college plus other costs of college. (Chapters 11 and 12 present formal methods for making such decisions over time.)

5. When comparing the costs and revenues of each feasible alternative, one is implicitly comparing opportunity costs.

a. Using the preceding example, the prospective college student could prepare an analysis of expected income levels from two alternatives: (1) begin a career after high school or (2) begin a career after college.

b. The net value of the alternative chosen (career after high school or after college) is its income over time less the opportunity cost (foregone income) of the other career not chosen.

> Before going on, be sure that you understand the concept of opportunity cost and how to include opportunity cost in decision making. Review the employment example in the textbook. What is your opportunity cost of studying managerial accounting today?

B. Managers often consider whether to make or buy product components or sub-assemblies or whether the company should operate its own support activities such as accounting, information systems, and legal services. These are called **make-or-buy** or *sourcing* decisions. ("In-sourcing" is making; "outsourcing" is buying.)

1. These decisions may depend greatly on *qualitative factors* such as maintaining good, long-term business relationships with suppliers or controlling the quality and timeliness of products and services.

2. However, the decision may depend partly on the *quantitative measurement* of the difference in future costs between the alternatives.

a. Understanding relevant fixed and variable cost behavior is crucial.

b. Identifying and using appropriate cost drivers to predict variable costs also is critical since inappropriate cost drivers will yield inaccurate cost predictions.

4. As in the decisions considered in Chapter 5, make-or-buy decisions should always first consider the company's productive capacity.

a. If there is idle capacity, some fixed costs will not change in the future as a result of the make-or-buy decision.

b. Conversely, if capacity is currently fully used, the make-or-buy decision may affect future fixed costs because making the part or component will require more capacity and capacity-related fixed costs.

5. Relevant costs of the make-or-buy decision are, as in the decisions in Chapter 5, those costs that will change in the future as a result of the decision.
   a. Relevant costs include future variable costs and *separable* or *avoidable* fixed costs.
   b. The most common problem in make-or-buy decisions is that managers may compare the absorption or unit cost of products made in-house with prices offered by suppliers.
   c. Absorption costs contain allocations of fixed costs, some of which are probably *unavoidable* fixed costs that are irrelevant to the decision.
   d. Another danger of using unit costs is that the fixed cost portion of the unit cost depends on the level of activity used to allocate fixed cost. Making or buying components or parts will affect activity levels and fixed cost allocations.
   e. It is better to remove all allocations of fixed costs from absorption costs since only variable costs per unit and *total avoidable* fixed costs are relevant to the make-or-buy decision.

6. Generally, the make-or-buy decision compares the costs of alternative uses of productive capacity:
   a. Use the facilities to make a given component or product.
   b. Buy the component or product and leave the facilities idle.
   c. Buy the component or product and rent out the unused facilities.
   d. Buy the component or product and use the facilities to make other components or products.
   e. If all qualitative factors are equal (and, therefore, irrelevant to the decision) the lowest cost source of the component or product is the preferred alternative.
   f. **Differential cost** is the difference in cost between two alternatives (e.g. making or buying).

> Before going on, study the make-or-buy example in the textbook. Do you see the similarity of the make-or-buy decision to the decisions in Chapter 5? For example, there is no fundamental difference between the analyses of whether to add or drop a product line and whether to make or buy a product.

C. When two or more products of relatively significant sales values are produced simultaneously by a single process (or a series of linked processes), they are called **joint products.**

1. The decision-making problem is whether to either sell joint products at the *point of split-off* or process the joint products further before sale.

2. Once again, the only relevant costs are the costs that will change as a result of this decision. This section analyzes which costs are relevant.

3. **The split-off point** is the stage of production at which the different joint products appear:

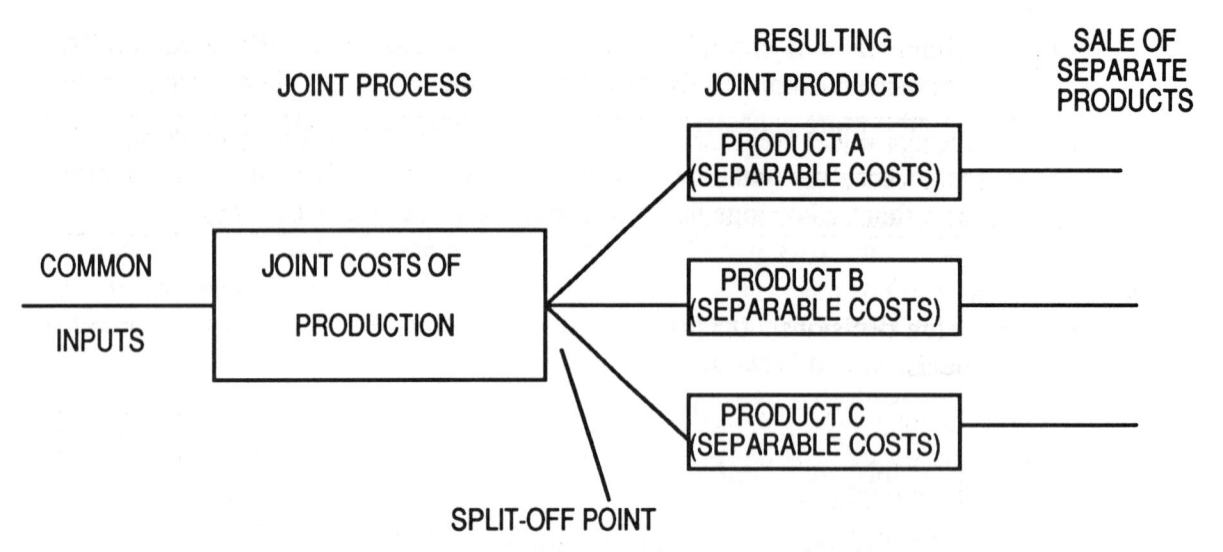

```
                                              RESULTING           SALE OF
                    JOINT PROCESS          JOINT PRODUCTS        SEPARATE
                                                                 PRODUCTS
                                          ┌──────────────────┐
                                          │    PRODUCT A     │
                                          │(SEPARABLE COSTS) │────────────
                                          └──────────────────┘
   COMMON       ┌──────────────────┐      ┌──────────────────┐
   ─────────    │   JOINT COSTS OF │      │    PRODUCT B     │
                │    PRODUCTION    │──────│(SEPARABLE COSTS) │────────────
   INPUTS       └──────────────────┘      └──────────────────┘
                                          ┌──────────────────┐
                                          │    PRODUCT C     │
                                          │(SEPARABLE COSTS) │────────────
                                          └──────────────────┘
                    SPLIT-OFF POINT
```

4. The only costs that are relevant to decisions whether to sell each joint product at split-off or after further processing are the *separable costs incurred after the split-off point*.

   a. **Separable costs** are *avoidable* costs of further processing, and are, therefore, relevant to the further-processing decision.

   a. Compare the contributions of each alternative: sales value at split-off *versus* sales value after further processing less separable (avoidable processing) costs.

   b. Alternatively, it is profitable to process an individual product beyond the split-off point if the separable costs are exceeded by the increase in revenue produced by such processing.

   > See textbook Exhibit 6-1

5. **Joint costs** include all material and production costs of common inputs incurred *prior* to the splitoff point.

   a. *Joint costs* are *unavoidable* costs of operating the joint process.

   b. Joint costs should not affect the decision to sell products at split-off or to process them further, but joint cost allocations may interfere with proper decision making.

   c. Allocation of joint costs to different products is customary for the purposes of costing inventory and goods sold for financial reporting (this is the same concept as allocating fixed factory overhead to products). However, joint cost and joint cost allocations are *completely irrelevant* to the question of whether the individual joint products should be sold at the split-off point or processed further before being sold.

   d. Joint costs will not change as a result of decisions to sell products at split-off or after further processing; therefore, joint costs are irrelevant for decision making, regardless of how they might be allocated to products. Allocations of joint costs can only confuse decision making by altering contributions to profit.

   > See textbook Exhibit 6-2

e. Either an analysis of the total joint process or a *differential analysis* produces the same analysis and either may be used to aid decision making.

> Do you recognize that decisions about joint products are fundamentally no different than those about accepting special orders, dropping or adding products, or make-or-buy decisions? In each case, determine the revenues and costs that will change.

D. As pointed out earlier, **past costs**, sometimes called **sunk costs**, *themselves* are not relevant to planning decisions. It is worthwhile to discuss this further in the context of some common decision-making examples.

1. Managers may face the issue of *what to do with goods already in inventory.* Should the goods be sold as regular product, scrapped, sold at well below variable cost, or reworked into salable products?
    a. A manager may be unwilling to dispose of the inventory in stock at less than its production cost, or at less than its variable production cost. This is a fallacy (particularly if disposal will not affect future sales).
    b. The historical cost of inventory is a past cost that is common to all decisions about disposal of the inventory. Production cost happened; it cannot be changed; it is *sunk*. Thus, it by itself cannot cause differences in expected profits from alternatives ways of disposing of the inventory.
    c. The only relevant data are the revenues that will result less any costs that would change as a result of the decisions to sell, scrap, discount, or rework. The past, historical cost of the inventory is irrelevant.

2. The *book value* of old equipment is also a past, sunk, or historical cost and is, therefore, irrelevant to *making replacement decisions*.
    a. However, the *disposal value* of old equipment is relevant because it is an expected future inflow that would usually differ among alternative replacement decisions.
    b. The gain or loss on disposal (the difference between book value and disposal value) is a combination of relevant and irrelevant costs and itself is not useful for making replacement decisions.
    c. The cost of new equipment is relevant, of course, because it is an expected future cost that will differ among alternative replacement decisions.

> See textbook Exhibits 6-3 and 6-4

3. That said, net book value of assets might be relevant to predicting future cash inflows that depend upon the *income tax effects* of the disposal of the assets.
    a. Disposing of assets at a loss (e.g., item 2b. above) often results in tax savings, which are counted as a contribution of the disposal alternative.
    b. Also relevant would be the tax benefits of continued depreciation of equipment that is not replaced.
    c. Chapter 12 formally analyses the effects of income taxes on equipment replacement decisions.

4. A serious incentive problem can exist when decision making using expected costs interacts with scorekeeping (performance evaluation) that uses past costs.
    a. Consider the equipment-replacement case in textbook Exhibit 6-3.

Relevant Information and Decision Making: Part Two   85

b. The analysis indicates a $2,500 total advantage of replacement during a four year period.
Question: Why might a manager nevertheless decide not to replace the equipment?
Answer: Because he might fear a poor performance evaluation when the $1,500 loss on disposal is *reported in the first year*.

c. Thus an organization could be denied a long-term benefit from replacing the equipment.

d. *This faulty decision is the result of using mismatched planning and scorekeeping information.*

e. The decision to replace the equipment affects multiple years, yet the performance evaluation is based on a single year, in this case the year when the loss is recognized and before significant benefits are realized.

f. This mismatching is a common problem in practice and may cause serious underinvestment in new equipment.

g. In many countries (especially in the U.S., some say) this problem has no easy solution because managers move often and are evaluated for their next positions on the basis of short-term results. Chapter 9 discusses this important topic in more detail.

PRACTICE TEST QUESTIONS AND PROBLEMS WITH SOLUTIONS

True or False Statements

Determine whether each of the following statements is True (T) or False (F) and enter your answer in the space provided.

__F__ 1. In general, all expected future fixed costs are irrelevant to planning decisions.

__F__ 2. Costs that are relevant to decisions to make or buy a critical component might include the cost of components currently in inventory.

__F__ 3. Rox Co. needs 8,000 units of a certain part. These can be purchased for $40 each, or they can be manufactured by Rox Co. by using some machinery that would otherwise be idle. This machinery has a net book value of $25,000. Amounts that are relevant to this decision include both the $25,000 and the $40.

__T__ 4. An example of opportunity costs could be the interest revenue that would have been received by us if we invested in savings bonds rather than in shares of stock.

__T__ 5. Opportunity costs do not require dollar outlays and are not ordinarily entered in the accounting records.

__F__ 6. Joint products are defined as two or more products that are combined to make another product.

__F__ 7. Determining whether to sell or to process beyond split-off point requires knowing each product's share of joint costs.

__T__ 8. The past production cost of inventories on-hand is irrelevant for choosing among alternatives for disposing of inventories, whether the inventory is obsolete or not.

__T__ 9. Amounts that could be relevant to choosing among alternative uses of certain materials on hand include their salvage value.

__F__ 10. The decision to process joint products individually beyond the split-off point should depend partly upon total joint processing costs. *Irrelevant.*

__F__ 11. Amounts that could be relevant to equipment-replacement decisions include both book value and disposal value.

__T__ 12. The gain or loss on disposal of old equipment can affect a manager's incentive to replace the equipment.

__F__ 13. In the comparison of fixed costs of available alternatives, it is best to compare the costs on a per-unit-cost basis. *F/C UNIT IRRELEVANT.*

__F__ 14. Since opportunity costs really do not require cash outlays, decision makers can safely ignore them.

__F__ 15. The various types of decisions covered in Chapters 5 and 6 are confusing because each requires such different information.

Multiple Choice Questions

For each of the following multiple-choice questions, select the best answer(s) and enter the identification letter(s) in the space provided.

__C__ 1. R. T. Jones presently earns an annual salary of $40,000 as an electrician. She accepts an invitation to join an electrical contracting partnership that promises an annual profit of $48,000 to Jones before the deduction of her $5,000 annual share of overhead costs. The opportunity cost of Jones' decision to join the partnership would be: (a) $5,000, (b) $8,000, (c) $40,000, (d) $43,000.

__D__ 2. See the preceding test item. The opportunity cost of Jones' decision to *not* join the partnership would be: (a) $5,000, (b) $8,000, (c) $40,000, (d) $43,000.

__B/C__ 3. Partha Company is considering buying a major assembly from one of its suppliers. Partha's expected costs of producing 1,000 assemblies include $5,000 fixed manufacturing overhead, $8,000 variable manufacturing overhead, $10,000 prime costs. The freed-up capacity would sit idle, but fixed costs are unavoidable. The relevant costs to compare with the supplier's price include: (a) $5 per unit fixed overhead, (b) $10 per unit prime cost, (c) $8 per unit variable overhead, (d) all of the above.

10 PRIME
8 VC
$18,000/1000 = 18

__C/D__ 4. Three products emerge from a joint process at a joint cost of $6,000, to be shared equally by the three products. Product C can either be sold for $5,000 after further processing costs of $7,000 or disposed of after split-off at a cost of $3,000. Amounts relevant to the decision about Product C include: (a) $6,000 joint cost, (b) $2,000 share of joint cost, (c) further processing cost of $7,000, (d) disposal cost of $3,000.

__B/C__ 5. Two products emerge from a joint process. Product H has no sales value immediately after split-off but would have a sales value of $15,000 after additional separable processing costs of $13,000 and allocated joint costs of $3,000. Product J could be sold at split-off for $4,000 or for $8,000 after further processing of $10,000 and allocated joint costs of $2,000. (a) Product H should be sold at the split-off point, (b) Product H should be separately processed after split-off before being sold, (c) Product J should be sold at the split-off point, (d) Product J should be separately processed after split-off before being sold.

$2000 H
SELL J

Relevant Information and Decision Making: Part Two **87**

__C__ 6. Obsolete inventory that cost $50,000 is on hand, but its scrap value is only $15,000. The inventory could be sold for $60,000 if converted into another form at an additional cost of $48,000. The *overall result* of converting and selling the inventory would be: (a) profit of $12,000, (b) profit of $27,000, (c) loss of $3,000, (d) profit of $15,000.

__B__ 7. See the preceding item. The decision should be: (a) do nothing, (b) sell the inventory for the $15,000 scrap value, (c) convert the inventory into another form and sell it for the $60,000, (d) hold the inventory at its $50,000 cost.

__A,B,C,D__ 8. An old machine has a net book value of $20,000 and a current salvage value of $7,000. It could be used for ten more years at an annual cash operating cost of $8,000, or it could be sold now and replaced by a new machine priced at $35,000 with a ten-year life and an annual cash operating cost of $5,000. Neither machine would have a salvage value in ten years. *Ignore income taxes and the time value of money.* Amounts that would be relevant to the replacement decision include: (a) $5,000, (b) $7,000, (c) $8,000, (d) $35,000.

__B__ 9. See item 6 above. If the old machine is replaced, there would be: (a) a gain of $7,000 on the sale, (b) a loss of $13,000 on the sale, (c) an overall benefit of $2,000, (d) an overall benefit of $30,000.

__C__ 10. See item 6 above. Assume the old machine was replaced. (Ignore depreciation and income taxes.) In the first year after the replacement of the machine, the overall effect on reported net income would be: (a) $13,000 decrease, (b) $3,000 increase, (c) $10,000 decrease, (d) $11,500 decrease.

Completion

Complete each of the following statements by filling in the blanks.

1. Future costs that are relevant to decisions can properly include both _____ and _____ types of costs if they are expected to change and differ among the alternative actions.

2. In an equipment-replacement situation, an incentive conflict can be caused by a possible _____ or _____ on the disposal of the old equipment because _____.

3. Relevant to equipment-replacement decisions is the old equipment's __salvage__ value, but not its __book value__ value.

4. It is usually not profitable to process a joint product beyond the split-off point if the _____ exceeds the _____.

5. _____ is a measure of the _____ foregone by choosing an alternative that excludes another alternative.

6. Relevant to decisions about the disposition of joint products is any _____ cost but not _____.

7. Decisions about the disposition of inventory on-hand depend on _____ and effects on future sales, but not _____.

88 Chapter 6

8. If inventory on-hand is obsolete and cannot be reworked into other products, any price greater than _____ is an acceptable sales price.

9. Separable costs are similar to _____ costs and joint costs are similar to _____ costs.

10. The dangers of using unit costs for decision making are _____ and _____.

Problems

1. Universal Products, Inc. incurs the following costs in making the basket element for its "Sun-Fun" line of picnic accessories:

	Total Cost for 20,000 Units	Cost per Unit
Direct materials	$100,000	$ 5
Direct labor	120,000	6
Variable factory overhead	40,000	2
Fixed factory overhead	140,000 (80)	7
Total costs	$400,000	$20

Another manufacturer offers to sell Universal the same basket for $17 per unit for 20,000 units. Determine whether Universal should make or buy the basket, assuming the capacity now used to make the basket would become idle if it were purchased and that $60,000 of the fixed overhead could be avoided by not making the basket.

2. Midwest Corp. owns and operates 713 retail stores. Expected annual operating results for one of these stores are as follows:

Sales revenues	$520,000
Cost of goods sold and other direct cash operating expenses	490,000

Use the opportunity-cost concept in deciding whether to continue operations of this store or to lease the store building to a noncompeting retailer for $4,000 per month. Building ownership costs are $19,000 per year.   48-RENT $29 vs $30

= $18

3. Nature's Way, Inc. annually produces non-toxic cleaning products T and W from a joint production process costing $195,000 per year. Each product can be sold at the split-off point or further processed before being sold:

Selling Prices per Unit

Product	Quantity	At Split-Off	At Completion	Separable Processing Costs after Split-off
T	20,000	$6	$9	$52,000
W	40,000	4	5	47,000

Analyze whether the individual products should be processed beyond the split-off point.

52 - 20,000(9-6) = 52-60 = $8 Process further

47 - 40(5-4) = 47-40 = $7 sell @ split

4. Celestial Tea Company presents the following data for a machine it owns:

Net book value	$32,000
Present scrap value	$12,000
Estimated remaining useful life	8 yrs
Predicted scrap value at end of useful life	none
Annual cash operating costs	$11,000

A new machine with the same productive capacity is available as follows:

Purchase price	$43,000
Estimated useful life	8 yrs
Predicted scrap value at end of useful life	none
Annual cash operating costs	$ 6,000

a. Ignoring income taxes and the time value of money, make computations on a *total cost basis* to determine which of the two alternatives the company should select: keep the old machine or replace it with the new machine.

	Eight Years Together	
	Keep	Replace
Cash operating costs:	$	$
Add: 11,000 × 8	88,000	
11,000 × 6		66,000
Disposal of old Machine		(12,000)
Purchase price of new machine		43,000
Total costs	$ 88,000	$ 79,000

Conclusion:

b. Use the differential cost approach to reach the same conclusions determined by the total-cost approach.

CHAPTER 6 SOLUTIONS TO PRACTICE TEST QUESTIONS AND PROBLEMS

True or False Statements

1. False — Some future costs may be separable or avoidable and, therefore, would be relevant to planning decisions. Unavoidable fixed costs are not relevant to planning decisions.

2. False — The cost of components in inventory is irrelevant to the make-or-buy decision. Past production costs, however, may be useful for predicting future production costs that are relevant to the "make" option.

3. False — Only the $40 purchase price is relevant to the sourcing decision. The book value (sunk cost) of the machinery is irrelevant since it cannot affect either the purchase cost or the cost of making the part.

4. True — If investing in savings bonds is our highest yielding alternative investment opportunity, foregone savings bond interest is the opportunity cost of investing in stocks. The stock investment must return at least as much as savings bonds to be attractive.

5. True — Opportunity costs are expected costs, but are real nonetheless. To turn the old adage around: "A penny not saved is a penny not earned."

6. False		Joint products are two or more products that are produced simultaneously from a common or joint process.
7. False		Neither the share of joint processing costs nor the total joint processing costs are relevant to the further processing decision. Of course, total joint processing costs are relevant to the decision to continue operating the joint process.
8. True		The past costs are sunk and cannot change or affect future costs of disposal. As in the special-order decision in Chapter 5, however, sales of current inventory below normal sales prices might affect future sales.
9. True		Salvage values are future effects of alternative disposal decisions and are relevant to the decisions.
10. False		Neither the total nor the shares of joint processing costs are relevant to further processing decisions.
11. False		Of the two, only disposal values are relevant to replacement decisions. Book values are useful, however, for predicting tax effects of replacement decisions.
12. True		A manager, who is evaluated on net income, may not replace equipment if the equipment will be sold at a loss because of the adverse effect on current income. Similarly, the manager may be motivated to sell productive equipment if it can be sold at a gain because of the one-time boost to net income. Future periods (without the benefit of the productive equipment) may be adversely affected, however.
13. False		For two reasons: Fixed costs per unit may include irrelevant costs, and fixed costs per unit across alternatives may be computed at different activity levels.
14. False		Managers may ignore them because they do not show up in accounting records, but they are real costs nonetheless. Because opportunity costs are not observable, some companies compare the performance (e.g., net income) of managers reasoning that the highest performing managers are doing a better job of considering opportunity costs.
15. False		The different decisions may be confusing, but it is not because they require different information. Each of these decisions uses remarkably similar information: capacity effects and future revenues and costs that will change because of decisions. Each of these decisions ignores unavoidable costs.

Multiple Choice Questions

1. b		By joining the partnership, Jones foregoes the $40,000 salary, which we assume is her highest-paying alternative. She expects to be $3,000 per year better off as a result.
2. d		The same reasoning applies. She gives up the $43,000 expected profit. She expects to earn $3,000 less by foregoing the $43,000 profit. Perhaps she is willing to give up the $3,000 as the price of security.
3. b, c		The relevant costs include the $10 prime (direct labor plus direct materials) and the $8 variable overhead costs per unit since these would be avoided if Partha purchases the part. The fixed cost of $5,000 is irrelevant in total or per unit because it is unavoidable.

4. c, d Both the further processing cost of $7,000 and the disposal cost of $3,000 are relevant to the disposition of product C. The joint process cost is irrelevant in total or allocated. Incidentally, note that the product would be processed further since the loss of $2,000 is less than the cost of disposal after split-off.

5. b, c The allocations of joint cost are irrelevant to the decisions about H and J. The net sales value of H after further processing is $2,000. The sale of J at split-off would generate $4,000 which is greater than the $2,000 loss that would be realized after further processing.

6. c Sale of the converted inventory would contribute $12,000 to profit, but the opportunity cost of this decision is the contribution foregone by not scrapping the inventory for $15,000. The overall effect is a loss of $3,000, though this figure would never show up on any accounting records.

7. b Selling the inventory for scrap has the higher contribution to profit by $3,000.

8. a, b, c, d The annual cash operating costs of $5,000 or $8,000 are relevant since they will change and differ between the alternatives. The $7,000 salvage value of the old equipment also is relevant, for the same reasons. The $35,000 purchase price of the new equipment is a future cost and is relevant. The $20,000 book value of the old equipment is irrelevant since it is a sunk cost and will not change.

9. b, c The loss on the sale of the old equipment is the salvage value less the book value, $7,000 - $20,000 = -$13,000. Ignoring the time value of money and taxes, the net benefit is $2,000: the $7,000 salvage value of the old equipment plus ten years of $3,000 operating cost savings less the $35,000 purchase price.

10. c Ignoring taxes and depreciation, the first-year effect would be a $10,000 decrease in income: the $13,000 loss on the sale of old equipment plus the $3,000 savings in annual operating costs.

Completion

1. fixed, variable
2. gain, loss, managers are evaluated on the basis of short-run income
3. salvage, book
4. separable cost, sales value
5. Opportunity cost, contribution to profit
6. separable, joint processing cost
7. revenues and costs of disposition, past production or purchase cost
8. zero or disposal costs, if any
9. avoidable, unavoidable
10. including irrelevant costs, computing unit costs at different activity levels

Problems

1. Universal Products, Inc.

   The relevant figures to compare with the $17 purchase price are:
Direct materials	$100,000
Direct labor	120,000
Variable factory overhead	40,000
Avoidable fixed factory overhead	60,000
Total	$320,000÷20,000 units = $16

   The difference in favor of making is $17 - $16 = $1 for 20,000 units or $20,000 total. The same total difference could, of course, also be obtained as follows: (20,000)x($17) - $320,000 = $340,000 - $320,000 = $20,000.

   Note that the unavoidable fixed overhead ($140,000 - $60,000 = $80,000) has been excluded from this analysis as being irrelevant to the decision, because it is not an expected future cost that will differ between the alternatives of making or buying the basket.

2. Midwest Corp.

Sales revenues		$520,000
Less costs:		
Cost of goods sold and other direct cash expenses	$490,000	
Opportunity cost of leasing: 4,000 x 12=	48,000	538,000
Difference in favor of leasing building to noncompeting retailer		$ 18,000

   (Building ownership costs are not relevant because they would be the same under each alternative.)

3. There are at least two equivalent solutions to Nature's Way, Inc.'s decisions:

   (a) Differential analysis:

   T: $52,000 - 20,000x($9 - $6) = $52,000 - $60,000 = $8,000 excess of expected benefit over related costs, *decision:* further process.

   W: $47,000 - 40,000x($5 - $4) = $47,000 - $40,000 = ($7,000) excess of expected costs over related benefit, *decision:* sell at split-off point.

   (b) Opportunity-cost analysis:

   T: (20,000 x $9) - (20,000 x $6) - $52,000

   $180,000 - $120,000 - $52,000

   $8,000, as above.

   W: (40,000 x $5) - (40,000 x $4) - $47,000

   $200,000 - $160,000 - $47,000

94 Chapter 6

($7,000), as above.

Note that the $195,000 joint costs are irrelevant under both of these approaches.

4. Celestial Tea Company

	Eight Years Together	
	Keep	Replace
Cash operating costs: $11,000 x 8	$88,000	-
$6,000 x 8	-	$ 48,000
Disposal value of old machine		(12,000)
Purchase price of new machine	-	43,000
Total costs for 8 years	$88,000	$79,000

Conclusion: Replace old machine because total costs are $9,000 lower for 8 years.

Note that the net book value of the old machine is irrelevant to the decision.

CHAPTER 7

The Master Budget: The Overall Plan

> **MAIN FOCUS AND OBJECTIVES**
>
> The keystone of successful planning and control systems is budgeting. We focus on the master budget, a coordinated set of detailed operating plans for all parts of an organization. This chapter is one of the most detailed so far and requires a basic understanding of financial statements. If you need a review, consult Chapters 18 and 19. Your learning objectives are to :
>
> - Distinguish between master budgets and long-range plans
> - Distinguish between operating and financial budgets
> - Identify advantages of budgets
> - Follow principal steps in preparing the master budget
> - Use cost drivers to prepare budgets
> - Prepare operating budgets and supporting schedules
> - Prepare the financial budget
> - Understand difficulties of sales forecasting
> - Anticipate problems of human behavior toward budgets
> - Use basic financial planning models
> - Use a spreadsheet to develop a budget

REVIEW OF KEY CONCEPTS

A. Budgets are quantitative plans for future operations and financial position targets.
    1. As we saw in Chapter 2, organizations may target certain levels of profit.
        a. Organizations may also target certain levels of cash flow or asset position.

- b. The important issue covered in this chapter is how organizations plan resources in order to achieve those targets.
- c. Most organizations that are successful in meeting their targets do so with the help of the formal planning mechanism called the *master budget*.
- d. This chapter discusses the organizational role, the components, and the preparation of the master budget.

2. Budgets quantitatively express the organization's plans to achieve targets over various time periods.
   - a. **Strategic plans** set overall, long-run goals and objectives of the organization.
   - b. **Long-range plans** set specific financial targets for a 5- or 10-year horizon.
   - c. **Capital budgets** detail capacity-related spending required by long-range plans.
   - d. **Master budgets** summarize the organization's planned activities in the form of *operating budgets* and *financial budgets* for periods of one year or less.
   - e. **Operating budgets** are plans for the basic activities of the organization necessary to support financial or other outcome targets.
   - f. **Financial budgets** are forecasted financial statements that demonstrate the planned achievement of financial objectives (also called **pro forma financial statements**).
   - g. **Continuous** or **rolling budgets** are annual master budgets expressed as 12 monthly targets, wherein as one month ends, another month is added to the budget. For example, the master budget may run from the beginning of June 19X2 to the end of May 19X3. As June 19X2 ends, the first month of the continuous master budget becomes *July* 19X2, and *June* 19X3 is added as the last month of the 12-month continuous master budget.

3. The operating budget consists of supporting plans for the activities of the organization which may include (depending on the nature of the organization):
   - a. Sales budgets (and other cost-driver budgets as necessary), which detail the levels of basic activities necessary to meet financial objectives
   - b. Purchases budgets, which plan resources to be acquired to support basic activities through cash outlays or credit purchases
   - c. Cost of goods or services sold budget, which compute the cost of goods sold expenses to be *recognized*
   - d. Operating expenses budget, which detail all the operating expenses to be *recognized*
   - e. Budgeted income statement, which reflects the effects of sales and other basic activities on income performance for the budget period (In a sense, this is a proof that successful implementation of the preceding plans will result in the targeted income.)

4. The financial budget includes budgets that demonstrate the effects of implementing the operating budget and the capital budget on cash and on financial position. The financial budget includes:

- a. Capital budget
- b. Cash budget, showing sources and uses of cash and ending cash balance
- c. Budgeted balance sheet, showing the period's ending financial position

> See textbook Exhibit 7-1

5. Advantages of budgets to organizations and individuals include:
   - a. Budgets force managers to face the task of planning, to anticipate changing conditions, and to formulate and implement organizational policies to deal with expected changes.
   - b. Budgets force managers to translate plans into explicit terms for evaluating actual performance in the future. Expectations are the best benchmark for evaluating actual performance.
   - c. Budgets force managers to communicate management plans, coordinate plans, and help carry them out.

> Before going on to the next section, be sure that you understand the components and benefits of the master budget.

B. Preparation of the master budget includes the following steps:

1. *The starting point is the ending balance sheet for the prior budget period.* Usually this, too, is a forecasted balance sheet because budgeting for the next period would not wait for the actual end of the current period -- that would be too late.
   - a. The beginning balance sheet shows the resources that the organization will begin the period with (cash, materials, work in process, finished goods, plant and equipment, and so on).
   - b. To meet the period's objectives, these beginning balances may not be sufficient, so subsequent parts of the operating budget detail which additional resources the organization must acquire.

2. Other *essential data* for beginning the master budget are the various *operating and financial characteristics and policies* of the organization. Among others these include:
   - a. Sales collection and bad debt expectations, including credit terms granted to customers
   - b. Payment policies for purchases, acquired services, and operating expenses, including credit terms granted by suppliers
   - c. Inventory policies, including required cash balance
   - d. Sources and terms of short-term financing
   - e. Planned additions or retirements of long-term assets and debt

3. Given the starting position and conditions, the *sales forecast and forecasts of other basic activities drive the rest of the master budget.*
   - a. These forecasts lead to sales budgets and other cost driver budgets. The sales budget identifies the expected pattern of sales during the budget period(s).

> See textbook steps 1a and 1b

b. The sales and cost driver budgets then lead to purchases and disbursements (payments) for purchases budgets for materials and for labor and services.

c. Each part of the operating budget is linked to the previous part by the organization's policies and by simple budget relationships of the form:

Start Desired ending balance of inventoried resource (skip for non-inventoriable resources such as labor and acquired services)
Plus Resources required for sales or cost driver activity
Equals Total resources needed on hand during the period
Less Beginning balance of inventoried resource (skip for non-inventoriable resources)
Equals Total resources to be acquired for the period (equals total resources needed on hand during the period for non-inventoriable resources)

> See textbook steps 1c and 1d

d. Purchases budgets and cost driver activity budgets then lead to operating expense budgets, which *match* costs of resources used to planned sales.

Note Not all expenses are cash outlays of the period. Some, such as depreciation are matching of past cash outlays to sales of the current period.

> See textbook steps 1e and 1f

e. Combining the sales budgets with operating expense budgets generates the budgeted income statement.

> See textbook step 2

f. The cash budget analyzes the period's cash flow and generate the ending cash balance by combining the following components:
The beginning cash balance
The cash portions of the operating budget
The capital budget and plans for long-term debt and equity (not covered here)
Short-term financing policies

> See textbook step 3a

g. The final step of the master budget is to combine the beginning balance sheet, the operating budget, and the cash budget to generate the ending or budgeted balance sheet of the period.

Note Some companies do not prepare budgeted balance sheets due to the size and complexity of the task. Omitting this final step can be a mistake because, by forcing total assets to equal total liabilities and equities, it forces your budget assumptions to be consistent. For example, the assistant controller of General Motors stated at a recent meeting that GM did not (as of 1992) budget balance sheets because to do so was too difficult. But GM would have caught a several hundred million dollar budgeting error before the bills came due if it had. One of the assistant

Master Budget: Overall Plan

controller's new tasks was to figure out how GM could budget balance sheets.

> Do you understand the the linked steps of the master budget process? If you are not sure, review the textbook example again.

C. Sales forecasting is a difficult and critical step in the master budgeting process.
1. A **sales forecast** is a prediction of sales under specified conditions (general economic trends, competitors' actions, advertising levels, and so on). As the underlying conditions change, sales forecasts will change.
    a. Nonprofit and government organizations would forecast demands for services, which would drive their budgets.
    b. Sales forecasts are generated using information from a wide variety of sources:
        - Past sales patterns
        - Sales force estimates
        - General economic conditions
        - Market research studies
        - Competitors' actions
        - Pricing alternatives
        - Product mix alternatives
        - Advertising and sales promotion alternatives
2. A sales budget is the forecast that the organization accepts as a target.
    a. This sales budget or target then determines the conditions that the organization can control -- the operating budget.

D. The budgeting process may seem to be mechanical, but it requires considerable human input to be successful.
1. Individuals realize that budgets serve as both planning tools and benchmarks for their own evaluations.
    a. Individuals may have incentives to disguise their true beliefs in order to make budgets easier to attain.
    b. Organizations, therefore, must design incentives to reinforce good planning, and effective and efficient implementation of budgets. (This important topic is explored further in Chapter 9).
    c. Problems are acute where budgets are used primarily to limit spending as in many government agencies.
2. It is believed that individuals will accept budgeting better and will set challenging objectives for themselves when they are permitted an active role in the budgeting process (called **participative budgeting**).

E. **Financial-planning models** combine cost-volume-profit models of the organization with sales forecasting and the master budget to create powerful, interactive planning tools.
1. Because financial planning models are complex and in order to provide timely advice, they usually are programmed for use on computers.
    a. This allows testing the **sensitivity** of income, cash flows and financial position to various decisions or alternative conditions.

b. These models quickly provide management with predicted effects of many combinations of possible choices and conditions.
c. Spreadsheet software for personal computers has evolved into a necessary tool for financial planning.
d. Spreadsheet software is easy to learn and extremely powerful (though probably not powerful enough yet to permit General Motors to budget its balance sheet).

2. Appendix 7 introduces the use of spreadsheet software for building financial planning models. You should learn how to do this. Virtually any PC-based spreadsheet software will do. Powerful software also is available for mainframe computers (one popular program is IFPS).

3. If possible, you should try to solve your homework problems or the practice test problems in this study guide with spreadsheet software and test the sensitivity to different sales assumptions. Note: this may be time consuming, but it is valuable practice.

> Before going on to the practice test, be sure that you can explain some of the difficulties of sales forecasting and human participation in the budgeting process. If it is possible, you should try to apply Appendix 7 to its example, to your homework, or to this practice test. Spreadsheet software is extremely important in today's environment -- learn to use it if you can.

PRACTICE TEST QUESTIONS AND PROBLEMS WITH SOLUTIONS

True or False Statements

Determine whether each of the following statements is True (T) or False (F) and enter your answer in the space provided.

____1. Pro-forma statements are prepared for comparison with actual financial statements at the conclusion of the budget year.

____2. Strategic planning sets the goals of the organization for the foreseeable future.

____3. The financial budget would include the budgeted balance sheet and the budgeted income statement.

____4. The operating budget would include the cash budget and the production budgets.

____5. As a general rule, the master budget should be based on the actual operating data for the preceding year or on an average of the data for the two or three most recent years.

____6. The main goals of budgets include limiting expenditures and identifying poor performance.

____7. Expected performance is generally considered to be a better basis for judging actual operating results than past performance.

____8. Cash collections from customers are composed of cash sales and (eventually) collections on all credit sales.

____9. In the preparation of a budget for merchandise purchases during a given period, consideration should normally be given to both the desired ending inventory for the period, and the beginning inventory for the period.

____10. The budget for disbursements for operating expenses plans for outlays such as materials, labor, and depreciation.

____11. Budgeted income statements combine sales budgets and operating expense budgets.

____12. Cash available before financing includes the beginning cash balance, cash receipts, and the minimum cash balance.

__T__13. Individuals are more likely to accept the discipline of budgeting if they have an active part in budget participation.

__F__14. Sales forecasting is one of the many skills mastered by managerial accountants.

__F__15. The term financial planning model refers to a computer model of an organization's master budget.

Multiple Choice Questions

For each of the following multiple-choice questions, select the best answer(s) and enter the identification letter(s) in the space provided:

__D__1. Budgets for individual projects requiring an extended period of years for completion are called: (a) rolling budgets, (b) operating budgets, (c) master budgets, (d) capital budgets.

__B__2. Budgets that plan a year's basic activities and the needed resources are called: (a) financial budgets, (b) operating budgets, (c) master budgets, (d) capital budgets.

__C__3. Budgets that plan the organization's ending financial position are called: (a) financial budgets, (b) operating budgets, (c) master budgets, (d) capital budgets.

__B__4. A company had sales last month of $60,000 and expects sales this month of $90,000. One third of all sales are cash sales. Two thirds of all sales are collected in the month following the sale. The company should expect cash collections from sales this month to equal: (a) $60,000, (b) $70,000, (c) $80,000, (d) $90,000.   40 + 30 = $70,000

__B__5. A merchandising company has $64,000 of accounts receivable at April 30. In May it expects to collect 75% of these receivables and 30% of the May sales on account. Its budgeted credit sales for May are $70,000. The budgeted accounts receivable at May 31 would be: (a) $69,000, (b) $65,000, (c) $37,000, (d) $97,000.   64,000 + 70,000 - .75(64,000) - .3(70,000) = 65K

__D__6 The pattern of collections of accounts receivable for a company is 20% in the month of sale, 50% in the following month, and 30% in the month after that. Sales on account were $80,000 for January and $60,000 for February. Budgeted sales for March are $70,000. Compute the budgeted *cash collections* in March: (a) $74,000, (b) $70,000, (c) $68,000, (d) $72,000.

__B__7. See the preceding test item. Compute the budgeted accounts receivable balance on April 1: (a) $56,000, (b) $74,000, (c) $68,000, (d) $80,000.

__A__ 8. A merchandising company forecasts $150,000 of sales for September. Its gross profit rate is 40% of sales, and its August 31 merchandise inventory is $112,000. Compute the budgeted purchases for September if the company wishes to budget an inventory of $112,000 for the end of September: (a) $90,000, (b) $70,000, (c) $80,000, (d) $100,000.

__D__ 9. See the preceding item and assume that all data are the same except that the company is moving to a JIT system and budgets an inventory of $12,000 for the end of September. The budgeted purchases for September would be: (a) $10,000, (b) $20,000, (c) $2,000, (d) zero.

__A__ 10. A company has a $7,200 cash balance at June 1. The budgeted cash transactions for June are receipts of $53,800 and disbursements of $67,500. If the company's minimum June 30 cash balance is $5,000, what is the budgeted amount to be borrowed during June? (a) $11,500, (b) $13,700, (c) $18,700, (d) $16,500.

```
                7200
               +53 800
               -67 500
               -6500
               -5000    (11,500)
```

Completion

Complete each of the following statements by filling in the blanks.

1. A budget that is regularly updated to show a one-year forecast by adding a month or quarter in the future as the month or quarter just ended is dropped is called a _____ budget.

2. The major types of budgets in *order of the length of time they generally cover* are: _____, _____, _____, _____.

3. The advantages to an organization of the budgeting process include: _____, _____, _____.

4. In general, it is usually best to start with forecasts of _____, _____ plus company _____ in constructing a master budget.

5. The operating budget usually consists of: the _____, _____, _____, _____.

6. The financial budget usually consists of the: _____ _____, and _____.

7. Budgeted merchandise purchases for a given period may be computed by adding _____ to budgeted cost of goods sold and subtracting the _____ from this total.

8. The budgeted income statement combines _____, _____ and _____.

9. The budgeted ending cash balance is generally _____ when borrowing is required.

10. The budgeted ending owner's equity should be found two ways:
    (a) _____
    (b) _____.

Master Budget: Overall Plan 103

Problems

1. Given for Maximo Co. (in thousands):

	April Actual	May Actual	June Budgeted	July Budgeted
Cash sales	$ 80	$ 50	$ 60	$ 80
Sales on account	320	200	300	280

Compute the budgeted cash receipts for June and July, assuming credit sales are collected as follows: 15% in month of sale, 60% in the following month, and 25% in the month after that:

JUNE = $60 + .25(320) + .60(200) + .25(80) + .15(300)$
    = $60 + 80 + 120 + 20 + 45$
    = $325 K

JULY = $80 + .15(280) + 300(.60) + 25(200)$
     = $80 + 42 + 180 + 50$
     = $352 K

2. Given for Boxes, Inc.

	April	July
Beginning merchandise inventory	$ 15,400	$ 33,900
Expected sales	160,000	180,000
Desired ending merchandise inventory	21,000	30,000
Expected gross profit rate on sales	30%	40%

Find the budgeted purchases for each month:

EXPECTED CGS (.7)(160K) $112,000 $108,000
         "   (.6)(180)

ADD DESIRED END. INV.   21,000   30,000
                          133,000   138,000

LESS BEGIN. INV.   15,400   33,900
                         $117,600 $104,100

3. Given the data below for Floor Veneer Products, complete the parts of the cash budget necessary to compute "borrowing" or "available for repayments"

	September	November
Beginning cash balance	$16,100	$15,600
Expected cash receipts	62,900	71,600
Expected cash disbursements	45,200	77,300
Minimum ending cash balance desired	12,000	14,000
BEGIN CASH BALANCE	16,100	15,600
RECIEPTS	62,900	71,600
TOTAL AVAILABLE	79,000	87,200
DISBURSEMENT	45,200	77,300
END. CASH BAL.	12,000	14,000
CASH NEEDED	57,200	91,300
a. Borrowing	$ 0	$ 4100
b. Available for repayments	$ 21,800	$ —

4. The Four-Sight Lens Company presented the following balance sheet at March 31, 19X4, the beginning of a budget period:

ASSETS			LIABILITIES AND OWNER'S EQUITY	
Current assets:			Current liabilities:	
Cash		$ 9,500	Accounts payable	$27,700
Accounts receivable		33,300	Accrued taxes payable	4,200
Merchandise inventory		66,600	Total current liabilities	$ 31,900
Total current assets		$109,400	Owners' equity	104,500
Plant and equipment		$45,000	Total liabilities and owners' equity	$136,400
Less accumulated depreciation		18,000		
Net plant and equipment		27,000		
Total assets		$136,400		

Master Budget: Overall Plan 105

The company's budgeted operations for the month of April 19X4 are shown below:

Cash receipts:		Other transactions and information:	
From cash sales	$14,800	Sales of merchandise on account	$25,000
From collections of accounts receivable	20,100	Purchases of merchandise (all on account)	18,500
Total	$34,900	Depreciation of plant and equipment	300
Cash disbursements:		Additional accrued taxes	1,200
For operating expenses	$14,500	Cost of goods sold	22,300
For payments on accounts payable	17,000	Minimum ending cash balance desired	9,000
Total	$31,500	Interest rate on borrowed funds	12%

Please resist the temptation to look at the solution until you have attempted your own solution. Using the forms provided below, prepare the following:

- The detailed budget schedules, (a) through (h), for April 19X4.
- The budgeted income statement for April 19X4.
- Budgeted statement of cash receipts and disbursements for April 19X4.
- The budgeted balance sheet at April 30, 19X4.

Detailed budget schedules:

(a) Sales for April 19X4:

Cash sales	14,800
Sales on account	25,000
Total budgeted sales for April 19X4	$39,800

(b) Cash balance at April 30, 19X4:

CASH MARCH	$9,500
BUDGETED APRIL CASH RECEIPTS	34,900
TOTAL	$44,400
LESS DISBURSEMENTS	31,500
BUDGETED CASH BALANCE	12,900

(c) Accounts receivable at April 30, 19X4:

A/R MARCH	$33,300
SALE OF MERCH ON ACC.	25,000
TOTAL	$58,300
LESS BUDGETED CASH COLLECT.	20,100
	38,200

(d) Merchandise inventory at April 30, 19X4:

MARCH END INV.	$66,600
BUDGETED PURCHASES	18,500
TOTAL	85,100
LESS CGS	22,300
BUDGET MERCH. INV. APRIL	62,800

(e) Accumulated depreciation at April 30, 19X4:

ACCUMULATED DEPRECIATION	18,000
BUDGETED DEPRECIATION	300
TOTAL DEPRECIATION	18,300

(f) Accounts payable at April 30, 19X4:

MARCH A/P	27,700
MERCH. PURCH ON ACCOUNT	18,500
TOTAL	46,200
LESS BUDGETED PAYMENTS	17,000
BUD A/P APRIL 30	29,200

(g) Accrued taxes payable at April 30, 19X4:

MARCH TAX PAY.	$4,200
ADD ADDITIONAL TAX	1,200
BUDGETED TOTAL TAX PAY	5400

(h) Owners' equity at April 30, 19X4:

OWNERS EQUITY	$104,500
NET INCOME	1,500
OWNER EQUITY	103,000

Budgeted income statement:

Sales (Schedule a)	$39,800
Less CGS	22,300
Gross Margin	$17,500
Less operating expenses: OP. EXP.	14,500
DEPRECIATION	300
TAXES	1,200
Total expenses	16,000
Net income	$1,500

Budgeted Statement of Cash Receipts and Disbursements

Cash balance, beginning	9,500
Cash receipts:	34,900
Collections from customers	34,900
Total cash available, before financing	44,400
Cash disbursements	31,500
Minimum cash balance	9,000
Total cash needed	40,500
Excess (~~deficiency~~)	+3,900
Financing:	∅
Borrowing	∅
Repayments	∅
Interest (at 12% per annum)	∅
Total Cash increase (decrease) from financing	∅
Cash balance, ending 44,400 - 31,500	$12,900

Budgeted balance sheet:

Current assets:	
Cash	12,900
Total current assets A/R + INV 38,200 + 62,800	101,000 $113,900
Plant and equipment	45,000
Less accumulated depreciation (Schedule e)	(18,300)
Net plant and equipment	$26,700
Total assets	$140,600
Current liabilities:	
A/P	29,200
TAX P	5,400
Total current liabilities	34,600
Owner's equity (Schedule h)	103,000
Total liabilities and owner's equity	$104,600

CHAPTER 6 SOLUTIONS TO PRACTICE QUESTIONS AND PROBLEMS

True or False Statements

1. True — But this is not the primary reason for preparing the pro-forma financial statements. These statements are prepared as part of the master budget process. Planning is the primary purpose of the statements.

2. True — Strategic planning is concerned with the long-run goals of the organization, but does not set immediate objectives.

3. False — The budgeted balance sheet is part of the financial budget, but, generally, the budgeted income statement is considered part of the operations budget.

4. False — Productions budgets are parts of the operations budget, but the cash budget is considered part of the financial budget.

5. False — The master budget should be based on expectations for the coming year. Past operating results are helpful only to the extent that they help the organization understand cost behavior, implementation problems, and help predict future events.

6. False — The main goals of budgets are planning, coordinating and communicating, as well as providing a benchmark for evaluating performance. Limiting expenditures is not a planning function, but in some organizations (particularly governmental) approved budgets are legal constraints on spending.

7. True — Expectations of future performance should be based on the best planning and forecasting that is feasible. Expectations state what should be achieved. Past performance may be completely unrelated to current performance.

8. False — Not all sales are collectible; you must make some allowance for uncollectible sales.

9. True — Budgeted purchases are equal to the required ending balance plus sales or production requirements less the beginning balance.

10. False — Materials and labor may require cash outlays, but depreciation is recognition of the use of past outlays.

11. True — The budgeted income statement collects plans for sales and subtracts all operating expenses, but also includes interest expense.

12. False — Cash available before financing does include the beginning cash balance and cash receipts, but the minimum cash balance is part of "total cash required."

13. True — Or at least this is what most studies have shown, and this conclusion is intuitively appealing. One would especially expect to see benefits from participative budgeting in organizations that are implementing JIT approaches, where employees at all levels must be involved in managing productive processes. Participative budgeting is still controversial, though.

14. False — Some management accountants may be skilled in sales forecasting, but this is not part of most management accountants' jobs. Management accountants take sales forecasts from forecasting experts as the starting point for building master budgets and analyzing actual results.

15. False — Financial planning models existed long before there were computers (if you can imagine such a time) in the form of manually prepared master budgets. Before computers, however, revising these manual models was extremely time consuming and was not done often. This may be the origin of the belief that the budget is an inflexible prescription of what future results must be; it was just too hard to revise plans in a timely manner. Now almost all financial planning models use some sort of powerful spreadsheet software.

Multiple Choice Questions

1. d. Capital budgets analyze the viability of individual, long-term projects. The cash flows from accepted capital budgets are inputs to the cash budgets of each period's master budget.

2. b — Operating budgets plan a year's basic activities and the needed resources. Financial budgets determine the effects of operations and other financing activities on cash and financial position. Master budgets combine operating and financial budgets.

3. c — Financial budgets determine the effects of operations and other financing activities on cash and financial position.

4. b — Cash collections should equal $1/3(\$90,000) + 2/3(\$60,000) = \$70,000$.

5. b The ending accounts receivable balance should equal the beginning balance plus credit sales less collections: $64,000 + $70,000 - .75 \times $64,000 - .30 \times $70,000 = $65,000.

6. d See the column total under March below.

Collections

Month	Sales	January	February	March	March A/R
January	80,000	16,000	40,000	24,000	
February	60,000	-	12,000	30,000	18,000
March	70,000	-	-	14,000	56,000
				68,000	74,000

7. b See the column total under March A/R (accounts receivable) above.

8. a The purchase amount is calculated as follows:

Desired ending balance	$112,000
Required for sales	
$150,000 x .6	90,000
Total required	$202,000
Less beginning balance	$112,000
Purchases	$ 90,000

9. d There is an excess of inventory, so no purchase is necessary, as shown below:

Desired ending balance	$ 12,000
Required for sales	
$150,000 x .6	90,000
Total required	$102,000
Less beginning balance	$112,000
Excess inventory	$ 10,000

10. a The amount of borrowing is the cash available less the cash required: $7,200 + $53,800 - $67,500 - $5,000 = the cash deficiency = $11,500.

Completion

1. continuous or rolling budget

2. strategic plan, long range plan, capital budget, master budget

3. formalizing planning, evaluating performance, coordinating efforts

4. sales forecasts or sales budgets, other cost driver activities, policies

5. sales budget, purchases budget, cost of goods sold budget, operating expenses budget, budgeted income statement

6. cash budget, capital budget, budgeted balance sheet

7. required ending balance, beginning balance

8. sales forecasts, sales budgets, operating expense budgets

9. the required minimum cash balance

10. (a) Beginning owners' equity plus net income plus capital contributions less dividends or withdrawals

(b) Total assets less total liabilities

Problems

1. **Maximo Co.**

June: 60 + 25%(320) + 60%(200) + 15%(300) = 60 + 80 + 120 + 45 = 305

July: 80 + 25%(200) + 60%(300) + 15%(280) = 80 + 50 + 180 + 42 = 352

2. **Boxes, Inc.**

	April	July
Expected cost of goods sold:		
70%(160,000)	$112,000	
60%(180,000)		$108,000
Add desired ending inventory	21,000	30,000
Total needs	$133,000	$138,000
Less beginning inventory	15,400	33,900
Budgeted merchandise purchases	$117,600	$104,100

3. **Floor Veneer Products**

	September	November
Beginning cash balance	$16,100	$15,600
Add expected cash receipts	62,900	71,600
Total available before current financing (a)	$79,000	$87,200
Expected cash disbursements	$45,200	$77,300
Add minimum ending cash balance desired	12,000	14,000
Total cash needed (b)	$57,200	$91,300
1. Necessary to borrow: (b) - (a)		$4,100
2. Available for repayment of loans and interest: (a) - (b)	$21,800	

4. **Four-Sight Lens Company**

Budget schedules:

(a) Sales for April 19X4:

Cash sales	$14,800
Sales on account	25,000
Total budgeted sales for April 19X4	$39,800

(b) Cash balance at April 30, 19X4:

Cash balance at March 31, 19X4	$9,500
Add total budgeted cash receipts for April	34,900
Total	$44,400
Less total budgeted cash disbursements for April	31,500
Budgeted cash balance at April 30, 19X4	12,900

(c) Accounts receivable at April 30, 19X4:

Accounts receivable at March 31, 19X4	$33,300
Add budgeted sales on account for April	25,000
Total	$58,300
Less budgeted cash collections on account for April	20,100
Budgeted accounts receivable at April 30, 19X4	$38,200

(d) Merchandise inventory at April 30, 19X4:

Merchandise inventory at March 31, 19X4	$66,600
Add budgeted purchases for April	18,500
Total	85,100
Less budgeted cost of goods sold for April	22,300
Budgeted merchandise inventory at April 30, 19X4	$62,800

(e) Accumulated depreciation at April 30, 19X4:

Accumulated depreciation at March 31, 19X4	$18,000
Add budgeted depreciation for April	300
Budgeted accumulated depreciation at April 30, 19X4	$18,300

(f) Accounts payable at April 30, 19X4:

Accounts payable at March 31, 19X4	$27,700
Add budgeted merchandise purchases on account for April	18,500
Total	$46,200
Less budgeted payments on accounts payable for April	17,000
Budgeted accounts payable at April 30, 19X4	$29,200

(g) Accrued taxes payable at April 30, 19X4:

Accrued taxes payable at March 31, 19X4	$ 4,200
Add additional accrued taxes budgeted for April	1,200
Budgeted accrued taxes payable at April 30, 19X4	5,400

(h) Owner's equity at April 30, 19X4:

Owners' equity at March 31, 19X4	$104,500
Add budgeted net income for April (from budgeted income statement for April)	1,500
Budgeted owners' equity at April 30, 19X4	$106,000

Budgeted income statement:

Sales (Schedule a)	$ 39,800
Less cost of goods sold	22,300
Gross margin on sales	$ 17,500
Less expenses:	
Operating expenses	$14,500
Depreciation	300
Taxes	1,200
Total expenses	16,000
Net income	1,500

Budgeted Statement of Cash Receipts and Disbursements:

Cashbalance, beginning	$9,500
Cash receipts:	
Collections from customers	<u>34,900</u>
Total cash available, before financing	<u>$44,400</u>
Cash disbursements	31,500
Minimum cash balance	<u>9,000</u>
Total cash needed	<u>$40,500</u>
Excess (deficiency)	$ 3,900
Financing:	
Borrowing	0
Repayments	0
Interest (at 12% per annum)	0
Total cash increase (decrease) from financing	0
Cash balance ending ($44,400 - $31,500)	<u>$12,900</u>

Budgeted balance sheet

Current assets:	
Cash (Schedule b)	$12,900
Accounts receivable (Schedule c)	38,200
Merchandise inventory (Schedule d)	<u>62,800</u>
Total current assets	<u>$113,900</u>
Plant and equipment	$45,000
Less accumulated depreciation (Schedule e)	<u>18,300</u>
Net plant and equipment	<u>26,700</u>
Total assets	<u>$140,600</u>
Current liabilities:	
Accounts payable (Schedule f)	$29,200
Accrued taxes payable (Schedule g)	<u>5,400</u>
Total current liabilities	$ 34,600
Owners' equity (Schedule h)	<u>106,000</u>
Total liabilities and owners' equity	<u>$140,600</u>

CHAPTER 8

Flexible Budgets and Standards for Control

MAIN FOCUS AND OBJECTIVES

This chapter develops budgeting systems for performance evaluation by utilizing the underlying activities that drive master budgets. By reformatting the master budget using *actual* driving activities that differ from budgeted activities, one creates a *flexible budget* that is a more informative benchmark for actual performance than the original master budget. Your learning objectives are to:

- Distinguish between flexible and master budgets
- Use flexible budget formulas
- Understand evaluation implications of master and flexible budgets
- Compute flexible budget and sales-activity variances
- Distinguish between expected and standard costs
- Compute price and usage variances

REVIEW OF KEY CONCEPTS

A. Master budgets are static, that is they do not change even if the underlying sales and other cost-driver activities do change.

    1. One of the major roles of the master budget is to provide a benchmark for evaluating actual performance.
        a. Recall from Chapter 1 the common form of the performance report:
Actual result - Expected result = Variance
        b. When the "expected result" is the master budget, say the budgeted income statement, the performance report variance is called the **master-budget variance**.
- When actual revenue exceeds master-budget revenue, the master-budget variance is "Favorable." (and vice-versa)
- When an actual cost or expense exceeds master-budget cost or expense, the master-budget variance is "Unfavorable." (and vice-versa)

> See textbook Exhibit 8-1

    c.   The shortcoming of the master-budget variance is that it is the net result of at least two underlying causes:
- Differences in underlying sales and other cost driver activity that cause total costs and revenue to differ from the master budget.
- Differences in revenue and costs per unit of activity that cause costs and revenue in total to differ from the master budget.

    d.   From the master-budget variance alone, managers cannot determine why actual results differed from the master budget. Since each cause has different control implications, it would be useful to separate their effects.

    e.   The *flexible budget* is used to attribute part of the master budget to different activity levels and the other part to differences in revenue and costs per unit of activity.

> Before going on to the next section, be sure that you understand that we have re-introduced the concept of a variance from Chapter 1 and have applied it to the master budget from Chapter 7. Can you explain two possible causes of a master budget variance?

B.   The **flexible budget** is part or all of a master budget that is prepared for the actual (or any) levels of sales and other cost driver activities.

    1.   Contrast with a master budget, which is tied to a single level of underlying activities

    2.   Obviously, use of a computerized financial planning model makes preparation of flexible budgets relatively easy because the model contains the quantitative relationships between activity levels and revenues or expenses, but flexible budgets can be prepared manually, too.

    3.   The relationships between activities and costs and revenues can be called *flexible-budget formulas*, but they are just the revenue and cost *functions* developed and used in previous chapters.

        a.   Recall for *strictly variable costs*, this formula is the *cost per unit of cost driver activity*, as shown in the upper part of Exhibit 8-2.

> See textbook Exhibit 8-2

        b.   For *fixed and step costs,* the flexible-budget formula is simply the total budgeted amounts per budget period, as illustrated in the lower part of Exhibit 8-2.

        c.   The relationship between these two formulas is identical to the relationships discussed in Chapters 2 and 3.

> See textbook Exhibit 8-3.

> Before going on to the next section be sure that you understand that by introducing the flexible budget we are combining concepts of CVP relationships, cost behavior, and the master budget. All the elements of the flexible budget should already be familiar to you.

C. The master budget variance can be split into two variances by "inserting the flexible budget between the master budget and actual results."

1. This is an important result because each variance can be attributed to differences in either activity levels or per unit revenues and variable costs and fixed costs per period.
    a. For simplicity, the textbook chapter and this studyguide chapter *assume that the only relevant activity level is sales activity.*
    b. In practice, multiple activity levels can be used for different portions of the master budget and flexible budget.
    c. The concept of what follows is applicable to activities other than sales.
    d. Note how the flexible budget is "inserted" between the master budget and actual results for a model income statement:

	Actual results at actual activity level	Flexible budget variances	Flexible budget for actual activity	Activity variances	Master budget
Units	xxx	xx	xxx	xx	xxx
Sales	xxx	xx	xxx	xx	xxx
Variable costs	xxx	xx	xxx	xx	xxx
Contribution margin	xxx	xx	xxx	xx	xxx
Fixed costs	xxx	xx	xxx	xx	xxx
Operating income	xxx	xx	xxx	xx	xxx

Total flexible-budget variances | *Total activity-level variances*

Total master-budget variances

  e. The variances are defined below.
  f. Another explanation follows:

Master budget	−	Actual result	=	Master-budget variance
(Master budget − Flexible budget)	−	(Actual result − Flexible budget)	=	Master-budget variance
Sales-activity variance	+	*Flexible-budget variance*	=	Master-budget variance

  g. Mathematically, the second line above, with the flexible budget inserted, is identical to the first (the flexible budgets "cancel out.")

2. The **sales-activity variance** is the difference between the master-budget amount and the flexible-budget amount.
    a. The underlying cause of the sales-activity variance is that actual sales activity was different than expected in the master budget.
    b. The sales-activity variance is the portion of the master-budget variance attributed to sales activity.

    > See textbook Exhibit 8-4

    c. The sales-activity variance can be split into various contributing causes, but that is beyond the scope of this textbook.

3. The **flexible-budget variance** is the difference between the flexible-budget amount and the actual result.

Flexible Budgets and Standards for Control 117

        a. The underlying cause of the flexible-budget variance is that actual fixed costs per period or per unit revenues or variable costs differed from expectations.
        b. The flexible budget variance is the portion of the master-budget variance attributed cost and revenue control.

> See textbook Exhibit 8-5

        c. Later we learn to split the flexible budget variance into several contributing causes.

> Do you understand how to split the master budget variance into a sales-activity effect and a flexible-budget effect? Do you understand what these two effects mean?

D. Master budgets and flexible budgets are constructed using *expected costs* or *standard costs*:

  1. An **expected cost** is the cost that is *most likely to be attained*.

  2. A **standard cost** is a carefully predetermined cost that *should be attained* (which may be the same as the expected cost).

  3. A **standard cost system** is an inventory valuation and control system that values inventories at standard costs only.
        a. Differences between standard costs and actual costs are charged to income.
        b. *Using standard costs for budgeting does not require using a standard cost system for inventories.*
        c. In practice, some companies use multiple cost systems for multiple purposes. This is because a single cost system that would support all decision making and financial reporting would be too expensive -- an application of the cost-benefit criterion.

> See the boxed example in the textbook

        d. In this textbook and studyguide, we consider only the budgeting and performance evaluation uses of standard costs.
        e. In budgeting and performance evaluation, the terms expected cost and standard cost are often used interchangeably.

  4. **Perfection standards,** also called **ideal standards,** are expressions of the absolutely minimum unit costs possible under the best conceivable conditions, using current specifications and facilities.
        a. These are not widely used for budgeting or performance evaluation.
        b. Perfection standards are thought to have adverse motivational effects since they can never be attained and always result in unfavorable cost variances.
        c. Perfection standards do direct attention to inefficiencies in the organization.

  5. **Currently attainable standards** represent costs that should be incurred under very efficient operations.
        a. These are widely used for budgeting and evaluation.

  b. These standards do make allowances for normal shrinkage, spoilage, lost time, and equipment breakdowns.

  c. Currently attainable standards usually have a *desirable motivational effect* on employees because, although difficult to reach, they are reasonable goals.

6. **Managers may trade-off variances.**

  a. For example, a manager may consider reducing material costs by buying lower quality materials even though this might cause higher labor costs due to more required rework of defective products.

  b. Trading off variances can be beneficial, but it is a dangerous practice since the tradeoff may be unfavorable.

  c. If standards or expectations are set carefully, they take into account the most favorable tradeoffs of various costs. Usually managers should try to change the standards rather than trying to informally change the tradeoffs.

7. Decisions to investigate variances balance the costs of investigating versus the costs of not investigating.

  a. Costs of investigating include managers' and other employees' time and downtime for equipment and processes.

  b. Costs of not investigating include allowing costs to be uncontrolled in the future.

  c. As discussed in Chapter 9, standard cost variances tend to not be very useful for control of operations where quick feedback is necessary -- more timely and relevant measures are available (e.g., defects, yields).

  d. Standard cost variances are more useful for periodic performance evaluations. Explanations of large variances serve to inform higher-level managers about the quality of lower-level managers -- how problems were resolved.

> Can you explain the different types of standards, their advantages and disadvantages? Which are the most widely used for budgeting and performance evaluation? Why?

E. Flexible-budget cost variances can be split into several effects: *price* of inputs and *usage* of inputs.

> See textbook Exhibit 8-6

1. We define **price variances** for direct materials, direct labor, and variable overhead items like supplies are computed as:

> Price variance = (Actual input) x (Expected price - actual price)

This is the portion of the flexible budget variance due to spending a different amount per unit for inputs than expected.

Flexible Budgets and Standards for Control

2. We define **usage variances** for inputs as:

> Usage variance = (Expected price)x(Expected input - actual input)

   a. This is the portion of the flexible budget variance due to using an amount of input different than expected.
   b. The "expected input" in the above formula is more formally known as the *standard input allowed for the output achieved.*
   c. Usage variances are also known as *efficiency* variances, but efficiency includes both spending and usage, so the term efficiency variance is misleading.

3. Flexible-budget variable overhead variances can be split similarly.

4. Another approach to computing price and usage variances is to split the flexible-budget variance into two complementary effects in much the same way as we split the master-budget variance.
   a. We split the master-budget variance by inserting the flexible budget between the master budget and the actual result.
   b. We can split the flexible-budget variance by inserting a *flexible budget based on actual inputs at expected prices*, between the previous flexible budget (which uses *expected inputs* for the outputs achieved *and expected prices*) and actual results.

> See textbook Exhibits 8-7 and 8-8

   c. For another explanation see below:

Actual result	−	Flexible budget (at expected inputs and expected prices)	=	Flexible-budget variance
(Actual result − Flexible budget at *actual* inputs and *expected* prices)	−	(Flexible budget at expected inputs and expected prices − Flexible budget at *actual* inputs and *expected* prices)	=	Flexible budget variance
Price variance	+	Usage variance	=	Flexible-budget variance

   c. Note that the two entries for *flexible budget at actual inputs and expected prices* cancel out in the second equation, leaving the first equation.
   d. The only difference between the actual result and the *flexible budget at actual inputs and expected prices* is the difference between actual and expected prices. Thus, the first part of the second equation is the price variance.
   e. The only difference between the two flexible budgets in the second part of the second equation is the difference between actual and expected usage of inputs. The second part of this equation is the usage variance.

> Before going on to the practice test, be sure that you understand how the flexible budget variance is split into price and usage effects. There are several ways to perform this analysis -- use the approach that makes the most sense to you -- they are equivalent.

PRACTICE TEST QUESTIONS AND PROBLEMS WITH SOLUTIONS

True or False Statements

Determine whether each of the following statements is True (T) or False (F) and enter your answer in the space provided:

__T__ 1. Comparisons between the master budget and the actual result obscure the effects of sales activity and efficiency.

__F__ 2. Using flexible budgets is really only feasible in large firms with computerized financial planning models.

__F__ 3. Multiplying actual levels of a direct input used by the flexible budget formula yields the flexible budget for that input which is compared to the master budget and the actual result.

__T__ 4. The sales-activity variance is the difference between the flexible budget and the master budget.

__T__ 5. The sales-activity variance is the difference between the master-budget variance and the flexible-budget variance.

__F__ 6. Flexible budgeting is only possible if one assumes that sales activity is the only cost driver.

__F__ 7. Flexible budget variances measure how effective an organization was in achieving its objectives. (EFFICIENCY OF OPERATIONS)

__F__ 8. Use of standard costs for budgeting and performance evaluation is really only feasible in companies that use standard cost systems.

__F__ 9. Currently attainable standards have little motivating impact because they require little or no effort to achieve.

__T__ 10. That some firms use multiple costs systems is evidence that current cost systems are not adequate for both decision-making and financial reporting needs.

__F__ 11. Perfection standards tend to have a positive effect on employee motivation because they direct attention to correctable inefficiencies.

__T__ 12. An unfavorable material usage variance could be calculated by multiplying the quantity of excess materials used by standard material unit prices.

__F__ 13. The labor usage variance is found by multiplying the actual labor cost per hour by the difference between the actual labor hours and the standard hours allowed for the actual number of product units produced.

__T__ 14. Labor price variances are usually the responsibility of the same manager who is in charge of labor usage.

__T__ 15. Generally, the cost variances that are more subject to immediate management control are usage variances.

Multiple Choice Questions

For each of the following multiple choice questions determine the best answer(s) and enter the identification letter(s) in the space provided.

__c__ 1. The master budget variance is the difference between: (a) flexible budget and master budget, (b) actual result and flexible budget, (c) master budget and actual result, (d) total costs at actual prices and actual inputs and master budget.

__A/D__ 2. The flexible-budget variance is the difference between: (a) flexible budget and actual results, (b) master budget and flexible budget, (c) actual results and master budget, (d) actual results and the budget at standard prices and standard inputs allowed for the outputs achieved.

__A__ 3. A summary of performance showed three amounts for variable costs: actual $180,000, master budget $185,000, and flexible budget $170,000. The sales-activity variance is: (a) $15,000 favorable, (b) $5,000 favorable, (c) $10,000 unfavorable, (d) $5,000 unfavorable.   185 - 170 = +15 F

__c__ 4. See the preceding test item. The flexible-budget variance is: (a) $15,000 favorable, (b) $5,000 favorable, (c) $10,000 unfavorable, (d) $5,000 unfavorable.
170 - 180 = -$10 (U)

__D__ 5. A summary of performance showed three figures for contribution margin: flexible budget $90,000, master budget $110,000, and actual results $92,000. The sales-activity variance is: (a) $2,000 favorable, (b) $2,000 unfavorable (c) $18,000 favorable, (d) $20,000 unfavorable.   M-F = 110-90 = 20(U)

__a__ 6. See the preceding test item. The flexible budget variance is: (a) $2,000 favorable, (b) $2,000 unfavorable (c) $18,000 favorable, (d) $20,000 unfavorable.

__c__ 7. There is no conceptual difference between a budget amount and a standard amount if standards are: (a) ideal standards, (b) perfection standards, (c) currently attainable standards, (d) flexible standards.

__D__ 8. The main flexible-budget variances are: (a) price and rate, (b) usage and efficiency, (c) usage and quantity, (d) price and usage.

__a__ 9. For most effective control, material price variances should be measured at the time materials are: (a) purchased, (b) used, (c) sold to customers, (d) issued to production.

__a__ 10. Data for a certain operation included a $9 standard wage rate per hour, a $10 actual wage rate per hour, 800 actual labor-hours used, 250 product units produced, and 3 standard labor-hours allowed per product unit. The labor price variance is: (a) $800 unfavorable, (b) $800 favorable, (c) $450 unfavorable, (d) $500 unfavorable.   (10-9)(800) = $800(U)

__c__ 11. See the preceding test item. The labor usage variance is: (a) $800 unfavorable, (b) $800 favorable, (c) $450 unfavorable, (d) $500 unfavorable.

(800 - 750) × 9 =
50 × 9 = 450 (U)

TYPO ≈ 130# ≠ 110#

__D__ 12. Data for a certain operation included a $20 standard material cost per pound, a $19 actual material cost per pound, 130 actual material pounds used, 30 product units produced, and 4 standard material pounds allowed per product unit. The material price variance is: (a) $190 favorable, (b) $200 unfavorable, (c) $200 favorable, (d) $110 favorable.   (20-19) × 110 = 110 F

__C__ 13. See the preceding test item. The material usage variance is: (a) $190 favorable, (b) $200 unfavorable, (c) $200 favorable, (d) $110 favorable.

(30×4) - 130 = -10 (20)
                   200 (U)

Completion

Complete each of the following statements by filling in the blanks.

1. Comparisons of actual results with _prior periods results_ are not as useful as comparisons with _the master budget_ or _flexible budget_.

2. The flexible-budget variance is the difference between the _static budget_ variance and the _flexible budget_ variance.

3. The master budget is also called the _static budget_ and the flexible budget is also called the _variable budget_.

4. The difference between a flexible-budget formula and a cost function is _nothing - they are the same_.

5. Standard costs that make no allowance for lost time, spoilage, shrinkage, or equipment breakdowns are called _perfect or ideal_ standards.

6. Activity-level variances are due to _differences in planned activity levels_.

7. The decision to investigate variances is a tradeoff between _cost of investigating_ and _cost of not investigating_.

8. Managers may _trade-off_ variances because the _performance_ in one area is linked to the _performance_ in another.

9. Material price variances are the responsibility of either the _purchasing agent_ or _production manager_.

10. The material price variance is computed as the difference between actual and standard _____ multiplied by _____.

Flexible Budgets and Standards for Control 123

Problems

1. Data-Bilt, Inc. presents the following data pertaining to its total manufacturing costs for a given month:

Master budget sales for 8,000 units	$800,000
Actual sales of 7,000 units	730,000
Actual variable costs of producing 7,000 units	248,000
Actual fixed costs of producing 7,000 units	220,000
Flexible-budget cost formula:	$200,000 plus $40 per unit

    Complete the following analysis:

    Use F for favorable variances and U for unfavorable variances.

	Actual results at actual activity level	Flexible budget variances	Flexible budget for actual activity	Activity variances	Master budget
Units	7,000	—	7,000	1,000 U	8,000
Sales	730,000	30,000 (F)	700,000	100,000 U	800,000
Variable costs	248,000	32,000 (F)	280,000	40,000 F	320,000
Contribution margin	482,000	62,000 (F)	420,000	60,000 (U)	480,000
Fixed costs	220,000	20,000 (U)	200,000	—	200,000
Operating income	262,000	42,000 (F)	220,000	60,000 (U)	$280,000

    Total flexible-budget variances: 42,000 (F)

    Total activity-level variances: 60,000 (U)

    Total master-budget variances: 18,000 (U)

2. Primordial Co., which uses standard costs and a flexible budget, provides the following data for its operations during last month:

Finished units produced	500 units
Standard material allowed per product unit	5 kg
Standard price per kilogram	$10
Actual price per kilogram	$11
Total material actually used	2,600 kg

Show calculation of material costs and variances in the format given below. Use F for favorable variances and U for unfavorable variances.

Actual cost: Actual inputs x Actual prices $(2600)(11) = \underline{28,600}$	Flexible budget: Actual inputs x Expected prices $(26,000)(10) = \underline{26,000}$	Flexible budget: Expected prices x Standard inputs allowed $(500)(5)(10) = \underline{25,000}$

2,600 (U) Material price variance	1,000 (U) Material usage variance

3,600 (U) Total flexible-budget variance for material

3. Superb Corporation, which uses standard costs and a flexible budget, provides the following data for its operations during the first week in April:

Finished product units produced	3,000 units
Direct material:	
Purchases	9,000 lb
Standard price per pound	$8
Actual price per pound	$7
Pounds used in production	7,000 lb
Standard quantity allowed per product unit	2 lb

Suppose the company is organized so that the purchasing manager bears the primary responsibility for the acquisition prices of materials, and the production manager bears the primary responsibility for the efficient use of materials but no responsibility for unit prices.

Show computations of direct material costs and variances in the analysis framework given below. Use F for favorable variances and U for unfavorable variances.

Control point	Actual cost: Actual quantity x Actual price	Actual quantity x Standard price	Flexible budget: Standard price x Standard quantity allowed for output achieved
Purchasing Department:	9,000 x 7 = 63,000	9,000 x 8 = 72,000	
		9,000 (F) Material price variance	
Production Department:		7000 x 8 = 56,000	(3000)(2)(8) = 48,000
			8,000 (U) Material usage variance

Flexible Budgets and Standards for Control 125

CHAPTER 8 SOLUTIONS TO PRACTICE TEST QUESTIONS AND PROBLEMS

True or False Statements

1. **True** — The difference between the master budget and the actual result is the master-budget variance, which may be due to either actual activities being different from the master budget or actual efficiency being different from master budget.

2. **False** — Effective flexible budgeting existed long before computers were readily available. It is true, however, that computers have made flexible budgeting much easier and much more responsive to managers inquiries.

3. **False** — The flexible budget for direct cost items to insert between the actual result and the master budget is the actual level of *output achieved* multiplied by the flexible-budget formula.

4. **True** — The sales activity variance is the difference between the flexible budget and the master budget. The only difference between the two budgets is sales activity (assuming that sales activity is the only appropriate cost driver).

5. **True** — The master-budget variance is the sum of the sales-activity variance and the flexible-budget variance. Therefore, the sales activity variance is the difference between the (overall) master budget variance and the flexible budget variance.

6. **False** — Different parts of the master budget may have different appropriate cost drivers. Flexible budgeting just requires that the appropriate cost drivers be used to compute the flexible budget, just as the the master budget does.

7. **False** — Flexible-budget variances are due to the efficiency of operations. Activity-level variances (e.g., sales-activity variances) measure effectiveness.

8. **False** — Standard costs are measures of what costs should be under desired conditions. They may be used for budgeting and performance evaluation even if the company does not use a standard cost system for financial reporting purposes.

9. **False** — Currently attainable standards may be set at different levels, requiring different levels of effort. These standards can motivate improved performance if incentives are present.

10. **True** — Ideally, one system would suffice for all an organization's needs. Currently, such a system may be too expensive compared to its benefits. The cost-benefit criterion may indicate that multiple cost systems are more efficient than a single system.

11. **False** — Most observers of company practice believe that perfection standards are de-motivators since these standards can never be achieved.

12. **True** — An excess of material means that actual material used was greater than the standard material allowed. This excess multiplied by standard or expected prices equals an unfavorable material usage variance.

13. **False** — The traditional calculation of usage variances multiplies the standard cost of the input times the difference in actual versus flexible-budgeted usage.

14. True — Generally, the manager who schedules the use of labor also controls which laborers, at their particular wage rates, will work. This is not always true, however, since company or union policy may dictate wage rates, leaving only labor usage under a manager's control.

15. True — In the very short-term, prices of inputs may not be as controllable as the usage of the input. Purchase contracts and union labor agreements may fix per unit prices for the short-term.

Multiple Choice Questions

1. c, d — The master budget variance is the difference between the master budget and actual results, the same as the difference between total costs at actual prices and actual inputs, which are actual results, and the master budget. The difference between the flexible budget and master budget is the activity-level variance. The difference between the actual result and flexible budget is the flexible-budget variance.

2. a, d — The flexible-budget variance is the difference between the flexible budget and actual results, or between actual results and the budget at standard prices and standard inputs allowed for the outputs achieved, which is the flexible budget.

3. a — The sales-activity variance is the difference between the master budget and the flexible budget: $185,000 - $170,000 = $15,000 F. The variance is labeled favorable because the flexible budget is less than the master budget, but it has no cost-control implications because it is due to sales activity.

4. c — The flexible-budget variance is the difference between the flexible budget and the actual result: $170,000 - $180,000 = $10,000 U. The variance is labeled unfavorable because the actual result is greater than the flexible budget. The implication is that productive activity was not efficient.

5. d — The sales-activity variance is the difference between the master budget and the flexible budget: $110,000 - $90,000 = $20,000 U. The variance is labeled unfavorable because flexible-budgeted sales are less than the master budget. The implication is that sales activity was not effective in meeting sales objectives.

6. a — The flexible-budget variance is the difference between the flexible budget and the actual result: $90,000 - $92,000 = $2,000 F. The variance is labeled favorable because actual contribution margin was greater than the flexible budget for the same sales activity. The implication is that operations were efficient through higher sales prices and/or lower variable costs.

7. c — Currently attainable standards are expected to be achieved given certain levels of effort; thus, they may be used for budgeting. Ideal or perfection standards cannot be achieved and would not be useful for budgeting. Flexible standards are not standards at all, but are probably just actual results.

8. d — Price and usage variances are the customary divisions of the flexible-budget variance. The other pairs are synonyms.

9. a — In some cases the person or department that purchases material is different from the person or department that uses the material. If so, it is better to isolate the

material price variance at the time of purchase so that current variances can be associated with current performance.

10. a   The labor price variance is the difference between the standard wage rate and the actual wage rate multiplied by the actual hours used: ($9 -$10) x 800 = $800 U. The variance is unfavorable since the actual wage rate exceeded the standard rate.

11. c   The labor usage variance is the difference between the standard hours allowed and the actual hours used multiplied by the standard wage rate: (3 x 250 - 800) x $9 = (750 - 800) x $9 = $450 U. The variance is unfavorable since actual hours used exceeded the standard hours allowed.

12. d   The material price variance is the difference between the expected price and the actual price multiplied by the actual material used (in this case): ($20 - $19) x 110 = $110 F. The variance is labeled favorable because the actual price was less than the standard price. Note that this may not be a beneficial outcome if the quality of material was lower than standard.

13. b   The material usage variance is the difference between the standard material allowed and the actual material used multiplied by the standard material price: (4 x 30 -130) x $20 = (120 - 130) x $20 = 200 U. The variance is labeled unfavorable because actual material used exceeded the standard allowed. Note that the tradeoff of price for usage resulted in an overall, unfavorable flexible-budget variance: $110 F + $200 U = $90 U.

Completion

1. prior periods' results, the master budget, the flexible budget
2. master-budget variance, flexible-budget variance
3. static budget, variable budget
4. nothing; they are the same
5. perfection or ideal
6. differences between the master budget and the flexible budget, which differ because of differences in planned activity levels
7. costs of investigating, costs of not investigating (or benefits of investigating)
8. tradeoff, performance, performance
9. purchasing agent, production manager -- depending on responsibilities
10. prices, material used or purchased -- depending on the control point

Problems

1. Data-Bilt, Inc.

	Actual results at actual activity level	Flexible budget variances	Flexible budget for actual activity	Activity variances	Master budget
Units	7,000	-	7,000	1,000 U	8,000
Sales	$730,000	$30,000 F	$700,000	$100,000 U	$800,000
Variable costs	248,000	32,000 F	280,000	40,000 F	320,000
Contribution margin	$482,000	$62,000 F	$420,000	$60,000 U	$480,000
Fixed costs	220,000	20,000 U	200,000	-	200,000
Operating income	$262,000	$42,000 F	$220,000	$60,000 U	$280,000

$42,000 F Total flexible-budget variances

$60,000 U Total activity-level variances

$18,000 U Total master-budget variances

2. Primordial Co.

Actual cost: Actual inputs x Actual prices	Flexible budget: Actual inputs x Expected prices	Flexible budget: Expected prices x Standard inputs allowed
2,600 kg x $11 = $28,600	2,600 kg x $10 = $26,000	(500 x 5 kg) x $10 = 2,500 kg x $10 = $25,000

$2,600 U Material price variance

$1,000 U Material usage variance

$3,600 U Total flexible-budget variance for material

3. Superb Corporation

Control point	Actual cost: Actual quantity x Actual price	Actual quantity x Standard price	Flexible budget: Standard price x Standard quantity allowed for output achieved
Purchasing Department:	9,000 lb x $7 = $63,000	9,000 lb x $8 = $72,000	

$63,000 - $72,000 = $9,000 F Material price variance

Production Department:		7,000 lb x $8 = $56,000	(2 lb x 3,000) x $8 = $48,000

$56,000 - $48,000 = $8,000 U Material usage variance

Flexible Budgets and Standards for Control

CHAPTER 9

Management Control Systems and Responsibility Accounting

MAIN FOCUS AND OBJECTIVES

A management control system combines knowledge of the types of key management decisions, cost behavior, budgeting, performance evaluation incentives, and motivation to help decision makers achieve organizational goals. Your learning objectives are to:

- Describe the importance of organizational goals and objectives for management control systems
- Understand responsibility accounting and cost, profit, and investment centers
- Understand how evaluations affect motivation, goal congruence, and effort
- Compare financial and nonfinancial performance
- Prepare segment income statements using contribution margins and controllable costs
- Measure performance against quality, cycle time, and productivity objectives
- Describe difficulties of management control in service organizations
- Explain the evolution of management control systems

REVIEW OF KEY CONCEPTS

A. A **management control system** integrates all the management accounting tools covered so far in this text to aid and coordinate management decision making and to motivate individuals to achieve organizational *goals*.

    1. Information from the accounting system alone usually is not sufficient to support a successful management control system.

        a. Many management concerns do not show up in the accounting system soon enough to prevent problems (such as warranty expenses, repeat sales).

        b. Some management concerns may never show up in the accounting system in a way that allows effective control (such as customer satisfaction, quality performance).

2. Design of the management control system begins with specifying *organizational goals*.
   a. An organization's **goals** are the purposes for the existence of the organization -- generally the goals of the founders, directors, shareholders, or major contributors of the organization.
   b. Some organizations never build effective management control systems because they either cannot identify goals or do not communicate them
   c. Organizations may fail to gain acceptance of goals in the organization; usually this is a problem of both communication and incentive problems.

3. Organizational goals are too vague to be helpful in planning, budgeting, and performance evaluation.
   a. Goals should be translated into observable, attainable **objectives** such as profit targets, standard costs, and so on.
   b. As shown in earlier chapters, managers can establish plans or budgets that will attain these objectives.
   c. Plans to attain objectives are the best benchmark for evaluating effectiveness and efficiency in actual performance.
   d. Objectives may be in conflict (e.g., short-term profit versus long-term profit), and balancing them can be the most difficult part of designing a management control system.

4. Most management control systems are designed for existing organizations.
   a. Though it may be desirable, it may not be possible to re-design both system and organization to be more effective and efficient.
   b. A key concern is the organization's structure which may be relatively fixed.

   > See textbook Exhibit 9-1

   c. Constrained resources may mean that the management control system is revised "piece-meal."
   d. No system is perfect, but should be the result of careful weighing of costs and benefits of possible improvements.

5. Motivation of employees to achieve organization goals may be a difficult task.
   a. **Goal congruence** exists when individuals aim at the same organizational goals.
   b. **Managerial effort** is exertion toward a goal or objective.
   c. **Motivation** is the amount of drive an individual has that creates effort toward meeting an objective. Motivation is a function of the organization's *incentives* and an individual's personal values and desires.
   d. An organization can supply incentives, which link rewards to actions and outcomes, but the individual must supply the desire -- that is why hiring decisions are so critical to an organization's success.

6. Because all the factors that affect the design of management control systems can change, system designers must be prepared to re-design the system over time.
   a. This may mean radical changes in relatively short periods of time.

- b. Standard cost systems have been around for over 50 years, yet only recently have some companies found that they are obsolete for management control puposes.
- c. It is likely that today's management control systems will be obsolete in the future, but much sooner than 50 years -- maybe 10 years at most.
- d. This means managers, accountants, and system designers must keep ahead of new developments and decision-making needs.

> Before going on to the next section, be sure that you can explain the links between goals, objectives, and management control systems. What is the relationship of management accounting to management control systems?

B. A **responsibility center** is a set of activities designated to be under the management control of a specific individual or group of individuals within an organization.

1. **Responsibility accounting** designs planning, scorekeeping, and attention-directing infomation that is consistent with the designation of responsibility centers.
   - a. Responsibility centers often have multiple objectives (financial and non-financial).
   - b. The usual form of responsibility center corresponds to *financial responsibility*.

2. There are three principal forms of responsibility centers:
   - a. **Cost centers**, usually departments that are responsible for efficient use of inputs and for which costs are accumulated and reported.
   - b. **Profit centers**, usually divisions that are responsible for both revenues and costs and for which income is reported.
   - c. **Investment centers**, which are responsible for their invested capital as well as for revenues and costs and for which income relative to the magnitude of the investment is reported (Chapter 10 covers this in more detail).

3. A key distinction in a responsibility accounting system is the *controllability* of an outcome; in particular, we will be concerned with costs.
   - a. A **controllable cost** is a cost that can be influenced by a specific responsibility center for a given period of time.
   - b. An **uncontrollable cost** cannot be affected by a specific responsibility center within a given time period.
   - c. Controllability is a matter of degree. For example, more costs are controllable at higher levels within an organization and/or as the time span increases.
   - d. Uncontrollable revenue may be changes in sales due to general economic conditions, yet there are arguments for not shielding managers from these uncontrollable forces -- how well did the manager react or perform relative to other managers in the same environment?

4. In many situations, a manager may have only a little influence over operating results.

a. Nevertheless, a responsibility accounting system identifies the person with the most day-today influence over a particular cost or revenue.
b. That person will then at least be responsible for explaining deviations of actual results from budgeted results.

> Can you explain the differences between the types of responsibility centers? between controllable and uncontrollable costs?

C. Measurement of financial performance

1. **Responsibility performance reports** provide managers of responsibility centers on each level with data concerning the items they have the authority and ability to influence.
   a. Many organizations measure performance using the contribution margin approach because it identifies expected and actual cost behavior more clearly than the absorption approach.
   b. The contribution margin approach is also consistent with CVP approaches to planning.
   c. Therefore, such reports often identify or exclude any revenues and costs beyond the control of the manager being evaluated.

2. The text develops a model income statement by segments at three different segment levels: divisions, product lines, and individual stores.

> See textbook Exhibit 9-2.

   a. Note how this income statement reports costs by *controllability* as well as by fixed or variable behavior.
   b. The **segment contribution margin** (line a in Exhibit 9-2) is the excess of revenues over controllable variable costs.
   c. The **contribution controllable by segment managers** (line b in Exhibit 9-2) is computed as the segment contribution margins less the fixed costs controllable by segment managers.
   d. The **contribution by segments** (line c in Exhibit 9-2) subtracts the additional fixed costs controllable by others (e.g., top management). This measures the financial performance of the entire segment.
   e. **Unallocated costs** (just before line d in Exhibit 9-2) are borne by the entire company and cannot be meaningfully distributed to segments.

> Can you construct a segment performance report and explain the importance of each element?

D. **Non-financial measures** of performance provide critical management control information that is not available from the accounting system.

1. Non-financial measures often "lead" financial measures of performance.
   a. Superior, *sustained* financial performance is usually the result of superior non-financial performance.
   b. Paying attention to only financial measures of performance may mean never getting at the root causes of poor financial performance or never appreciating the reasons for superior financial performance.

c. Important areas of non-financial performance include: *quality*, *cycle time*, and *productivity*.

2. **Quality control** is the effort to insure that products and services meet customer requirements.
   a. Emphasis now is on **Total Quality Management**, which motivates all members of the organization to satisfy customers and clients.
   b. In order to gauge the quality control efforts, some companies measure their costs of quality.
      - **Quality costs** include defect prevention, appraisal, internal failure and external failure costs.
      - Employees should be able to shift resources from appraisal, internal failure, and external failure (which are non-value-added activities) to prevention.
      - Costs of quality draw attention to the financial impact of quality problems.
      - If employees can see how costly poor quality is, they can be motivated to improve quality.

      > See textbook Exhibit 9-3.

   c. Quality control charts are used to monitor quality on a "real time" basis and provide information much more quickly than a cost variance report could.

      > See textbook Exhibit 9-4

3. **Cycle time** is the time it takes from beginning to completion of a product or service.
   a. Improvements in cycle time are possible only with high quality products and processes.
   b. Reducing cycle time exposes more quality and process problems which must be solved to obtain further improvements.
   c. Companies monitor cycle time with flexible-budget-type reports and with control charts.

      > See textbook Exhibit 9-5

4. **Productivity** is a measure of the efficiency of an operation based on ratios of key outputs to related inputs.
   a. Improved productivity is a key to surviving global competition, and is often due to improvements in quality and cycle time.
   b. Faulty management control systems have been blamed for U.S. companies continuing to lag companies in other countries improvements in productivity.
   c. Properly designed productivity measures should help managers by identifying inefficient operations.
   d. In contrast, poorly thought-out productivity measures may be quite misleading.

> See textbook Exhibit 9-6

> Why is controlling nonfinancial performance so important? How are quality, cycle time, and productivity related?

E. Management control systems are more difficult to design and implement in nonprofit and governmental organizations.

1. Management control in these organizations is critical to all of us since they comprise the large majority of the U.S. economy.

2. In concept, management control in these organizations is no different than in a manufacturing firm, only more difficult.

3. Management control in service and govenment organizations is more difficult because:
   a. Goals and objectives are less clear.
   b. Professionals in these organizations are less receptive to control and may have different motivations.
   c. Labor is more important both as a share of total costs and as the point of contact with customers and clients.
   d. There are fewer objective measures of performance (e.g., what is a "good unit of output" in a government organization?)
   e. There is less competitive pressure to improve.
   f. Budgeting may be less planning than negotiating for larger appropriations.

> Before going on to the practice test, be sure that you can explain the difficulties of designing management control systems in service and nonprofit organizations.

PRACTICE TEST QUESTIONS AND PROBLEMS WITH SOLUTIONS

True or False Statements

Determine whether each of the following statements is True (T) or False (F) and enter your answer in the space provided. Note that concepts in this chapter are especially difficult to classify as true or false -- many of the correct anwers could be, "True, but..." or "False, but...."

_____1. A management control system is another name for the master-budget process.

_____2. Profit centers exist in nonprofit and government organizations.

_____3. Senior managers state that the firm's primary objective is to improve cycle time. In the same firm, middle managers state that meeting delivery schedules and reducing defectives are the primary objectives. Workers on the assembly lines say that their most important objectives are improving their attendance and cooperation with each other. What we have here is a failure to communicate.

_____4. There is no practical difference between a profit center and an investment center.

_____5. Properly designed incentives will motivate employees to achieve organizational goals.

_____ 6. Net income before income taxes is the total contribution by segments less unallocated costs.

_____ 7. A contribution income statement by segments is aimed at reporting costs by cost behavior and segment controllability.

_____ 8. Managers are supposed to take risks even though they may have limited control over outcomes; therefore, responsibility accounting measures only the controllable performance of managers.

_____ 9. Segment contribution is the complete measure of a segment's achievement of company objectives.

_____ 10. Usually, the same criteria should be used in evaluating (a) the performance of a division as an investment by the company and (b) the performance of the division manager.

_____ 11. Successful management control systems allow managers to balance competing goals as best they can.

_____ 12. Measurement of segment contribution is consistent with financial reporting rules.

_____ 13. U.S. companies cannot hope to match the quality of Japanese companies because U.S. workers are unwilling to be involved in total quality management.

_____ 14. Productivity measures of organizational efficiency relate goods and services sold to customers to the inputs required to produce them.

_____ 15. There is little sense in studying today's management control systems since they will be obsolete before I graduate from college.

Multiple Choice Questions

For each of the following multiple-choice questions, select the best answer(s) and enter the identification letter(s) in the space provided.

_____ 1. Usually the management control system should incorporate (a) financial reporting rules, (b) organizational goals, (c) short-term objectives, (d) the master budget.

_____ 2. A large company's responsibility centers might include: (a) cost center, (b) profit center, (c) investment center, (d) shopping center.

_____ 3. The focus of responsibility accounting is: (a) accounting accuracy, (b) rewarding managers, (c) identifying blame or fault, (d) information gathering and reporting.

_____ 4. Responsibility accounting basically asks, "Who in the organization is in the best position to: (a) control the outcome, (b) explain why the outcome occurred, (c) predict the outcome, (d) take the blame for the outcome."

_____ 5. The smallest segment of activity or area of responsibility for which costs are accumulated is called: (a) a mini-center, (b) a profit center, (c) a cost center, (d) an investment center.

_____ 6. Managers should focus their attention on the parts of performance reports that do not reflect smoothly running aspects of operations. This is called: (a) exceptional management, (b) management by perception, (c) perceptional management, (d) management by exception.

_____7. The contribution margins by segment are most helpful in measuring: (a) long-run segment profitability, (b) short-run performance of division managers or product managers, (c) effects on segment net income of long-run changes in activity, (d) long-run earning power of the entire company.

_____8. The following data (in thousands) appeared for a certain segment of a company in the contribution approach income statement: Variable expenses $500, Fixed costs controllable by others $80, Fixed costs controllable by segment managers $110, Unallocated costs $50, Net sales $690. The segment contribution margin is: (a) zero, (b) -$50, (c) $190, (d) $80.

_____9. See the preceding test item. The contribution controllable by segment managers is: (a) zero, (b) -$50, (c) $190, (d) $80.

_____10. Ram Co. prepared a contribution margin income statement that included the following data (in thousands) for one of its segments: Fixed costs controllable by segment managers $240, Fixed costs controllable by others $150, Variable expenses $300, Net sales $750. The financial performance of the segment is measured best as: (a) $60, (b) $210, (c) $450, (d) $540.

_____11. Quality costs may include (a) inspection costs, (b) rework costs, (c) lost sales, (d) redesign of the production process.

_____12. Total quality management involves whom in creating customer-oriented quality? (a) top management, (b) middle managers, (c) sales representatives, (d) factory workers.

Completion

Complete each of the following statements by filling in the blanks.

1. Organizational _____ are generally too _____, so companies express _____ as _____.

2. Because most management control systems are redesigned for existing organizations a new system often must be consistent with the existing organization _____ and _____.

3. The most common types of responsibility centers in government organizations could be characterized as _____.

4. A segment is a set of activities which _____.

5. The contribution controllable by segment managers is the excess of the _____ margin over the _____.

6. The contribution of segments is the excess of the contribution _____ over the _____.

7. Many companies are finding that the most effective control of quality is through _____.

8. The more a manager's evaluation and rewards are linked to _____ the more _____ there is to _____.

Management Control Systems and Responsibility Accounting 137

9. _____ due to poor product quality may be far greater than _____ costs reported on quality cost reports.

10. Productivity in general is measured by dividing a measure of _____ by _____.

Problems

1. From the following data for Homer Equipment Company (in thousands), prepare a contribution approach income statement by segments:

	Company Total	Beta Division	Gamma Division
Net sales	$850	$500	$350
Fixed costs:			
Controllable by division managers	140	60	80
Controllable by others	70	10	60
Variable costs:			
Manufacturing cost of sales	450	300	150
Selling and administrative expenses	130	60	70
Unallocated costs	45	-	-

	Company Total	Beta Division	Gamma Division
Net sales			
Less			
Income before taxes			

2. From the following data evaluate the The Burns Company's cost of quality and productivity during April 19X4. The Burns Company could sell all of its output at market prices. Defective units are detected at the end of the manufacturing process.

Master-budgeted production	4,600 units
Sales revenue	$82,000 @ $20/unit
Total good production	3,500 units @ $7 variable cost/unit
Defective units -- scrapped	500 units
Defective units -- reworked	600 units (reworked at additional $2 cost/unit)
Sales warranty expense	$6,000
Number of employees	50
Redesign of product to reduce future defectives	$ 5,000
Quality control personnel salaries	$ 6,000
Operation and depreciation of quality test equipment	$ 8,000
Total fixed manufacturing cost	$20,000
Direct labor cost	$ 4,000
Quality training costs for direct labor to detect defectives earlier in the future	$10,000

Cost of Quality Report:

Analysis of productivity:

CHAPTER 9 SOLUTIONS TO PRACTICE TEST QUESTIONS AND PROBLEMS

True or False Statements

1. False — The master-budget process is *part* of a successful management control system. Though in some companies, it may be the only part.

2. True — A profit center could be operated with a targeted income of zero or breakeven. Many nonprofit and government organizations sell services to the public at prices designed to just cover their costs. Managers of these organizations have responsibility for both revenues and expenses, and are managers, therefore, of profit centers.

3. False — Individuals at different levels of the organization may properly perceive different objectives based on controllability. It is disturbing though that workers do not perceive a quality-related objective that is as important as attendance or cooperative behavior.

4. False — In many cases, however, this is true due to sloppy terminology. An investment center has responsibility and authority over the investment in plant, equipment, and other long-term assets, whereas a profit center does not have authority over its investment.

5. False — If only it were that easy (and even that is difficult). External incentives are part of motivation, but individuals may be motivated by other, internal desires that conflict with the organization's objectives. Incentives that are sufficient to overcome most base desires (e.g., effort-aversion) plus hiring internally motivated employees may result in motivated workers.

6. True — Total contribution by segments includes contribution margin, less fixed costs controllable by managers, less fixed costs controllable by others. All that remains is unallocated costs.

7. True — By combining cost behavior (contribution margin approach) and responsibility (by segment), this approach provides useful feedback information for both performance evaluation and planning.

8. False — Separating controllable from uncontrollable events can never be 100% successful. Responsibility accounting, when it cannot report by pure controllability, assigns outcomes to the individual or group best able to explain the outcomes.

9. False — Segment contribution measures only the past period's financial performance. Non-financial performance is an important component of segment performance not captured by the income statement by segments.

10. False — Some segment events are not controllable by managers, and for clarity probably should be separated from controllable events. For example, credit policy and investment may not be controllable by managers, so their costs should be reported separate from more controllable items.

11. False — In general, the more guidance (possibly through incentives) given to managers about the organization's desired tradeoffs, the more likely it is that managers will achieve organizational goals. Some argue that the performance of profit centers should be based on the "bottom line" only and that good managers will figure out

how to improve that number, to the benefit of the organization as a whole. This assumes, however, that managers will be in place long enough to experience the long-term effects of their actions.

12. False — The revenue portions of segment contribution are probably consistent with financial reporting, but the cost or expense portions are not. Financial reporting measures expenses by operational function, whereas segment contribution measures expenses by cost behavior. Because of the effects of inventories there may be sizable differences in expenses between the two approaches.

13. False — Though Japanese companies are not content to rest on past success, many U.S. companies are matching Japanese quality by educating and involving workers in total quality management. Japanese companies operating in the U.S. with U.S. workers have been especially successful. Thus, the problem is more a management problem than a worker problem.

14. True — But this is an incomplete definition. Many measures of productivity are possible before goods and services are sold to customers.

15. False — Though current management controls may be obsolete in only a few years, there are principles of management control that will be valid for many years. Though it is helpful to be aware of current practice, be sure that you are learning basic principles.

Multiple Choice Questions

1. b, c, d — The management control system includes these items (and others) but is not bound by financial reporting rules. In some organizations, however, the financial reporting system is a major part of the management control system. Some critics of accounting practice believe that this causes serious decision-making errors.

2. a, b, c, d — Of course, the first three are responsibility centers. The inclusion of "shopping center" may seem like a feeble joke, but a real estate holding company, for example, could own a shopping center that it operates as a profit or investment center.

3. d — Accounting accuracy is desirable, but not as desirable as relevance. Rewarding managers for excellent performance may be an outcome of using responsibility accounting, but management bonuses are the responsibility of top management or the board of directors. Identifying blame or fault may occur as a result of investigating poor performance highlighted by responsibility accounting, but information gathering and reporting is the primary function of responsibility accounting.

4. a, b, c — The most general assignment is on the ability to explain outcomes. However, this person or persons works closest with the operations of the responsibility center and may also be in the best position to control and/or predict outcomes.

5. c — A cost center is the most basic level of financial responsibility, but this by no means that all cost centers are small or their operations simple. The U.S. Department of Defense is essentially a cost center, and it certainly is neither small nor simple.

6. d   Management by exception is facilitated by well-designed reports that direct attention to unusual outcomes.

7. a, c   The contribution margin by segment is the contribution to profit after all identifiable fixed costs and is the best measure of the overall profitability of the segment. At the budgeting stage, knowledge of cost behavior and the relevant range of segment activities can help predict changes in segment profitability over the long run.

8. a   The segment contribution margin is contribution after all but unallocated costs: $690 - $500 - $110 - $80 = 0.

9. d   The contribution margin controllable by managers is the contribution margin less controllable fixed costs: $690 - $500 - $110 = $80.

10. a   The segment contribution margin, which includes all but unallocated costs, is the best overall measure of segment financial performance: $750 - $300 - $240 - $150 = $60.

11. a,b,c,d   Quality costs include all of these, and more. Inspection costs are classified as appraisal costs. Rework costs are internal failure costs. Lost sales are external failure costs. And redesign of the production process is a prevention cost.

12. a,b,c,d   For total quality management to succeed, all employees must be involved in creating customer-oriented quality.

Completion

1. goals, vague, goals, tangible objectives
2. goals, structure (other possibilities: information system, management, ???)
3. cost centers
4. has been designated the responsibility of an individual or group
5. contribution margin, fixed costs controllable by managers
6. contribution margin controllable by managers, fixed costs controllable by others
7. total quality management
8. objectives, incentive, attain objectives
9. lost sales, external failure
10. output, a measure of input

Problems

1. Homer Equipment Company

	Company Total	Beta Division	Gamma Division
Net sales	$850	$500	$350
Less variable costs			
Manufacturing cost of sales	$450	$300	$150
Variable selling and admin. expenses	130	60	70
Total variable costs	$580	$360	$220
Contribution margin	$270	$140	$130
Less fixed costs controllable by managers	140	60	80
Contribution controllable by managers	$130	$80	$50
Less fixed costs controllable by others	70	10	60
Contribution by segments	$60	$70	$(10)
Less unallocated costs	45		
Income before taxes	$15		

2. The Burns Company

Cost of Quality
  Prevention cost
    Product redesign $5,000
    Employee training   10,000 $15,000
  Appraisal cost
    Quality control salaries $6,000
    Test equipment operation   8,000 $14,000
  Internal failure cost
    Scrapped units   500 x $7 $3,500
    Reworked units   600 x $2   1,200 $4,700
  External failure cost
    Warranty expense $6,000
    Lost sales contribution*   500 x $13   6,500 $12,500
  Total $46,200

*Note that other, future sales may have been lost due to defective units.

These are only some of the possible productivity measures:

Non-value-added quality cost as a percentage of sales revenue (all but prevention costs)	($46,200 - $15,000) ÷ $82,000	$38%
Sales revenue per employee	$82,000 ÷ 50	$1,640 per employee
Production per employee	(4,600 - 500 - 600) ÷ 50	70 units per employee
Direct labor cost as a percentage of sales revenue	$4,000 ÷ $82,000	4.9%
Direct labor cost as a percentage of manufacturing costs	$4,000 ÷ $(20,000 + 7 x 4,600 + 2 x 600)	7.5%
Product yield (first-time good units as a percentage of total units)	3,500 ÷ (3,500+500+600)	76%

Note: These are only useful if compared to Burns' competitors or over time for Burns.

Chapter 10

Management Control in Decentralized Organizations

MAIN FOCUS AND OBJECTIVES

To complete the basic description of management control systems, this chapter covers the closely related topics of transfer pricing and alternative measures performance in decentralized organizations. The discussion of transfer prices raises problems common to all organizations with responsibility centers that share outputs. There are a number of transfer pricing policies; each has advantages and disadvantages. This chapter covers transfer pricing based on cost, market prices, and negotiation. The discussion of alternative measures of decentralized performance extends Chapter 9's discussion of evaluating investment centers. This chapter covers return on investment, residual income, and various ways of measuring the components of each. Your learning objectives are to:

- Understand decentralization and its costs and benefits
- Distinguish between profit centers and decentralization
- Understand transfer pricing methods and issues
- Identify issues of multinational transfer pricing
- Understand the links between rewards, incentives, and risk
- Compute and contrast ROI and residual income
- Understand the relative merits of alternative methods of measuring invested capital

---

REVIEW OF KEY CONCEPTS

A. **Decentralization** is the delegation of decision-making authority to segment managers.

1. Decentralization implies more segment autonomy than merely designating a subunit as a responsibility center.
   a. Decentralized segments are operated more as separate businesses than as just a division of the parent company.
   b. Decentralization implies the ability to set major policies and make major investment decisions at the segment level.

2. Decentralization seeks to have the best of two worlds:
   a. Decentralized segments must compete with other, autonomous businesses and so managers must develop competitive practices, products, and services to survive.
   b. Affiliation with the parent company provides access to capital and other business services that may not be available to truly separate businesses, except at much higher cost.
   c. Other benefits of decentralization include:
      - Better and more timely decisions because of managers' closeness to problem areas
      - Improvement of skills in the pool of company managers that will benefit the company as a whole
      - Improved motivation of managers who have enhanced status and who see rewards tied closely to their performance

3. Decentralization has disadvantages as well:
   a. Managers may focus narrowly on their own segment performance
   b. Managers may be unaware of all relevant information regarding other segments and the parent company
   c. Segments may duplicate costly central services
   b. Overall information costs may rise

4. As a result of these disadvantages, decentralization tends to be most successful when segments are relatively independent of each other.
   a. An additional criterion for designing and evaluating a successful control system in decentralized organizations is respect for **segment autonomy.**
   b. This means allowing segment managers to make decisions without interference from top managers.

5. Decentralization is not equivalent to the use of profit centers.
   a. *Decentralization* is the delegation of the authority to make decisions.
   b. *Profit centers* are responsible for revenues and expenses of segments.
   c. Thus, profit centers are designations of the scope of *responsibility*, but not necessarily *authority*.
   d. Some profit centers have far more *decentralized authority and autonomy* than others, and even some cost centers may have more decentralized authority and autonomy than some profit centers.

> Before going on, be sure that you can can describe the difference between a decentralized segment and a responsibility center. What are the advantages and disadvantages of decentralization?

B. **Transfer prices** are the amounts charged for the exchanges of goods and services among the decentralized segments of a company.
   1. Transfer prices exist to communicate information that promotes goal congruence.
      a. If segments are evaluated on some basis of income (as discussed in later sections), then transfer prices charged will influence where and how much managers will pay for goods and services.
      b. Transfer pricing and performance evaluation are closely tied together.

c. If transfer prices did not affect evaluations of segments and segment managers, then transfer pricing policies would not cause so many problems in decentralized companies.

2. Organizations have three general transfer pricing policies, each of which may be appropriate under different circumstances:
   a. *Cost-based transfer prices* use some measure of cost -- variable cost, full cost, full cost plus markup, and any of these using standard or actual cost.
   b. *Market-based transfer prices* rely on competitive market prices.
   c. *Negotiated transfer prices* rely on negotiations between autonomous segment managers who may consider costs and market prices in their negotiations.

3. *Transfer prices based on costs* other than strictly variable cost depend heavily on the process of *cost allocation* of fixed costs, which is covered in detail in Chapter 15.
   a. Allocation of fixed costs is arbitrary and coupled to transfer pricing increases opportunities for disagreements among segment managers.
   b. Arguments are over appropriate cost drivers, cost driver levels, identification of avoidable versus unavoidable costs, appropriate markups, use of actual or expected costs, and so on.
   c. Suffice to say, cost-based transfer prices cause considerable headaches.

4. Using *market prices* for transfer prices is usually appropriate when decentralized segments are profit centers.
   a. The problems of disagreements, goal congruence, managerial effort, and segment autonomy are minimized when market prices are used.
   b. If market prices do not exist, some organizations try to imitate market prices with "cost-plus-a-profit," but these are just cost-based transfer prices and introduce all their problems.

5. Segment managers make supplying and sourcing decisions regarding other segments of the same company in just the way described in Chapter 5.
   a. These are special-order and make-or-buy decisions, and the decisions among autonomous segments revolve around *transfer prices*.
   b. Managers of segments who are evaluated on some basis of income will want to charge as much as possible to supply other segments and pay as little as possible when buying from other segments -- just as they would if dealing with an outside company.
   c. The same concerns exist for utilization of capacity within segments.
   d. Review make-or-buy and special order decisions if they are not fresh in your memory.

6. Negotiating transfer prices can consume considerable time and energy, but may resolve an important area of conflict. Further, this conflict-resolution process may carry over into other areas of conflict.
   a. Conflicts are inevitable, but well-designed incentives will steer managers toward making decisions that benefit the company as a whole.
   b. Negotiations that stray from what top management would prefer are one of the costs of decentralization.

> See textbook Exhibit 10-1

7. A company may choose to use different transfer prices for different purposes: motivation, performance measurement, taxation, and domestic and international government regulation.

> Can you explain why transfer pricing causes conflicts among decentralized segments? What are the alternative transfer pricing policies? What are their advantages and disadvantages?

C. A common goal of profit-seeking organizations is to achieve competitive profits. To give segment managers guidance, this goal is translated into *profit objectives, usually related to capital invested in the segment*. These measures are most appropriate for investment centers:

1. A widely used measure is the rate of return on investment (ROI).
    a. ROI can be computed as:

    > ROI = Income ÷ Invested capital

    b. An alternative computation is:

    ROI = (Income ÷ Revenue) x (Revenue ÷ Invested capital), or

    ROI = Return on sales x Capital turnover

    c. Subdividing ROI into its basic components as shown in (b) helps identify strategies for improving ROI. For example, reducing expenses (which increases income and return on sales) or reducing investment in assets (which increases capital turnover) will improve ROI.

2. *Residual income* (RI) is another measure of performance that relates segment profit to invested capital.
    a. **RI** is the excess of income over the *opportunity cost* of the invested capital.
    b. A segment manager evaluated on RI would expand the segment only if the expansion would earn at least the charge for invested capital (the minimum desired rate of return).

    > See the textbook example

3. Evaluation of segments based on ROI may lead to managers' rejecting projects that promise more than the required rate of return but less than the current ROI.
    a. If managers' performances are compared across the company, a manager would be unwilling to decrease his or her ROI even if the company as a whole would benefit.
    b. In contrast, a manager evaluated on RI would be better off (as would the company) by accepting any project that earned more than the required rate of return.
    c. Most companies, however, use ROI, but add growth and profit objectives.

> Can you explain the two main measures of investment center performance? What are their components?

D. To apply either the ROI or RI approach to measuring segment performance, the company must choose how to measure both income and invested capital.

1. As discussed in Chapter 9, the contribution margin approach is the preferred measure of income.
   a. The contribution margin approach highlights cost behavior and controllable versus uncontrollable costs.
   b. Many companies, however, use the absorption approach because it is the method required for financial reporting.
      - Segment incomes "roll up" into overall reported income
      - Multiple cost systems are not used (though perhaps they should be for decision making)

2. Different bases can be used for measuring *invested capital*. Alternatives include:
   a. *Total assets* -- the most inclusive measure, appropriate if managers have authority over all assets
   b. *Total assets employed* -- appropriate if managers are required to maintain some unused capacity
   c. *Total assets less current liabilities* -- appropriate if mangers control short-term credit policy and bank loans
   d. *Stockholders equity* -- appropriate only if managers have control of short-term and long-term debt (unlikely)

> See the textbook example

3. Expect managers to try to reduce assets counted and increase liabilities deducted. The definition of the asset base should be sure to include only those assets that managers should be able to reduce or expand, likewise with liabilities.

4. Of crucial importance is the *valuation base* for measuring assets.
   a. For the routine measurement of assets included in the investment base, the most frequently used valuation is *historical cost* because it is the cheapest measure to obtain -- it is already in the accounting system.
   b. Some argue that *replacement* or *disposal* values are more relevant, but they are more costly to obtain, which makes their use usually not feasible, except for special decisions.
   c. When historical cost is used as an investment measure, some prefer **net book value** of assets (cost less accumulated depreciation) *because it is consistent with conventional reporting of assets and net income.*
   d. But others prefer **gross book value** (undepreciated cost) *because it facilitates comparisons among divisions, and because ROI and RI does not increase merely with the passage of time* (as it may with net book value)
   e. Managers evaluated on a base of gross book value will tend to replace assets sooner than those using net book value (whose asset base declines and ROI and RI increase as assets age).

Management Control in Decentralized Organizations

> Before going on to the practice test, be sure that you understand the effects that alternative investment and valuation bases can have on ROI and RI. When is each most appropriate?

PRACTICE TEST QUESTIONS AND PROBLEMS WITH SOLUTIONS

True or False Statements

Determine whether each of the following statements is True (T) or False (F) and enter your answer in the space provided.

_____1. Two main criteria for designing and evaluating decentralized control systems include obtaining managerial effort and respecting segment autonomy.

_____2. Decentralization tends to be least successful when the segments of an organization are extremely independent.

_____3. The amount of an organization's decentralization depends on the existence of profit centers within the organization.

_____4. Segment autonomy means the freedom of each organization segment to define its job or function.

_____5. The costs of decentralization can include poorer training for managers and dysfunctional decision making.

_____6. The benefits of decentralization can include improved management motivation and decreased costs of gathering and processing information.

_____7. Disadvantages of transfer prices based on total actual cost include reduction of incentive of managers of supplying divisions to control their costs.

_____8. Transfer pricing is a form of cost allocation.

_____9. When a producing segment has idle capacity and future sales and transfers will not be affected, it may be willing to transfer its output to another segment at variable cost.

____10. Firms have more incentive to control their costs of production when cost-based transfer prices are set using standard costs than when they are set using actual costs.

____11. It is better to use an arbitrary basis for allocating asset costs to segments than to not allocate asset costs to divisions at all.

____12. In general, for evaluating the operating performance of managers, it is more appropriate to use an asset total reduced by long-term debt as an investment base than an asset total not reduced by long-term debt.

____13. If segment managers are supposed to maximize rate of return on investment (ROI), they will sometimes reject projects that, for the welfare of the total organization, should be accepted.

____14. When historical cost is used as an investment measure, it is more appropriate to use gross book value than net book value.

____15. The use of stockholders' equity as an investment base would be just as appropriate for evaluating owners' returns as management performance.

Multiple Choice Questions

For each of the following multiple-choice questions, select the best answer(s) and enter the identification letter(s) in the space provided:

____1. Decentralized segments may be: (a) cost centers, (b) profit centers, (c) investment centers, (d) government agencies.

____2. Defining characteristics of a decentralized segment include: (a) manufacturing capability, (b) profit responsibility, (c) autonomous decision making, (d) physical separation from parent company.

____3. Benefits of decentralization include: (a) market-like competition within the company, (b) freedom to set goals at the segment level, (c) improved training for future top executives, (d) ease of control of operations by top management.

____4. Costs of decentralization include: (a) the need to use summary performance measures like ROI, (b) dysfunctional decision making, (c) required measurement of segment profit, (d) duplication of services.

____5. Transfer prices are most like: (a) consulting fees, (b) cost allocations, (c) transportation charges, (d) interest payments.

____6. The most beneficial basis for transfer prices when an organization has profit centers is: (a) full cost, (b) variable cost, (c) market price, (d) negotiated price.

____7. The Pampas division of Argentine Co. has an idle capacity of 1,000 units per month for producing an element that it usually makes at a unit cost of $120 variable and $80 fixed. If another division of Argentine were to buy 1,000 units of the same element at a market price of $130 from an outside supplier, there would be a per-unit effect to Argentine as a whole from buying inside the company of: (a) $10 advantage, (b) $70 advantage, (c) $10 disadvantage, (d) $70 disadvantage.

____8. See the preceding test item. If the element could be purchased on the outside at a market price of $110, there would be a per-unit effect to Argentine as a whole from buying inside the company of: (a) $10 advantage, (b) $90 advantage, (c) $10 disadvantage, (d) $90 disadvantage.

____9. The critical test of the profitability of a decentralized segment is: (a) the absolute amount of profit, (b) the relationship of profit to sales, (c) the relationship of profit to the number of employees, (d) the relationship of profit to invested capital.

____10. An investment center is a business segment that relates its net income to its: (a) sales, (b) total assets, (c) stockholders equity, (d) invested capital.

____11. ROI is return on sales multiplied by: (a) revenue, (b) income, (c) capital turnover, (d) total assets.

____12. Given for a division of Phaeton Co.: $32,000 operating income, $800,000 revenues, and a capital turnover of five times. Compute ROI: (a) 4%, (b) 5%, (c) 10%, (d) 20%.

Management Control in Decentralized Organizations 151

____13. Astin Corporation turned its capital six times and earned an operating income of 2.5% of sales. Compute ROI: (a) 6%, (b) .4%, (c) 15%, (d) 10%.

____14. Given for a division of Bugatti Co.: 18% ROI, 6% return on sales, and $2 million of invested capital. Compute total revenues: (a) $360,000, (b) $6 million, (c) $120,000, (d) $480,000.

____15. Other factors remaining the same, the rate of return on investment may be improved by: (a) increasing investment in assets, (b) increasing expenses, (c) reducing sales, (d) decreasing investment in assets.

____16. Residual income is the excess of an investment center's income over: (a) operating expenses, (b) dividends to stockholders, (c) imputed interest on average capital invested, (d) opportunity cost of capital.

____17. Maserato Co. has $10 million of operating assets and an operating income of $2 million. What is residual income if the opportunity cost of capital is 14%? (a) zero, (b) $400,000, (c) $600,000, (d) $2 million.

Completion

Complete each of the following statements by filling in the blanks.

1. _____ of an organization occurs when sets of activities are designated as _____.

2. The degree of decentralization is a function of _____.

3. Decentralization is more popular in profit-seeking organizations than in nonprofit organizations because _____.

4. Transfer pricing are of three general types: _____, _____, _____.

5. Managers of segments that are evaluated on the basis of income and that must buy parts from other segments or outside companies consider the transfer pricing decision in the same way as a _____ decision.

6. ROI is _____ divided by _____.

7. Capital turnover is _____ divided by _____.

8. Residual income is _____ less _____.

9. The residual income calculation subtracts _____ from net income because _____.

10. _____ of assets may be better than _____ as valuation basis for measuring assets included in the investment base because _____ does not increase with just the passage of time.

Problems

1. Complete the calculations for three divisions of EarthWise Brands Inc.:

	Maritime Division	Farm Division	Industrial Division
Invested capital	$250,000	$200,000	

152 Chapter 10

Revenues (sales)	$750,000		$450,000
Net income	$37,500		$13,500
Capital turnover			4.5 times
Income percentage of revenue		5%	
Rate of return on investment		10%	

2. Given for the real estate division of the Continental Corporation:
   Capital invested in operating assets $3,000,000
   Net income $540,000
   Revenues $2,700,000

a. What is the division's ROI? _____

b. If Continental can earn 16% (before tax) on other investments, what is the division's residual income (RI)?_____

c. A project is available to the division that promises a 17% return on a $200,000 investment. Could it make a difference whether the division manager is evaluated on ROI or RI? Show why.

d. Continental is considering increasing the required rate of return to 20%. If ROI is used, by how much would revenues have to be increased in the real estate division to meet this new requirement? _____

Independently, by how much would expenses have to be reduced to meet this new requirement?_____

Independently, by how much would investment have to be reduced to meet this new requirement?_____

3. Given for the Ozone Regeneration Division of Mother Earth Company:

Cost of manufacturing 2,000 units of a thraxadyne assembly

	Total	Per Unit
Variable costs	$120,000	$60
Fixed costs	$ 60,000	$30

Find the total advantage (or disadvantage) to the company if there are at least 2,000 units of idle capacity in the Ozone Division, *and* if the Global Cooling Division of the same company purchases 2,000 units of this assembly from an outside supplier at a market price of:

a. $63 per unit

b. $58 per unit

CHAPTER 10 SOLUTIONS TO PRACTICE TEST QUESTIONS AND PROBLEMS

True or False Statements

1. True — Since decentralized segments are given decision-making autonomy, the incentive system must be designed so that managers have incentive to achieve the overall organization goals. A control system that does not respect segment autonomy renders decentralization ineffective.

2. False — Just the opposite is true, because increased independence reduces the likelihood that conflicts among segments will occur.

3. False — Decentralization does not depend on the form of responsibility center, but it does depend on the degree of decision-making authority.

4. False — Decision-making authority usually is constrained to maintain the purpose of the segment.

5. False — Though dysfunctional decision making is a possible cost, managers should receive improved training in a decentralized organization.

6. False — Though improved motivation is a benefit of decentralization, information costs likely will increase.

7. True — When transfers are made at actual cost, the supplying division is able to pass on its inefficiencies to the purchasing divisions.

8. True — When transfer prices are based on cost (rather than market prices), forming the transfer prices faces the same difficulties as cost allocation.

9. True — This is just like the special-order decision covered in Chapter 5. The minimum acceptable price, when there is idle capacity and no effect on future sales, is variable cost.

10. True — When transfers are based on standard costs, supplying divisions cannot transfer unfavorable cost variances to purchasing divisions. Suppliers, therefore, have more incentive to control their costs.

11. False — If it is not possible to trace costs to divisions, it is probably better to leave the costs as unallocated costs.

12. False — Managers of segments rarely can control long-term debt, but they can control the utilization of assets.

13. True — There may be projects that have returns greater than the minimum required rate of return for the company but less than the segment's current ROI. Accepting these projects would reduce the segment's ROI and may not be desirable to the segment.

14. True — But opinions vary. Gross book value remains constant over the life of the asset and does not inflate ROI or RI the way that net book value does.

15. False — Stockholders' equity is a measure of owner's investment in a company, but using it to evaluate a manager's performance confuses the financing of a segment with the operations of a segment.

Multiple Choice Questions

1. a,b,c,d — A decentralized segment may be any type of responsibility center, even a government agency.

2. c — Of those listed, only autonomous decision making defines a decentralized segment. A segment does not have to be a manufacturer, manage profits, or be physically separated.

3. a, c — Decentralization can foster a market atmosphere with its disciplining forces and can provide a valuable proving ground for future executives. Companies rarely allow segments to set their own goals, and top management cannot (and should not) control segment operations.

4. b, d — Dysfunctional decision making -- decisions that work against the benefit of the company as a whole -- and duplication of services are possible costs of decentralization. Measurement of profit and use of summary performance measures are not necessary.

5. b — Determining transfer prices based on full costs require some allocation of fixed or common costs.

6. c — Market prices are objective and utilize the information processing of the market to determine the value of resources. The other possibilities are more subjective and prone to challenge.

7. c — Every unit purchased outside the company costs $10 more than the incremental costs incurred by the Pampas division. Just as in the special order decision, the fixed costs are irrelevant since there is idle capacity.

8. c — The situation is reversed from the previous item. Every item made in the company costs $10 more than it would cost to purchase outside.

9. d — All are measures of productivity or efficiency, but the best measure of the segment's profitability as an investment is profit related to invested capital.

10. b, d — Performance is measured as income to invested capital, which may be measured as total assets.

11. c   ROI = return on sales x capital turnover. ROI may be increased by increasing return on sales or capital turnover or both.

12. d   Capital turnover = Revenue/Invested capital
           5 = $800,000/Invested capital
           Invested capital = $800,000/5
           Invested capital = $160,000
      ROI = $32,000/$160,000 = 20%

13. c   ROI = return on sales x capital turnover = .025 x 6 = 15%

14. b   ROI = return on sales x capital turnover
         .18 = .06 x (Revenue/$2,000,000)
    Revenue = (.18/.06) x $2,000,000 = $6,000,000

15. d   Decreasing invested capital increases capital turnover and ROI. The other actions will decrease ROI.

16. c, d   Residual income is segment income less a charge equal to the imputed interest on average capital invested, which is the opportunity cost of the capital -- what the capital could earn in other investments.

17. c   RI = income less opportunity cost of capital
    RI = $2,000,000 - .14 x $10,000,000
    RI = $2,000,000 - $1,400,000 = $600,000

Completion

1. decentralization, the responsibility of an individual or group
2. autonomy of decision making
3. profit-seeking firms have more reliable measures of efficiency
4. cost-based, market price, negotiated
5. make-or-buy
6. net income, invested capital
7. revenue, invested capital
8. net income, imputed interest on invested capital or opportunity cost of capital
9. imputed interest, that is what the invested capital could be earning if invested elsewhere
10. gross book value, net book value of assets, return on investment or residual income

Problems

1. EarthWise Brands, Inc.

	Maritime Division	Farm Division	Industrial Division
Invested capital	$250,000	$200,000	$450,000÷4.5 = $100,000
Revenues (sales)	$750,000	$20,000÷.05 = $400,000	$450,000
Net income	$37,500	.10 x $200,000 = $20,000	$13,500÷$450,000 = 3%
Capital turnover	$750,000÷$250,000 = 3 times	$400,000÷$200,000 = 2 times	4.5 times
Income percentage of revenue	$37,500÷$750,000 = 5%	5%	$13,500
Rate of return on investment	$37,500÷$250,000 = 15%	10%	$13,500÷$100,000 = 13.5%

2. Continental Corp.

   Find for the real estate division:

   a. ROI = $540,000 ÷ $3,000,000 = <u>18%</u>

   b. RI = $540,000 - .16 x $3,000,000 = <u>$60,000</u>

   c. Yes. It would be beneficial to the company as a whole because it earns additional residual income of (.17 - .16) x $200,000 = $2,000. However, the manager would find it unattractive on an ROI basis because overall ROI would decline:
   ROI(new) = ($540,000 + .17 x $200,000) ÷ ($3,000,000 + $200,000)
   ROI(new) = $574,000 ÷ $3,200,000 = <u>17.9%</u>

   d. The ROI would have to increase to 20%
   Revenues:
       Current expenses = $2,700,000 - $540,000 = $2,160,000
       ROI[new] = .20 = (Revenues[new] - $2,160,000) ÷ $3,000,000
   Revenues[new] = .20 x $3,000,000 + $2,160,000 = <u>$2,760,000, an increase of $60,000</u>
   Expenses:
       ROI[new] = .20 = ($2,700,000 - Expenses[new]) ÷ $3,000,000
   Expenses[new] = $2,700,000 - .20 x $3,000,000 = <u>$2,100,000, a decrease of $60,000</u>
   Investment:
       ROI[new] = .20 = $540,000 ÷ Investment[new]
       Investment[new] = $540,000 ÷ .20 = <u>$2,700,000, a decrease of $300,000</u>

Management Control in Decentralized Organizations

3. Ozone Regeneration Division of Mother Earth Company:

	(a)	(b)
Outside market price per unit	63	58
Variable cost per unit	$60	$60
Advantage (disadvantage) per unit	($3)	$2
Multiply by number of units	2,000	2,000
Total advantage (disadvantage) to the company	($6,000)	$4,000

(The fixed costs are irrelevant.)

CHAPTER 11

Capital Budgeting: An Introduction

MAIN FOCUS AND OBJECTIVES

Capital budgeting is the process of arriving at decisions regarding investments in projects covering several years. The leading model for capital-budgeting analysis is discounted cash flow (DCF). This model is based on the concept of time value of money and discounting expected future cash flows. We focus on the two DCF models for selecting and evaluating long-term investments: net present value (NPV) and internal rate of return (IRR). We discuss the limitations and possible benefits of two other models that are sometimes used for analysis of long-term projects: payback period and accounting rate of return. Your learning objectives are to:

- Compute projects' NPVs and IRRs
- Identify the assumptions of these DCF models
- Apply the decision rules for DCF models
- Use sensitivity analysis in evaluating projects
- Use both the total project and differential approaches
- Identify relevant cash flows for DCF analysis
- Use payback and acounting rate of return models
- Understand conflicts between using a DCF model for project selection and accounting income for performance evaluation

---

REVIEW OF KEY CONCEPTS

A. **Capital budgeting** is the process of selecting and evaluating investments in longterm projects.

    1.   There are three steps in preparing a capital budget:
        a.   Identifying potential investments
        b.   Selecting investments to undertake

c. Follow-up or "post-audit" to compare outcomes with expectations (this is a source of valuable feedback, but, unfortunately, this is the least-followed step in practice)

2. Accounting information plays a significant role in the second and third steps, and may play a role in the initial screening step. *This chapter focuses on the second step.*
    a. Note that *capital budgeting is project-oriented*, in contrast to the organization-oriented budgeting we have focused on in earlier chapters.
    b. Recall that a segment of an organization can be characterized as a set of activities. Another way of characterizing a segment is a *set of capital projects* under the management of an individual or group.

3. The conceptually superior approaches to selecting the best projects from those available are **discounted cash flow (DCF)** models because they explicitly and systematically weigh the **time-value (or opportunity cost) of money.**
    a. Money that is tied up in particular projects is not available for other productive purposes. DCF models account for the opportunity cost of money tied up over time.
    b. At a minimum money could be earning interest in the bank, so any project evaluated on financial criteria should do at least as well as money in the bank. In this example, the opportunity cost of capital tied up in projects is at least (expressed as a percentage) the interest rate the money could be earning.
    c. Since any decision is about the future, one could argue that all financial decisions should consider the time value of money. If the time period of a project is short, the time value of money can be ignored (unless interest rates are very high).
    d. The foregone opportunities are *compounded* over time.

    > If you are not familiar with the effects of compounding, please review textbook Appendix B.

    e. Note that DCF models are concerned with cash inflows and outflows, not net income. The reason is that cash could be used (consumed or reinvested), whereas net income may not (e.g., depreciation is an expense but is not a cash outflow).
    f. The initial investment in an asset is typically treated as a single outflow of cash at the start of a project (DCF models easily allow subsequent actual investment).
    g. Therefore, to also deduct periodic depreciation from periodic cash inflows would be a double-counting of this cost over the life of the project and confusing the timing of actual cash outflows.

4. The major information requirements of the DCF models are:
    a. *Predicted cash flows*. Most models assume that cash inflows and outflows are expected to occur at definite times and amounts. These cash flows are the tangible costs and benefits of investing in the future. Usually benefits are more difficult to measure than costs.

b. *The minimum desired rate of return.* This is also called the opportunity rate, required rate of return, interest rate, cost of capital, hurdle rate, discount rate, or the time-value of money. Alternative interest rates abound, but theoretically it is difficult to specify which one is appropriate for a given project.

> Before going on to the next section, be sure that you understand the nature of capital budgeting and are familiar with the theory and mechanics of compound interest.

B. Two DCF models are most commonly used in capital budgeting: the *net-present-value* model and the *internal-rate-of-return* model. In most applications, they are equivalent.

Note: In practice, the mathematics of capital budgeting is accomplished with computer programs, particularly spreadsheet software for PCs. The textbook chapter and this study guide discuss manual approaches to capital budgeting because we believe that once you are familiar with the arithmetic involved, you can use computer programs with the assurance that you are providing the correct inputs. The easy part of capital budgeting is the arithmetic, which is performed quickly by computers, eliminating computational effort. The difficult management task, which computers cannot do, is to develop the cash flows and required rate of return. To confidently develop the proper information and interpret the results, you need to know how the models work. It will reinforce your learning if you also work the examples in the text using a spreadsheet, but only after you understand the manual steps.

1. The **net-present-value (NPV) model** uses a minimum desired rate of return for *discounting* cash outflows and inflows to the present time.
    a. Because future cash flows could be obtained by investing an amount now at some interest rate, we *discount* future cash flows to a present equivalent -- what we would have to invest now to have the expected future cash flow.
    b. For example, if we expect a project's future cash inflow will be $110 one year from now, and our opportunity rate is 10%, how much would we have to invest now in our other opportunities to have the same future cash flow? It is easy to tell that $100 invested today at 10% interest would earn $10, and we would have $110 a year from now. Therefore, our project's expected cash flow of $110 a year in the future is equivalent to $100 today. This is the essence of *discounting*.

> If you are uncomfortable with the concept of discounting, please review textbook Appendix B

    c. The NPV model *discounts* the expected future cash flows of each project to their *present equivalents* or *present values* so that the projects' *net present values* can be compared.
    d. *Net present value* is the sum of the present values of the expected future cash inflows and outflows.
    e. *If the net present value of a project is zero or positive, the project is acceptable. If capital is constrained, choose the projects with the highest net present values first.*

2. The arithmetic of NPV analysis is not difficult, but it pays to be methodical and to be sure that all relevant information is used.
   a. The first step (manual or with spreadsheet software) is to display the relevant cash flows in a diagram. (Just entering cash flows in a spreadsheet effectively builds a diagram of cash flows.)

   > See textbook Exhibit 11-1

   b. The next step is to compute the present value of each cash flow. The manual approach, which you should try until you are comfortable with NPV analysis requires looking up appropriate present value factors in the tables of Appendix B. These factors depend on when cash flows are expected and the appropriate discount rate.
   c. The last step is to sum the present values of the individual cash flows to compute the net present value of the project. Specifying the ranges of cash flows and locations of other parameters of a spreadsheet's present value functions accomplishes this and the previous step automatically.

   > Work through the textbook example in Exhibit 11-1

2. **The internal rate of return (IRR)** is the rate of return (discount rate) that makes the net present value of a project equal to zero.
   a. The IRR approach treats the NPV of a project as known (zero) and treats the discount rate as the unknown -- the IRR process is just the inverse of the NPV process.

   For example, what is the IRR of a project that costs $100 now and will have a cash inflow of $110 one year from now? It is easy to see that this project earns $10 or 10% on the investment in one year; that is, its IRR is 10%.

   What you did in your head, we could prove mathematically by solving the following equation for the unknown IRR:
   $$\$110 = \$100 + \$100 \times IRR$$
   $$\$110 = \$100 \times (1 + IRR)$$
   $$(1 + IRR) = \$110 \div \$100 = 1.10$$
   $$\therefore IRR = 1.10 - 1 = .10 = \underline{10\%}$$

   b. As shown in the example above, the essence of the IRR process is conceptually not difficult, but when the pattern of cash flows is complex, the arithmetic can be messy.
   c. If the IRR equals or exceeds the minimum desired rate of return, accept the project; if not, reject the project. If capital is scarce, choose the projects with the highest IRRs first.

3. The IRR approach to capital budgeting follows these steps:
   a. The first step of the IRR approach is identical to the first step of the NPV approach -- diagram the pattern of cash flows.

   > See textbook Exhibit 11-2

b. The second step is to find the interest rate that makes the NPV of the project equal to zero. The manual approach is to use a *trial-and-error* search (another name for systematically guessing the IRR):
- Choose an interest rate
- Multiply the expected cash flows by the appropriate discount factors in Appendix B
- See whether the sum of all the present values (NPV) of the cash flows equals zero.
- If the NPV is positive, you have not discounted enough, so choose a higher interest rate and repeat.
- If the NPV is negative, you have discounted too much, so choose a lower interest rate and repeat
- Repeat the process until the NPV is close enough to zero.

c. The best approach in practice is to use a spreadsheet program (or programmable calculator) IRR function, which itself is just a computer program to conduct a trial and error search.

d. However, do not use a spreadsheet program to find the IRR until you are comfortable with the arithmetic involved.

> Work through the example in textbook Exhibits 11-2 and 11-3

4. The attractiveness of two projects can be compared by two, equivalent NPV methods or by comparing IRRs.
  a. The total project NPV approach:
  - Calculate the NPV of each of the two projects.
  - Find the difference between these NPVs.
  b. The differential NPV approach:
  - Find the differences between the cash flows of each of two projects in each time period.
  - Calculate the NPV of these differences.

> See textbook Exhibit 11-4

> Before going on to the next section be sure that you are comfortable with the concepts and the computations of the NPV and the IRR approaches to capital budgeting analysis.

C. There is always some *uncertainty* whether cash-flow predictions will actually be realized.

1. Some ways to recognize this uncertainty is to become more conservative in the measurement of the inputs to the NPV or IRR models:
  a. Use higher discount rates when uncertainty is greater.
  b. Predict lower cash inflows and higher cash outflows when uncertainty is greater.
  c. Reduce expected lives when uncertainty is greater.

2. Perhaps a better way to model uncertainty is to use *sensitivity analysis*, introduced in Chapter 7. A popular form of sensitivity analysis prepares three possible NPVs or IRRs:

       a. Make and compare three separate sets of predictions for each possible project: *pessimistic, expected,* and *optimistic.*
       b. Determine how much the optimistic and pessimistic NPVs or IRRs differ from the expected NPV or IRR for each project.
       c. *Riskier* projects have a wider range of NPV and IRR from the expected values.
       d. By identifying the risk of projects, managers can make tradeoffs between the expected NPV or IRR of a project and its risk. For example, a manager may choose a project with a lower IRR if higher IRR projects have unacceptably high risk. This tradeoff is a personal one, but, as discussed in Chapter 9, incentive systems may be designed to align managers' goals with owners' goals.

3. Summary of typical concerns in analyzing expected cash-flows:
       a. *Current* disposal values of old assets are most conveniently handled by offsetting them against the gross cash outlays for new assets at time zero.
       b. All initial investments (including receivables, inventories, intangibles) are typically regarded as cash outflows at time zero, and their *terminal* disposal values (if any) are treated as cash inflows at the end of the project's useful life.
       c. Errors in forecasting future disposal values are usually not crucial because the combination of relatively small disposal values and long time periods tends to produce rather small present values.
       d. In the relevant-cost analysis of factory overhead, the only pertinent cost is avoidable overhead.
       e. A reduction in an operating cash outflow is the same as a cash inflow.
       f. Depreciation and book values are ignored because they are cost allocations, not cash flows.
       g. When comparing projects with unequal lives, make the projects have equal lives by either imposing the shorter life on both or assuming reinvestment in the shorter-life project.
       h. Income taxes and inflation do affect cash flows, but consideration of their effects is postponed until the next chapter.

4. It is important to recognize that not adopting new technology could result in lower future cash flows than were predicted for the current process. The status quo actually may decline from the present course because of the advantages new technology will give to competitors.

Do you have an appreciation for the difficulties of measuring future cash flows? This is what causes managers and budget analysts the most problems and where subjectivity is the greatest. Sensitivity analysis may be crucial to making good capital budgeting decisions.

D. DCF models are recommended for capital-budgeting decisions but several other approaches are still used in some businesses:
1. The crisis-response or emergency-persuasion method uses no formal planning but seems to be based mainly on urgency caused by procrastination and neglect (not recommended!).
2. The **payback model** measures the estimated number of years before cash inflows return the initial cash investment.
   a. If cash flows are uniform, the initial cash investment is divided by the annual cash inflow; if cash flows are not uniform, a cumulative approach is used.
   b. Though this method ignores the profitability of investment, it is a popular way for providing a rough estimate of riskiness -- longer paybacks imply greater risk.
3. The **accounting rate-of-return** is the predicted amount of future average annual net income divided by the initial (sometimes average) amount of the required investment.
   a. This model ignores the time value of money.
   b. However, it is used because it measures profit by conventional accrual accounting methods, and because it is easy to evaluate the performance of projects by comparing actual accounting income to expected income.
   c. It is also used because it is constructed the same way as the return-on-investment (ROI) figure used to evaluate decentralized profit centers as a whole (Chapter 10).

PRACTICE TEST QUESTIONS AND PROBLEMS WITH SOLUTIONS

True or False Statements

Determine whether each of the following statements is True (T) or False (F), and enter your answer in the space provided.

_____1. If a capital-budgeting project has a zero net present value, this would indicate that the project is acceptable.

_____2. If a capital-budgeting project has a negative NPV, this would measure the amount of prospective loss on the project.

_____3. The main purpose of post-audits of capital-budgeting projects is to verify that the accounting records accurately reflect the actual transactions of the projects.

_____4. The internal rate of return is the discount rate that produces a zero NPV.

_____5. If a project has a negative NPV, the IRR would be higher than the discount rate used to compute NPV.

_____6. A project has a positive NPV using a 15% discount rate. Its IRR would be greater than 15%.

_____7. The present value of $50,000 due five years from now would be higher if computed at a discount rate of 6% than at 12%.

___8. Two projects promise the same amounts and timing of cash inflows, but Project A requires an immediate cash outflow of $100,000 while Project B requires a $50,000 cash outflow now and a $50,000 cash outflow one year from now. The project with the larger NPV is Project A.

___9. The use of the discounted-cash-flow approach requires that periodic depreciation expense be deducted from cash inflows.

___10. Discounted-cash-flow techniques are designed to measure the opportunity cost of investments.

___11. Generally, in DCF analysis, we should ignore book values.

___12. The profitability of an investment is ignored by the payback model.

___13. The time value of money is ignored by the accounting-rate-of-return model.

___14. The adoption of the DCF approach to capital-budgeting decisions tends to be hindered by the continued use of conventional accrual accounting methods for performance evaluation.

___15. A follow-up or postaudit of a capital-budgeting decision is facilitated by the capital budgeting use of the accounting-rate-of-return model.

Multiple Choice Questions

For each of the following multiple-choice questions, select the best answer(s) and enter the identification letter(s) in the space provided.

___1. DCF models include: (a) NPV, (b) IMA, (c) ARR, (d) IRR.

___2. Present value annuity factors are (a) applied to terminal disposal values, (b) equal to the sum of the same number of year's present value factors, (c) applied to equal cash inflows over a number of periods, (d) applied to equal cash outflows over a number of periods.

___3. Bon Co. is considering the purchase of a special-purpose machine for $48,000. The machine has a twelve-year estimated life, a zero salvage value, and expected cash operating savings of $11,000 per year. Compute the payback period: (a) 4.4 years, (b) 7.6 years, (c) 4.8 years, (d) 6.9 years.

___4. See the preceding test item. Compute the accounting rate of return on the initial investment using straight-line depreciation: (a) 20.8%, (b) 22.9%, (c) 14.6%, (d) 13.2%.

___5. See the Bon Co. data in item 4 above. Present-value tables at 16% show 0.168 and 5.197, respectively, for present values of $1 and an annuity of $1. Compute NPV: (a) $5,007, (b) $9,167, (c) $4,167, (d) $6,327.

___6. See the Bon Co. data in item 4 above. The project's IRR is closest to: (a) 14%, (b) 16%, (c) 18%, (d) 20%.

___7. In a capital-budgeting project, risk can be recognized by: (a) decreasing predictions of cash inflows, (b) increasing the discount rate to be used, (c) decreasing the predicted useful life of the project, (d) comparing the NPV of optimistic and pessimistic predictions of cash flows.

_____ 8. Mot Co. is considering the purchase of equipment for $10,000. The company anticipates annual cash savings of $4,000 for four years with no residual value. Compute NPV at a 10% discount rate. A table shows the annuity discount factor to be 3.170. NPV is: (a) $2,680, (b) $12,680, (c) $6,000, (d) $1,680.

_____ 9. See the preceding test item. Compute the annual cash inflow that would make the net present value equal to zero: (a) $3,170, (b) $13,170, (c) $6,830, (d) $3,155.

_____ 10. A project requires an immediate investment of $50,000 cash, and it promises cash returns at the end of each year as follows: first year $10,000, second year $12,000, third year $13,000, fourth year $15,000, fifth year $20,000, and sixth (and final) year $30,000. The payback period in years is: (a) two, (b) three, (c) four, (d) five, (e) six.

_____ 11. A project requires an immediate investment of $60,000 in some new equipment with an estimated useful life of ten years and no residual value. If predicted annual savings of cash operating expenses are $15,000, what is the accounting rate of return based on the initial investment? Use straight-line depreciation and ignore income taxes: (a) 25%, (b) 20%, (c) 15%, (d) 10%.

Completion

Complete each of the following statements by filling in the blanks.

1. Identify each of the following:
   DCF _____
   PV _____
   NPV _____
   IRR _____
   ARR _____

2. What the terms above have in common is: _____
   _____

3. The primary difference between IRR and ARR is _____
   _____.

4. When a project has a negative NPV, the present value of the _____
   _____ is _____ than the present value
   of the _____.

5. A proposed project should be accepted if the internal rate of return is
   _____ than the _____.

6. If the NPV is negative, the _____ return is greater than the
   _____ return.

7. Depreciation is not deducted from future cash flows in DCF analysis because though depreciation is an _____ it is not a
   _____ at the time depreciation is recognized as an
   _____.

8. _____ is the process of varying assumptions about cash flows and project lives to test the
   _____ of NPV or IRR to those assumptions.

Capital Budgeting: An Introduction **167**

9. If expected annual cash flows are uniform, the payback period can be computed by dividing _____ by _____ ; otherwise a _____ approach must be used.

10. The major difference between ARR and ROI is that ARR measures _____ _____ and ROI measures _____.

Problems

1. Given for Solar Production Corp.:

Old machine: book value now $60,000, salvage value now	$ 8,000
New replacement machine:	
Price now	$110,000
Predicted useful life	13 years
Predicted residual value at end of useful life	$ 20,000
Predicted annual savings in cash operating expenses (increase in annual cash operating income)	$ 15,000
Minimum desired rate of return	10%
Present value of $1 due 13 years from now, using a 10% interest rate	$0.29
Present value of $1 per year due at the end of *each* of 13 years from now, using a 10% interest rate	$7.10

Should the old machine be replaced with the new machine? Show supporting computations:

2. Given for GeoTherm Equipment Co.:

Initial cost of investing in a special-purpose machine	$540,000
Predicted useful life (no terminal disposal value)	15 years
Predicted annual savings in cash operating expenses	$ 90,000
Present value of an annuity of $1 for 15 years:	
Using a 8% interest rate	$8.559
Using a 10% interest rate	$7.606
Using GeoTherm's opportunity cost of capital, 12%	$6.811
Using a 14% interest rate	$6.142
Using a 16% interest rate	$5.575

a. What is the NPV of this investment project?

b. Is the IRR greater or less than GeoTherm's minimum, required rate of return? Explain.

c. Manually find the project's IRR to the nearest tenth of a percent, ignoring income tax effects (hint: begin by computing the payback period):

Capital Budgeting: An Introduction 169

3. Given for TidalSurge Company

Initial cost of proposed new equipment	$130,000
Predicted useful life	10 years
Predicted disposal value at end of useful life	$10,000
Predicted savings per year in cash operating expenses	$24,000
Present value of $1 due 10 years from now, using a 10% interest rate, which is TidalSurge's required rate	$0.385
Present value of $1 per year due at the end of *each* of 10 years from now, using a 10% interest rate	$6.145

Manually compute each of the following for this project, ignoring income tax effects:

a. NPV

b. Payback period

c. Depreciation expense per year by straight-line method:

d. Predicted increase in future annual net income:

e. ARR based on initial investment:

f. GeoTherm Company is an autonomous division of Consolidated Energy Corp, evaluated as an investment center, an currently has an ROI of 15%. Would the managers of GeoTherm be inclined to accept or reject this project? Explain.

CHAPTER 11 SOLUTIONS TO PRACTICE TEST QUESTIONS AND PROBLEMS

True or False Statements

1. **True** — If the NPV of a project is zero, the project just earns the minimum required rate of return and is acceptable.

2. **True** — The amount of the negative NPV is the amount of the *opportunity loss* taken if the project is accepted -- that much less could be invested in other projects to attain the same pattern of cash flows over time. This does not measure the amount of accounting loss that might occur.

3. **False** — The capital budgeting post-audit process is similar to flexible-budgeting variance analysis. The purpose is to assess the quality of planning and implementation of capital projects and to determine whether continued investment is worthwhile.

4. **True** — This is the definition of internal rate of return. This IRR would be compared to the required rate of return to determine project acceptability.

5. **False** — A negative NPV means that the project is earning less than the required rate of return, or the IRR is less than the discount rate.

6. **True** — A positive NPV means that the project is earning more than the required rate of return; in this case the IRR is greater 15%.

7. **True** — Higher interest rates discount future cash flows more than lower rates because at less would have to be invested now to grow to the same future amount. At 6% the present value of $50,000 five years from now is .747 x $50,000 = $37,350, which means that $37,350 could be invested now at 6%, and five years later the investment would have grown to $50,000. In contrast, at 12% the present value of $50,000 five years from now is only .567 x $50,000 = $28,350, because only $28,350 need be invested now at 12% to have $50,000 after five years.

8. **False** — Because half of the cost of Project B is not due for a year, its NPV is greater. Looking only at the investment costs, the present value of the cost of Project A is $100,000 because it is paid immediately. The second cash outflow of Project B, however, is discounted. For example, at a 10% discount rate the present value of the cost of Project B is $50,000 + .909 x $50,000 = $50,000 + $45,450 = $95,450. Because the present value of the investment cost of Project B is $4,550 less, its NPV will be $4,550 greater.

9. **False** — Periodic depreciation is not a cash outflow, so it is not deducted from cash inflows when using DCF techniques.

10. **True** — By using an individual's or organization's opportunity cost of capital as the discount rate, DCF techniques measure either the value of a project in terms of equivalent investment required to earn the same cash flows (NPV) or the rate of return foregone if a project is not accepted (IRR).

11. **True** — Book values of assets really have no relevance for decisions regarding future cash flows, except as they might impact gains or losses for tax purposes.

12. **True** — All the payback model does is compute the number of years it would take to recover the initial investment, ignoring both the time-value of money and the

profitability of the project. By coincidence, however, in the case of an investment with equal cash flows over time the payback period is also the annuity factor of the IRR of the project.

13. True   The ARR model is the expected net income divided by the average value of the investment; it has nothing to say about the time-value of money.

14. True   It is possible that projects which look attractive using DCF methods could cause reductions in accrual accounting measures of net income at the same time as the investment base would increase. Both of these effects would reduce a segment's ROI. Thus, a manager might prefer to use ARR or payback to make capital budgeting decisions rather than the more appropriate (from the company's point of view) DCF methods.

15. True   Post-audit is easier when the ARR method was used to choose capital projects because the information to compute ARR (and ROI) are readily available from the accounting system.

Multiple Choice Questions

1. a, d   NPV (net present value) and IRR (internal rate of return) are both DCF (discounted cash flow) models. IMA is the Institute of Management Accountants; and ARR is accounting rate of return (a non-DCF approach to capital budgeting).

2. b, c, d   Annuity factors are applied to both equal cash inflows and equal cash outflows. They are also equal to the sum of the individual present value factors over the same sequence of periods.

3. a   The payback period is $48,000 ÷ $11,000 = 4.36 years or approximately 4.4 years.

4. c   The ARR = ($11,000 - $48,000÷12) ÷ $48,000 = $7,000 ÷ $48,000 = 14.6%

5. b   The NPV is $11,000 x 5.197 - $48,000 = $9,167.

6. d   The NPV is positive, so the IRR is greater than 16%. Since the cash flows are equal, the payback period is the same as the annuity factor at the IRR. A look at the annuity table in textbook Appendix B along the 12-year row shows that 4.36 is closest to the annuity factor for 20%.

7. a,b,c,d   The first three approaches make the analysis more conservative, but there is much subjectivity involved. The last approach, sensitivity analysis, may be the best because it is more systematic.

8. a   The NPV is $4,000 x 3.170 - $10,000 = $2,680.

9. d   The annual cash inflow would be computed as: C x 3.170 -10,000 = 0; C = 10,000 ÷ 3.170 = $3,155.

10. c   The payback period is computed as the number of years to recover the initial investment: $50,000 = $10,000(1st yr) + $12,000(2nd yr) + $13,000(3rd yr) + $15,000(4th yr).

11. c   The ARR is computed as: ($15,000 - $60,000÷10) ÷ $60,000 = 15%.

Completion

1. DCF = discounted cash flow; PV = present value; NPV = net present value; IRR = internal rate of return; ARR = accounting rate of return.
2. All the terms refer to capital-budgeting models.
3. IRR incorporates the time-value of money, whereas ARR does not.
4. cash inflows, less, cash outflows (or cash outflows, greater, cash inflows)
5. greater, required (or opportunity) rate of return.
6. required rate of, internal rate of
7. expense, cash outflow, expense.
8. Sensitivity analysis, sensitivity or variation
9. the initial investment, the annual cash flow, cumulative
10. the accounting rate of return of projects, the accounting rate of return of segments.

Problems

1. Solar Production Corp.

Present value of new machine's disposal value:
$20,000 x 0.29 $ 5,800

Present value of annual savings:
$15,000 x 7.10   106,500

Total present value $112,300

Less required investment:
$110,000 - $8,000   102,000

Net present value of replacement $ 10,300

Decision: replace old machine ($60,000 book value is irrelevant)

2. GeoTherm Equipment Co.

a. NPV = $90,000 x 6.811 - $540,000 = $72,990

b. The IRR is greater than the minimum rate of return. If the IRR were 12% the NPV would be zero. The NPV is positive which means that the project earns more than 12%.

c. Payback period is $540,000 divided by $90,000   6 years

Since the IRR is greater than 12%, note that the payback period, which is the annuity factor of the IRR lies between the annuity factors for 14% and 16%.

<u>Present-Value Factors</u>

Rate of return		
14%	6.142	6.142
True rate		6.000
16%	<u>5.575</u>	<u>- .</u>
Differences.	<u>.567</u>	<u>.142</u>

The IRR can be approximated by linear interpolations (which usually is close enough, as shown below):

IRR = 14% + (.142 ÷ .567) x 2% = 14% + .25 x 2% = 14.5%

The estimate of IRR from a spreadsheet program is 14.4721%

3. TidalSurge Company
   a. NPV $24,000 x 6.145
           + $10,000 x .385
           - $130,000   <u>$21,330</u>

   b. Payback period: $130,000 ÷ $24,000   <u>5.4 years</u>

   c. Depreciation expense per year: $130,000 ÷ 10 years   <u>$13,000 per year</u>

   d. Predicted increase in future
      annual net income: $24,000 - $13,000   <u>$11,000</u>

   e. Accounting rate of return based on initial investment: $11,000 ÷ 130,000   <u>8.5%</u>

   f. GeoTherm would be inclined to reject this project because the ARR is less than the current ROI. Thus, accepting the project would reduce the segment's ROI, at least in the early part of the project. This is contrary to the advice from the NPV model which is to accept the project.

CHAPTER 12

Capital Budgeting: Taxes and Inflation

> **MAIN FOCUS AND OBJECTIVES**
>
> This chapter deals with *income tax effects*, principally involving depreciation, on capital-budgeting decisions, which the preceding chapter ignored. Your primary objective is to be able to make a capital budgeting analysis that includes income tax effects. Note that most countries' tax regulations are very complex, and this chapter is only a brief introduction to the effects of taxation on capital budgeting. This chapter also considers how to incorporate expectations about inflation in capital-budgeting analyses. The main learning objectives are to:
>
> - Determine the after-tax cash flow from operations
>
> - Compute after-tax NPVs using straight-line and accelerated depreciation methods
>
> - Compute the after-tax effects of disposing of assets
>
> - Assess the impact of inflation on capital-budgeting decisions

REVIEW OF KEY CONCEPTS

A. Both the *amount* and *timing* of cash flows are directly affected by taxation of income of profit-seeking firms.

    1. Payments for income taxes are cash outflows in the year paid; therefore, reductions in tax payments are cash savings, equivalent to cash inflows ("a penny saved ....").

    2. Deferral of tax payments results in payments at a later time, which because of the time-value of money are discounted (i.e., their present value is less than their future amount).

    3. Depreciation is a *noncash* expense that *reduces* what taxable income would otherwise be.
        a. Although depreciation itself is not a cash flow, it has important cash-flow consequences because it is a deduction from taxable income.
        b. Depreciation is an important **tax shield**, so-named because it protects income from taxation. The tax shield effects of depreciation are meant to provide incentive to invest through lowered tax payments.

c. The amount of the tax shield is the amount of taxes saved, which is the amount of income shielded multiplied by the tax rate.

> See textbook Exhibits 12-1 and 12-2

4. Depending on the depreciation method used, depreciation expense can also affect the *timing* of tax savings.
    a. Because these tax savings from depreciation occur over the life of a capital project, they have a present value.
    b. Alternative depreciation methods may be used to compute taxable income.
    c. Different depreciation methods affect the timing of depreciation expense, and therefore affect the timing of tax savings and the *present value of tax savings*.

5. The two types of depreciation are straight-line and *accelerated* depreciation.
    a. Straight-line depreciation per year, as introduced earlier in the text is the initial investment less terminal salvage value, divided by useful life.
    b. **Accelerated depreciation** is a depreciation method that recognizes more expense early in the life of the capital project compared to straight-line depreciation (note: total depreciation expense over the life of the project is the same using any method).
    c. With accelerated depreciation, also early in the life of the project: taxable income is less, tax savings are greater, and tax payments are less.
    d. Because of the time-value of money, *the present value of tax savings is greater using accelerated depreciation than using straight-line depreciation*.

6. A widely used form of accelerated depreciation is **double-declining balance (DDB)**. The method is applied as follows:
    a. Divide 100% by the number of years in the investment's depreciation life.
    b. For a five-year life, this would be 100% ÷ 5 = 20% per year (this is also the straight-line rate per year).
    c. Double this to get 40% as a constant rate to apply each year to the *undepreciated balance* of the investment. Ignore terminal salvage values to compute the depreciable amount.
    d. Toward the end of the life of the investment, switch to straight-line depreciation for the remainder of the life when the DDB depreciation would drop below the straight-line amount.
    e. To ease the use of DDB, use the schedule in Exhibit 12-3. This shows DDB annual depreciation rates for selected investment lives.

> See textbook Exhibit 12-3

Example 1: Assume a project initially costs $1,000, has no disposal value, and has an expected life of 4 years. The project promises operating cash savings of $500 per year. The cost of capital is 8%, and the tax rate is 40%(a) Compute the NPV of the project using straight-line depreciation, (b) compute the NPV of the project using DDB depreciation.

(a) Straight-line depreciation:

	Present value at 8%	1	2	3	4	total
Cash savings		$500	$500	$500	$500	$2,000
Less depreciation		250	250	250	250	1,000
Income		$250	$250	$250	$250	$1,000
Taxes at 40%		100	100	100	100	400
Income after tax		$150	$150	$150	$150	600
Add back depreciation		250	250	250	250	1,000
After-tax net cash flow	$400 x 3.312 = $1,325	$400	$400	$400	$400	$1,600
Less investment cost	$1,000					
Net present value	$325					

(b) DDB depreciation using Exhibit 12-3:

	Present value at 8%	1	2	3	4	total
Cash savings		$500	$500	$500	$500	$2,000
Less depreciation		500	250	125	125	1,000
Income		$ 0	$250	$375	$375	$1,000
Taxes at 40%		0	100	150	150	400
Income after tax		$ 0	$150	$225	$225	$600
Add back depreciation		500	250	125	125	1,000
After-tax net cash flow		$500	$400	$350	$350	$1,600
PV factors	$1,341	.926	.857	.794	.735	
Less investment cost	$1,000					
Net present value	$341					

Difference in NPV = $16 in favor of DDB

Note: (1) Depreciation is added back to net income after tax to obtain net cash flow after tax because though depreciation reduced income, it is not a cash outflow.

(2) The total incomes, depreciations, taxes, and net cash flows are the same over the 4-year life, regardless of depreciation method

(3) *The NPV of the project is higher using DDB depreciation because of the timing of the tax savings is earlier using DDB.*

Example 2: Assume the same facts as the previous example, but compute the present values of the tax savings using either straight-line or DDB depreciation.

Straight line depreciation

	1	2	3	4	total
Annual depreciation	$250	$250	$250	$250	$1,000
Tax savings at 40%	100	100	100	100	400

Present value of tax savings $100 x 3.312 = $331

DDB depreciation

	1	2	3	4	total
Annual depreciation	$500	$250	$125	$125	$1,000
Tax savings at 40%	200	100	50	50	400

Present value of tax savings $347   .926 .857 .794 .735

Difference $16

Note: (1) The difference in the present value of the tax savings is exactly the same as the difference in NPVs using the alternative methods.

(2) Again, though the total depreciation and tax savings are the same over the investment's 4-year life, the difference in present values is due to the *timing* of tax savings.

7. In the U.S. MACRS depreciation is the allowed accelerated method for taxation for most investments. Schedules similar to Exhibit 12-3 are available for MACRS.

8. When a depreciable asset is sold, the amount of the after-tax cash inflow from the disposal is the sales proceeds:
   a. *Minus* the income tax on the gain, or
   b. *Plus* the tax savings from the loss on sale.

> See the textbook example.

> Before going on to the next section, be sure that you understand (1) how depreciation increases after-tax cash flow through tax savings and (2) how different depreciation methods affect the timing of tax savings and the net present values of projects. Remember: depreciation is not a cash outflow, nor is it a cash inflow -- it has beneficial cash flow effects because it reduces tax payments.

B. In most cases, DCF models should be adjusted for the effects of price inflation (the decline in the general purchasing power of money).

1. Inflation is the condition of eroding purchasing power of money over time; that is, when prices have risen in unison, it costs more to buy the same goods and services now than it did in the past.
   a. If inflation is expected, operating expenses (*except depreciation*) should be predicted to rise with inflation.
   b. Note that since depreciation is an allocation of a past cost to future periods, tax laws usually do not permit adjusting depreciation expense for the effects of inflation.

c. If inflation is expected, sales revenues also should be expected to rise -- a difficult prediction is whether sales prices will increase at the same rate as operating expenses.
d. Because interest rates are the costs of money, they can be expected to rise as well.
e. Even modest rates of inflation can have very large compounded effects after a number of years. Of course, in parts of the world with 3-digit inflation rates, the problem is critical.

2. The **nominal** (or market) discount rate includes an element that is the real rate of interest and another element representing the expected rate of inflation.
   a. If nominal, market rates are used in DCF models, future cash flows must also be adjusted for expected inflation.
   b. If only the real rate of interest is used, then do not adjust future cash flows for expected inflation, use estimates in today's costs.
   c. The key is consistency in either using an inflation element in both the discount rate and the predicted operating cash flows or in neither.

> See textbook Exhibit 12-5

3. Operating expenses or revenues are adjusted for expected inflation by multiplying current amounts by an index that measures percentage changes expected prices.
   a. For example, if an operating cost today is $100 and 10% inflation is expected each year for the next 3 years, adjusted expenses will be
      now $100
      in 1 year   110
      in 2 years   121
      in 3 years   133
   b. Note that continued inflation has the same mathematical impact as compound interest.
   c. Many different price indexes that measure past levels and rates of inflation are available for use, but it is not always clear which one to use. In practice, analysts use either a very general (economy-wide) price level index or a very specific (product, region, or industry) index.

> Before going on to the practice test, be sure that you understand why and how to adjust DCF models for the anticipated effects of inflation.

PRACTICE TEST QUESTIONS AND PROBLEMS WITH SOLUTIONS

True or False Statements

Determine whether each of the following statements is True (T) or False (F) and enter your answer in the space provided.

____1. The income tax rate to be used for capital-budgeting analysis is a company's average effective rate.

____2. Assume, as in the textbook Exhibit 13-1, that all transactions involve cash except depreciation. If the income tax rate is 40%, depreciation in the amount of $5,000 would produce a cash tax savings of $2,000.

____3. An investment tax credit would enhance the net present value of a project because it would increase the deductions allowed against revenues.

____4. In the U.S., the choice of depreciation method for financial reporting is restricted to the method used for tax reporting.

____5. The benefit of accelerated depreciation is that it moves tax payments earlier in the life of an investment and gets them over with sooner.

____6. The depreciation method to be used for capital-budgeting analysis is the method used by a company for its reports to its stockholders.

____7. Examples of tax shields include depreciation of equipment, salaries of employees, and interest expense.

____8. Net book values and depreciation can be relevant to predicting future cash flows.

____9. The present value of a depreciation tax shield is the tax rate multiplied by the present value of the depreciation stream.

____10. Straight-line depreciation could be characterized as a "single-declining-balance" method.

____11. The gain or loss on the disposal of depreciable equipment is the disposal value less the net book value of the equipment.

____12. The gain or loss on the disposal of depreciable equipment is a cash flow in the year of disposal.

____13. A World Bank budget analyst uses the pure rate of interest to evaluate the acceptability of a 50-year dam project in an under-developed country. Because inflation rates have been and are expected to be near 100% per year for the foreseeable future, the analyst must adjust future cash flows for the enormous expected inflation.

____14. The expected future cash flows caused by income tax savings from depreciation should be adjusted by the rate of inflation before being discounted to the present.

____15. The "nominal rate" to use for DCF computations under inflationary conditions is the sum of the business-risk element and the inflation element.

Multiple Choice Questions

For each of the following multiple-choice questions, select the best answer(s) and enter the identification letter(s) in the space provided.

_____ 1. Assume that the income tax rate is 60%. Depreciation in the amount of $5,000 would produce a cash tax savings of: (a) $5,000, (b) $3,000, (c) $2,000, (d) $2,500.

_____ 2. See item 1. Assume also $60,000 of sales and $40,000 of cash expenses. Net income is: (a) $15,000, (b) $9,000, (c) $6,000, (d) $20,000.

_____ 3. See items 1 and 2. The total after-tax cash inflow from operations is: (a) $9,000, (b) $11,000, (c) $5,000, (d) $8,000.

_____ 4. Assume two expenses of a business: cash advertising $20,000 and depreciation $20,000. If the income tax rate is 30%, the after-tax effects on cash would be: (a) inflow $6,000 for advertising and inflow $6,000 for depreciation, (b) inflow $14,000 for advertising and inflow $14,000 for depreciation, (c) outflow $6,000 for advertising and inflow $14,000 for depreciation, (d) outflow $14,000 for advertising and inflow $6,000 for depreciation.

_____ 5. Given for a certain company: sales $200,000, depreciation expense $20,000, other expenses $150,000, income tax rate 40%. All amounts are for cash except depreciation. Compute net income: (a) $30,000, (b) $18,000, (c) $12,000, (d) $20,000.

_____ 6. See the preceding test item. Compute the after-tax cash flow from operations: (a) $32,000, (b) $40,000 (c) $50,000, (d) $38,000.

_____ 7. See item 5 above. Compute the after-tax effect of depreciation on cash inflow: (a) $8,000, (b) $12,000, (c) $20,000, (d) $30,000.

_____ 8. Appropriate Company acquired a depreciable asset for $72,000. It has an estimated life of eight years with an $8,000 terminal salvage value. First-year depreciation expense by the DDB method would be: (a) $36,000, (b) $16,000, (c) $18,000, (d) $8,000.

_____ 9. See item 8. If the income tax rate if 40%, what is the tax-saving effect of using the DDB method instead of the straight-line method for the first year? (a) $6,000 less tax, (b) $6,000 more tax, (c) $4,000 more tax, (d) $4,000 less tax.

_____ 10. Pow Co. sold for $44,000 cash an old piece of equipment. It was purchased 8 years ago for $130,000 and was being depreciated on a straight-line basis over a useful life of 10 years with an expected terminal scrap value of $10,000. What was the gain or loss on the sale before income taxes?(a) $20,000 gain, (b) $18,000 loss, (c) $10,000 gain, (d) $16,000 loss.

_____ 11. See the preceding test item. Compute the after-tax cash effect of the sale transaction only, assuming a 40% tax rate: (a) $40,000, (b) $17,600, (c) $26,400, (d) $32,000.

_____ 12. To compensate for the effects of inflation, one should adjust the DCF model by: (a) increasing the market rate and reducing the cash operating inflows, (b) reducing the market rate and keeping the cash operating inflows at current costs, (c) reducing the market rate and increasing the cash operating inflows, (d) using the market rate and increasing the cash operating inflows.

Capital Budgeting: Taxes and Inflation 181

Completion

Complete the following statements by filling in the blanks.

1. The _____ income tax rate is the rate that will be charged on additional income that is expected from new investment.

2. Inflation is the _____ of the monetary _____.

3. Though depreciation is not a _____ it has _____ effects through its shielding of income.

4. The benefit of accelerated depreciation is that it _____ earlier than straight line depreciation.

5. DDB or _____ depreciation is an example of _____.

6. DDB depreciation ignores _____ values and switches to _____ depreciation when _____.

7. A gain or loss on the sale of depreciable equipment is equal to _____ less _____.

8. The problem with adjusting depreciation for expected inflation in capital-budgeting analysis is _____.

9. If expected future cash flows are not adjusted for expected _____, then use the _____ rate of interest in DCF models.

10. The nominal rate of interest, also called the _____ rate of interest is the _____ rate plus the _____ rate.

Problems

NOTE: Ignore any possible tax credits in these problems.

1. Given for Sun Flower Energy Corporation's 19X5 operations:

Sales	$700,000
Straight-line depreciation expense	30,000
Other operating expenses, including cost of goods sold	600,000
Income tax rate	60%

    a. Compute net income

    b. Compute the annual value of the income tax savings from depreciation:

    c. Compute the after-tax net cash inflow from operations:

2. Using the data below for Gasahol Co., compute the NPV of the investment:

Purchase price of special equipment	$120,000
Predicted useful life	8 years
Predicted annual savings in cash operating costs	$ 30,000
Predicted disposal value (terminal scrap value)	none
Depreciation method:	straight-line
Minimum desired *after-tax* rate of return	8%
Marginal income tax rate	30%
Present value of annuity of $1 for eight years at 8%	$5.75

Capital Budgeting: Taxes and Inflation **183**

3. Zephyr Energy Company has just purchased a special piece of electrical generation equipment for $450,000. It is estimated to have a depreciable life of five years and a terminal scrap value of $30,000. Compute the following:

   a. Depreciation for the first year:

   Straight-line method

   DDB method

   b. Depreciation for the second year by DDB

   c. Income tax saving effect of DDB compared with the straight-line method for the second year, assuming a 30% income tax rate

4. Parachute Oil Shale Co. sold for $90,000 cash some of its old equipment. This machinery was purchased five years ago for $280,000. It was being depreciated on a DDB basis over a useful life of ten years with an estimated terminal salvage value of $40,000.

   Compute the after-tax cash effect of the sale transaction only, assuming a 30% income tax rate.

5. Wildcat Company's discount rate of 24% for capital budgeting includes an 8% inflation element. Use .806 as the discount factor for one year at 24%. Assume a 40% income tax rate and compute the present value of:

   a. A $400,000 pretax cash operating inflow one year from now.

   b. The income tax savings of a $140,000 depreciation expense one year from now.

CHAPTER 12 SOLUTIONS TO PRACTICE TEST QUESTIONS AND PROBLEMS

True or False Statements

1. False — New investment will produce incremental income; therefore, the proper income tax rate to use is the marginal rate, not the average rate.

2. True — The cash tax savings is the amount of income shielded multiplied by the tax rate that would have been paid on that amount: $5,000 x .4 = $2,000.

3. False — Technically, this is not correct. Tax credits reduce income tax payments directly in the amount of the credit. The credit is not deducted from revenues as is depreciation.

4. False — Though this is true in some countries, in the U.S. companies can use different depreciation methods for financial reporting and tax reporting.

5. False — Just the opposite is true: accelerated depreciation is beneficial because it moves tax savings earlier in the life of the investment. There would be an adverse effect to moving tax payments earlier.

6. False — Some U.S. companies use the same method for both, but this is not required. The more common practice is to use straight-line depreciation for financial reporting and an accelerated method for tax reporting.

7. True — Any deduction from revenues for the calculation of taxable income is technically a tax shield. Though tax *shelters* have gotten a bad name in recent years because of some abuses, there is nothing inherently wrong with taking advantage of legal tax shields.

8. True — This is their only relevance to capital budgeting. Net book value can help predict taxable gains or losses on disposal of equipment. Depreciation can help predict after tax cash flows from operations.

9. False — The correct computation is the present value of the product of the tax rate times the depreciation stream.

10. True — Though no one calls it that, straight-line depreciation applies the single rate (100% ÷ life) to the undepreciated balance.

11. True — The definition of the gain or loss on the disposal of depreciable equipment is the disposal value less the net book value of the equipment.

12. False — The gain or loss on the disposal of depreciable equipment has cash tax implications that affect tax payments in the year of disposal that are a function of but are not equal to the gain or loss.

13. False — If you use the pure rate of interest it does not have an inflation component. To be consistent, do not adjust future cash flows for expected inflation, regardless of how bad you expect it to be. You might question whether using the pure rate without addition of a business risk adjustment (to get the "real" rate) is appropriate in this case. Many would argue that it is not appropriate and such low rates contributed to overinvestment in this type of project. Most government bodies now must use a real rate of interest.

14. False   At least in the U.S., depreciation expense for tax purposes is considered to be an allocation of past expense and cannot be adjusted for inflation. Therefore, the amount of the cash savings from depreciation will not be affected by inflation. This represents a loss of purchasing power in the tax savings.

15. False   This is an incomplete definition. The nominal rate or market rate is the sum of the "pure" or riskless rate plus a business-risk element plus an inflation element.

Multiple Choice Questions

1. b   The tax savings is the amount of income shielded times the tax rate: $5,000 x .6 = $3,000.

2. a   Net income = $60,000 - $40,000 - $5,000 = $15,000.

3. b

Net income	$15,000
Tax at 60%	$ 9,000
Income after tax	$ 6,000
Add back depreciation	$ 5,000
Cash flow after tax	$11,000

4. d   The after-tax cash cost of advertising is its amount less the amount of its tax shield: $20,000 - .3 x $20,000 = $14,000 outflow. The tax shield from depreciation (not a cash cost) is .3 x $20,000 = $6,000 inflow.

5. a   Net income is $200,000 - $20,000 - $150,000 = $30,000.

6. d

Net income	$30,000
Tax at 40%	12,000
Income after tax	$18,000
Add back depreciation	20,000
After-tax cash flow	$38,000

7. a   The depreciation tax shield is $20,000 x .4 = $8,000 inflow

8. c   The straight-line rate is 100% ÷ 8 = 12.5%. The double-declining rate is then 25%. First-year depreciation (ignoring salvage value) is .25 x $72,000 = $18,000.

9. d   Straight-line depreciation would be .125 x ($72,000 - $8,000) = $8,000. The first-year advantage to using DDB depreciation is the increase in shielded income times the tax rate: ($18,000 - $8,000) x .4 = $4,000 less tax.

10. c   The amount of gain or loss is the proceeds less the net book value. The net book value is the initial price less accumulated depreciation: $130,000 - 8 x ($130,000 - $10,000) ÷ 10 = $34,000. The gain on sale is $44,000 - $34,000 = $10,000.

11. a   The after-tax effect is the proceeds less tax paid on the gain: $44,000 - .4 x $10,000 = $40,000.

12. b, c To be consistent either (1) reduce the market rate to the real rate and do not adjust expected future cash flows or (2) use the market rate and adjust future cash flows for expected inflation. Either of the other approaches is inconsistent.

Completion

1. marginal
2. erosion, purchasing unit
3. cash inflow or outflow, cash flow
4. recognizes depreciation expense for tax purposes
5. double-declining-balance, accelerated
6. terminal disposal, straight-line, the DDB depreciation would be less than straight-line depreciation.
7. proceeds of the sale, net book value
8. that it is not allowed for tax purposes, so that would overstate the tax shield
9. inflation, real
10. market, real, expected inflation

Problems

1. Sun Flower Energy Corporation

    a. Sales $700,000
    Less:
      Depreciation expense $ 30,000
      Other operating expenses   600,000   630,000
    Income before income taxes $ 70,000
    Less income taxes at 60%   42,000
    Net income $28,000

    b. Depreciation $30,000
    Multiply by income tax rate   60%
    Annual value of income tax savings from
    depreciation $ 18,000

    c. Sales $700,000
    Less:
      Other operating expenses $600,000
      Income taxes, from (1) above   42,000   642,000
    After-tax net cash inflow from operations $ 58,000

Alternative computational methods for (c):

(a) Net income, from above	$ 28,000
Add back depreciation	30,000
After-tax net cash inflow from operations	$ 58,000
(b) Sales	$700,000
Less other operating expenses	600,000
Cash inflows from operations before taxes and the depreciation effect	$100,000
Less applicable income tax outflow at 60%	60,000
After-tax effect of cash inflow from operations before the depreciation effect	$ 40,000
Add annual value of tax savings from depreciation: 60% of $30,000	18,000
After-tax net cash inflow from operations	$58,000

2. Gasahol Co.

Annual savings in cash operating costs	$ 30,000
Less income taxes at 30%	9,000
After-tax effect of expected annual cash savings in operating costs	$ 21,000
Annual depreciation: $120,000/8 years	$15,000
Multiply by income tax rate	30%
Value of expected annual income tax savings from depreciation	4,500
Total expected annual increase in after-tax cash inflow	$ 25,500
Multiply by present value of annuity of $1 at 8%	5.75
Total present value of expected annual increase in after-tax net cash inflow	$146,625
Less cost of the investment	120,000
Net present value of the investment	$ 26,625

3. Zephyr Energy Company

   a. straight-line
   ($450,000 - $30,000) ÷ 5 = $84,000

   DDB (ignore terminal value)
   100% ÷ 5 = 20%; 2 x 20% = 40%; 40% ($450,000) = $180,000

   b. DDB second year
   40% ($450,000 - $180,000) = $108,000

   c. ($108,000 - $84,000) x 30% = $24,000 x 30% = $7,200 increased savings using DDB

4. Parachute Oil Shale Co.

    From Exhibit 12-3 the cumulative DDB depreciation factors for five years of a 10-year depreciation schedule are: .2 + .16 + .128 + .102 + .082 = .672. Thus, 67.2% of the investment cost has been depreciated leaving 32.8% undepreciated as the net book value.

Net book value when sold, $280,000 x .328	$91,840
Sold for cash	90,000
Loss on sale	($1,840)
Tax savings: $1,840 x 30%	$552
Plus proceeds	$90,000
After tax cash effect	$90,552

5. Wildcat Company

    a. The after tax amount of the cash inflow is:
        $400,000 - .40 x ($400,000) = $240,000;
        Adjusted for 8% inflation and discounted at 24% the present value of the cash inflow is:
        $240,000 x 1.08 x .806 = $208,915

    b. The tax savings of depreciation is:
        $140,000 x .40 = $56,000
        Discounted at 24% (and not adjusted for inflation!) the present value of the tax savings is:
        $56,000 x .806 = $45,136

CHAPTER 13

Cost Allocation and Activity-Based Costing

MAIN FOCUS AND OBJECTIVES

This chapter focuses on purposes and methods for allocating indirect costs to products and organization segments. It is important to realize that cost allocations can affect behavior and decision making and that it is worthwhile to carefully consider how to perform cost allocations. After studying this chapter you should:

- Be able to explain the major purposes for allocating indirect costs

- Allocate variable and fixed costs of service departments to other departments

- Allocate central costs to segments

- Use direct and step-down methods for cost allocation

- Use traditional approaches to allocate costs to products and services

- Use activity-based costing to allocate costs to products and services

- Use physical units and relative sales value to allocate costs to joint products

---

REVIEW OF KEY CONCEPTS

A. The assignment of costs to cost objectives is called **cost allocation.** The process of cost allocation is fundamental to managerial accounting. It can be done arbitrarily or based on careful reasoning; obviously, we are more interested in the latter approach.

   1. The basic conceptual approach of cost allocation is twofold:
      a. Group similar costs together in a *cost pool*. Costs are similar if they have the same *cost driver(s)* that plausibly link costs with objectives (e.g., from analysis of cost behavior, as discussed in Chapter 3).
      b. Use cost driver activity as an **allocation base**; that is, divide each cost pool by its allocation base to obtain the **allocation rate**. If budgeted costs and budgeted cost driver activity are used, the rates are budgeted rates.
      c. Allocate costs to the cost objective based on that objective's *actual* level of cost-driver activity.

2. Major purposes of cost allocation are:
   a. To measure costs and profits of segments and individual products and projects
   b. To help determine output prices or reimbursements that are based on costs
   c. To promote goal congruence and managerial effort, and thus to obtain desired motivation of managers
   d. To predict the economic effects of planning and control decisions
3. The first two purposes of cost allocation will be accomplished (for better or worse) with any arbitrary cost allocation scheme. Carefully designed cost allocations may promote reliable measures of cost and profitability. Only carefully prepared cost allocations can accomplish the last two purposes.
4. Basic types of cost allocations include:
   a. Allocation from central cost pools to responsibility centers for measuring costs of responsibility center operations, as discussed in Chapter 9
   b. Reallocation from one center to other centers via transfer prices for services or products, as discussed in Chapter 10
   c. Allocation to products or services for sale to customers and clients, as discussed in Chapters 4, 14, 15, and 16

> See textbook Exhibit 13-1

> Before going on, be sure that you understand the purposes and types of cost allocation.

B. Guidelines for allocating costs are:
1. Allocate costs and evaluate actual results using budgets.
2. If possible, divide the costs of each service department into *two pools:* variable and fixed, with appropriate cost drivers for each cost pool.
   a. Allocate the variable-cost pool to other segments by multiplying the budgeted variable-cost rate by the actual activity level.
   b. The use of predetermined cost rates protects the using departments from operational inefficiencies of service departments and subsequent price changes.
   c. Allocate the fixed-cost pool in lump sums to other segments by multiplying the budgeted total fixed costs by the *budgeted proportions of cost driver capacity available to users*.
      - This predetermined *lump-sum* allocation prevents the allocations to user departments from being affected by the actual usage of other departments.
      - Thus, motivational effects of allocation are less likely to be dysfunctional.
   d. Many critics of current cost allocation practice argue that the allocation base level should be the *practical capacity* of the activity and allocation should be on the basis of activity used, *not* as a lump sum.
      - That way, any unallocated costs, because operating segments did not utilize the capacity, are an indication of the costs of *excess capacity*.

- Using practical capacity also avoids the so-called "death spiral" where decreasing utilization leads to higher budgeted rates, higher costs, higher prices and then lower utilization because demand decreases and even higher rates, and so on until the service or even the company cannot recover its costs and disappears.

3. Communicate the method and rationale for cost allocation to all affected parties.
   a. Managers will have the opportunity to respond and plan accordingly.
   b. Allocations are more likely to be viewed by managers as fair and will be less likely to cause undesirable motivational effects.

4. Organizations typically incur many **central costs** such as expenses of corporate headquarters and various company-wide expenses.
   a. Because of the lack of a plausible allocation scheme, many companies do not allocate such costs.
   b. However, if these costs are to be allocated, an undesirable motivational effect can usually be avoided by using the same approach described above for allocating the fixed costs of a service department.

5. There are general methods for allocating service costs to other segments: *direct*, *step-down*, and *reciprocal methods*.
   a. The **direct method** service costs are allocated directly to segments without consideration of *reciprocal* services among service departments.
   b. The **step-down** method first ranks service departments according to their generality of service. The most general service costs are allocated to other service centers and segments and so on until all service costs have been allocated to segments. This method recognizes some reciprocal services, but only from the more general to the less general.

> See and work through textbook Exhibits 13-3, 4, and 8

   c. The **reciprocal cost** method explicitly recognizes the interaction of service centers with simultaneous equations. It is the least used method, probably because few accountants understand how to solve simultaneous equations or if they do, they feel uncomfortable explaining the results to others.

> Before going to the next section, review again the guidelines and procedures for allocating service center costs to operating segments.

C. An important reason to allocate costs is to determine costs for financial reporting or for pricing outputs of tangible products or intangible services. Costs of operating departments, which include costs allocated from service departments, are often allocated to products or services of the operating departments.

1. Indirect costs of a product or a service are allocated using bases that explain how the indirect costs are incurred. Note these should be the same as the cost drivers discussed in Chapter 3. Common allocation bases include:
   a. machine hours
   b. direct labor hours or cost
   c. number of transactions to complete a product or service

d. number of components of a product or service.
2. Activity-based costing is the approach to assigning (or *attributing*) costs to outputs that relies specifically on using cost driver activities as allocation bases.
   a. Traditionally, costs have been allocated in many companies on the basis of some volume activity such as sales or direct labor input that is directly proportional to unit volume.
   b. Because of changing technology and competitive pressures, firms are finding that other activities such as complexity and time-related activities actually drive costs.
   c. Because segments are evaluated as cost or profit centers, better decisions are being made with activity-based costs.
   d. Activity-based costing first accumulates costs into cost pools corresponding to basic activities (i.e., driven by the same cost drivers).
   e. The second step is to apply costs from the activity-based pools to products and services based on actual usage of cost driver activity.
   f. In concept, this is not a different approach to cost allocation, but it is a different approach to identifying cost pools and allocation bases.

   See textbook Exhibits 13-5 and 13-6

3. Different allocation bases can lead to greatly different product costs and may lead to greatly different *transfer-pricing* and production decisions by managers who are evaluated by segment margins. (Recall the presentations in Chapters 9 and 10)

4. Joint production costs are often allocated to joint products:
   a. using physical units
   b. using relative sales value
   c. more recently, using other cost driver levels
   d. Note that by-products do not receive allocations of joint costs.

   See the texbook examples of joint cost allocation

Cost Allocation and Activity-Based Costing

PRACTICE TEST QUESTIONS AND PROBLEMS WITH SOLUTIONS

True or False Statements

Determine whether each of the following statements is True (T) or False (F) and enter your answer in the space provided.

_____1. The term *cost driver* is just another name for *cost allocation base*.

_____2. Prior to allocation, costs are gathered in to cost pools primarily for convenience so that the same cost driver can be used.

_____3. If a cost cannot be allocated to certain segments on a meaningful basis, it should be excluded from the income statement.

_____4. One problem with the step-down method of allocating service department costs is that only the most-general service costs get allocated to operating segments.

_____5. The primary reasons why the reciprocal cost method is not used more in practice is that it is too difficult to gather the necessary information and too difficult to implement.

_____6. The direct method of allocating service department costs ignores all services rendered by service departments to other service departments.

_____7. Bases for allocating indirect costs to products are completely arbitrary since the products cannot be observed causing the costs.

_____8. Acceptable ways of dealing with the central costs of an organization include not allocating to organization segments, or allocating by an activity-based-cost approach.

_____9. In order to prevent the variable-cost charges to a given operating department from being distorted by changes in the costs or efficiencies of service departments, one can use allocation rates based on budgeted hours and costs.

_____10. The step-down method of allocating service department costs ignores the reciprocal services among service departments.

_____11. The capacity or peak needs of central service departments would provide the most suitable base for allocating the fixed element of service costs.

_____12. Fixed costs should be allocated as a lump sum based on budgeted use so that costs of excess capacity are evident.

_____13. Allocations of some central costs on the basis of either budgeted or actual sales is unfair because the allocations indicate ability to pay for central costs, not usage of central costs.

_____14. If costs in a particular cost pool are found to not be caused by its assigned cost driver, the cost should be placed in the unallocated cost pool.

_____15. Activity-based costing represents a fundamentally different approach to cost allocation that will lead to better decision making.

Multiple Choice Questions

For each of the following multiple-choice questions, select the best answer(s) and enter the identification letter(s) in the space provided.

_____1. The major purposes of cost allocation include: (a) obtaining a basis for setting output prices, (b) measuring income and asset valuations, (c) aiding in making planning and control decisions, (d) motivating employees.

_____2. Basic types of cost allocations include (a) allocation of costs to segments, products, and services, (b) determining inputs for CVP models, (c) establishing cash flows for capital budgeting analyses, (d) reallocation of costs among service departments.

_____3. It is recommended that variable costs be allocated separately from fixed costs because (a) fixed and variable costs have different cost drivers, (b) managers react differently to allocations of fixed costs than they do to allocations of variable costs, (c) allocations of fixed costs should be on the basis of budgeted activity, but allocations of variable costs should be on the basis of actual activity, (d) the separate allocations highlight differences in cost behavior that managers should recognize in planning and pricing activities.

_____4. Reciprocal services are recognized in allocating costs using the: (a) direct method, (b) step-down method, (c) reciprocal cost method, (d) activity-based cost method.

_____5. A service department in a large company presents the following data:
- budgeted variable costs per direct labor-hour $1.50;
- actual direct labor hours: 8,000 for Producing Dept. A, 12,000 for B;
- budgeted labor-hours: for A 9,000, for B 11,000;
- long-run expected direct-labor hours: for A 11,000, for B 9,000.

Compute the allocation of variable costs to A if actual variable costs are $40,000: (a)$16,000, (b) $12,000, (c) $18,000, (d)$13,500.

_____6. The long-run demand hours of Producing Department A-5 are 10% of the capacity of a certain service department, but A-5 actually used 20% of the output of the service department during a certain period. The budgeted fixed costs of the service department for that period were $90,000, but the actual fixed costs were $100,000. The lump-sum allocation of fixed costs to A-5 should be: (a) 10% of $90,000, (b) 10% of $100,000, (c) 20% of $90,000, (d) 20% of $100,000.

_____7. Service Departments A and B each have $80,000 of overhead to be allocated. They render 20% of their services to each other. Producing Department C receives 10% of the service of A and 30% of the service of B. Use the step-down method to compute the total overhead to be allocated to C from A and B. Begin with Department B. (a) $32,000, (b) $40,000, (c) $34,000, (d) $36,000.

_____8. Service Department P has $70,000 of overhead to be allocated. It renders 30% of its service to other service departments, 10% to Producing Department Q, and the remainder to all the other producing departments. The cost to be allocated from P to Q by the direct method is: (a) $7,000,(b) $11,667, (c) $49,000, (d) $10,000.

_____9. Bonzo Company has two service departments, S1 and S2, and two operating segments, P1 and P2. Department S1 is the more general service center and provides 20% of its services to S2, the remainder equally to P1 and P2. If the direct costs of S1 and S2 are $30,000 and $9,000, respectively, after the first stage of the step-down method the costs to be allocated from S2 to P1 and P2 total: (a) $30,000, (b) $9,000, (c) $39,000, (d) $15,000.

____10. See the preceding test item. If S2 provides 10% of its service to S1, 60% to P1, and 30% to P2, the cost allocated from S2 to P1 after the second stage of the step-down method is: (a) $15,000, (b) $9,000, (c) $10,000, (d) $5,000.

____11. A joint process that cost $6,000 results in two products: 100 units of A and 50 units of B. Using a physical units basis the allocated cost per unit is: (a) A: $60, B: $120, (b) A: $20, B: $20, (c) A: $40, B: $40, (d) A: $80, B: $80.

Completion

1. A convincing or plausible link between costs and cost objectives is called a _____.

2. Before allocating costs, one should usually group like costs into _____ that are determined by _____.

3. The contribution margin by segments is _____ less _____.

4. In the allocation of costs of such services as power, the variable-cost element may be distributed by a _____ and the fixed cost element may be distributed as a _____.

5. In order to prevent the fixed-cost charges to a given operating department from depending on the quantity of services actually consumed by other operating departments, one can use allocation amounts based on _____ hours and costs.

6. Using a cost allocation base that reflects the _____ of indirect costs can promote _____.

7. By-products of joint processes never _____.

8. The new cost allocations in the case of Schrader Bellows in the text are based on _____.

9. See item 8. The new allocation base should lead to _____ because _____.

10. Decisions about joint products should never _____.

196 Chapter 13

Problems

1. Bush Company's power plant provides electricity for its two producing departments, X and Y. The 19X3 budget for the power plant shows:

Budgeted fixed costs $70,000
Budgeted variable costs per kilowatt hour (KWH) $ 0.18

Additional data for 19X3:	Dept. X	Dept. Y
Long-run demand (KWH)	420,000	280,000
Budgeted for 19X3 (KWH)	310,000	200,000
Actual for 19X3 (KWH)	320,000	160,000

Actual power plant costs for 19X3 are:
Fixed $78,000
Variable $90,000

Compute the 19X3 allocation of power plant costs to Departments X and Y:

    a. Fixed   b. Variable
Dept. X $ $

Dept. Y $ $

2. Expert Innovations, Inc. provides the following information:

	Service Dept. 1	Service Dept. 2	Production Dept. X	All Other Production Depts.
Overhead costs before allocation	$4,000	$4,500	$5,000	$51,000
Proportions of service furnished by Dept. 1	-	20%	30%	50%
Proportions of service furnished by Dept. 2	10%	-	40%	50%

    a. Use the *direct method* to allocate costs and determine the total overhead of Dept. X after allocation.

	Dept. 1	Dept. 2	Dept. X	Others
Overhead costs before allocation	$4,000	$4,500	$5,000	$51,000

Cost Allocation and Activity-Based Costing

b. Use the *step-down method* to allocate costs and determine the total overhead of Dept. X after allocation. *Begin with Dept. 2.*

	Dept. 1	Dept. 2	Dept. X	Others
Overhead costs before allocation	$4,000	$4,500	$5,000	$51,000

3. Lewis Company uses a $5,000 joint process to produce X, Y, and Z. Use the following data to compute the cost per unit of each product using (1) physical units and then (2) relative sales value.

Product	Units	Sales price per unit	Separable costs after split-off
X	500	$12.00	$1,000
Y	700	$ 5.00	$3,000
Z	50	$ 1.00	0

a. Physical units:

b. Relative sales value:

4. TunnelView Services has three basic service products, Alpha, Beta, and Gamma. Overhead is applied to products on the basis of 150% of direct design cost. The controller of TunnelView has determined from activity analysis that overhead costs should be split in at least three separate cost pools and allocated according to separate cost drivers.

The following information is now available:

	Alpha	Beta	Gamma	New overhead rates
Direct design cost	$900	$2,000	$1,000	@20% of design cost
Computer time	8 hours	14 hours	3 hours	@ $65 per hour
Systems integration	10 hours	26 hours	5 hours	@ $110 per hour

a. Compute the cost of each product using the old overhead rate of 150% of direct design cost.

b. Compute the cost of each product using the new overhead rates.

c. Discuss the implications of the differences in product costs.

CHAPTER 13 SOLUTIONS TO PRACTICE QUESTIONS AND PROBLEMS

True or False Statements

1. False — The term cost driver implies a cause and effect relationship between a particular cost and an underlying activity. A cost allocation base can be any arbitrary basis for assigning costs. It is believed that using cost drivers as allocation bases will result in better decision making because the allocated costs will more closely represent "true" cost behavior.

2. False — The issue is more than convenience. Each cost pool should contain costs that can be affected by different usage of the assigned cost driver.

3. False — If a cost cannot be allocated to segments, it still should be shown on the income statement as "unallocated" cost that must be covered by contribution margins by segments.

4. False — All service department costs eventually get allocated to operating segments using the step-down method. Problems with the step-down method include determining the order of the steps and not recognizing two-way reciprocal services between service departments.

5. False — The information to implement the reciprocal cost method is usually available, and the method is no more difficult to implement than other methods. In fact, using matrix algebra makes the reciprocal cost method easier than the others. The primary problem is understanding and communicating the use and results of the method.

6. True — The direct method allocates all service department costs directly to operating segments. If there are significant interdependencies among service departments, this could lead to somewhat different cost allocations than using the step-down or reciprocal cost methods.

7. False — Because indirect costs cannot be observed as they are incurred, there is some element of subjectivity in allocating them. However, the techniques of activity analysis, discussed in Chapter 3, can go a long way in making the process of allocating indirect costs more objective -- effectively transforming indirect into direct costs.

8. True — If cost drivers cannot be identified, then perhaps it is best not to allocate central costs. However, if appropriate cost drivers can be identified, planning and control of central costs are enhanced by allocating them to operating segments. Some believe that central costs should be allocated if only to make operating segments aware of the magnitude of central costs and so that they will complain if central costs seem to be greater than necessary.

9. True — If actual variable costs are allocated to operating segments, the service centers have little incentive to control costs unless operating segments are free to purchase services externally. Organization by responsibility centers and decentralization of some sourcing decisions are necessary for this market pressure to control service center costs.

10. True — The step-down method recognizes one-way services among service departments, but not true reciprocal services.

11. True — Using the practical capacity or peak capacity of central service departments sets the allocation base at the originally planned level of usage. Allocations of these fixed costs according to actual usage of capacity may leave some central cost unallocated. This unallocated portion of cost indicates excess capacity.

12. False — Allocations of fixed costs as lump sums on budgeted use prevents distortions of cost allocations due to other departments' usage. However, this does not indicate the magnitude of excess capacity. Allocations on a unit of capacity used basis might leave some capacity costs unallocated, which would indicate excess capacity.

13. True — Few central costs are *caused* by segment sales levels; thus most allocations based on either budgeted or actual sales levels are based on a "deep pockets" approach to allocation. These allocations are unlikely to fulfill the purposes of cost allocation.

14. False — This is one response, but a better one would be to try find the appropriate cost driver. Failing that, the cost may be assigned to the unallocated pool.

15. False — The activity-based approach is not a fundamentally new one, the cast of likely cost drivers and therefore cost-pool organization are different, but the process is not. The *hope* is that activity-based allocations will lead to better decisions, but we do not have much evidence that this is true. Hopefully, we will soon.

Multiple Choice Questions

1. a,b,c,d — All of these are purposes of cost allocations; whether cost allocations succeed depends on the care and effort taken to design the allocations.

2. a,d — Cost allocations are not suitable for either CVP modeling or capital budgeting; for these purposes, costs should be separated by cost behavior only. Allocations are intended to assign costs to segments, products, and services and to reallocate costs among service centers for income measurement, pricing, and motivational purposes.

3. c,d — Fixed and variable costs of a single type have the same cost driver, but the time perspective may be different. Variable costs are driven by short-run usage of an

activity; whereas fixed costs are driven by long run activity capacity -- e.g., the level of the relevant range. If both fixed and variable costs are allocated on a per unit basis, managers will react to them the same -- as if they both were variable costs. The usual recommendation to split the costs is based on the desire that one department's usage of a cost driver should not affect the costs of another using department. Separate allocations do reinforce the use of CVP planning models and appropriate cost behavior.

4. c   The direct method ignores reciprocal service costs, and the step-down method recognizes only one-way relationships. Activity-based methods may be direct, step-down, or reciprocal.

5. b   The allocation of variable costs to operating departments should be at budgeted rates and actual usage: $1.50 \times 8,000 = $12,000$.

6. a   Usually, the lump sum allocation of fixed costs to the operating department should be 10% of $90,000. The $10,000 unfavorable spending variance should be borne by the service department unless it can be shown that A-5's excess usage required the service department to acquire additional capacity. In that case, the entire variance should be charged to A-5 along with its budgeted share of budgeted costs.

7. d   Use the following approach:

	A	B	C	Others
Overhead	$80,000	$80,000		
Allocate B (.2, .3, .5)	16,000	(80,000)	$24,000	$40,000
Allocate A (1/8, 7/8)	$(96,000)		12,000	84,000
Totals			$36,000 (d)	$124,000

8. d $100\% - 30\% = 70\%; 10\% \div 70\% = 1/7, \$70,000 \times 1/7 = \$10,000$ (d)

9. d   Use the following approach:

	S1	S2	P1	P2
S1	-	.20	.40	.40
S2	.1	-	.6	.3
Cost	$30,000	$9,000		
Allocate from S1:	($30,000)	$6,000	$12,000	$12,000
Allocate from S2:		($15,000)(d)	$10,000	$5,000
Totals allocated			$22,000	$17,000

10. c   See above.

11. c   Using the only physical basis available in this problem, number of units, the joint cost per unit is $6,000 \div 150$ units $= \$40$ per unit.

Completion

1. cost driver or cost allocation base
2. cost pools, common cost drivers
3. net sales, variable costs

Cost Allocation and Activity-Based Costing **201**

4.   budgeted (or standard) rate per unit of services consumed, lump-sum predetermined monthly charge

5.   predetermined (or budgeted)

6.   cause or cost driver, improved cost control and decision making

7.   receive allocations of joint costs

8.   the number of transactions

9.   better decision making, product costs more closely reflect how costs are incurred

10.   be based on allocated joint costs.

Problems

1. Bush Company

    a. Use long-run demand to allocate budgeted fixed costs
    (total KWH: 420,000 + 280,000 = 700,000):
    Dept. X: (420,000/700,000) x $70,000 = $42,000
    Dept. Y: (280,000/700,000) x $70,000 = $28,000

    b. Use predetermined rates and actual KWH to allocate variable costs:
    Dept. X: 18cts x 320,000 = $57,600
    Dept. Y: 18cts x 160,000 = $28,800
    (Unallocated actual costs for 19X3 may be written off to expense at end of year.)

2. Expert Innovations, Inc.

    a. direct method

	Dept. 1	Dept. 2	Dept. X	Others
Overhead costs before allocation	$ 4,000	$ 4,500	$5,000	$51,000
Dept. 1 costs allocated, 3/8 and 5/8	($4,000)		1,500	2,500
Dept. 2 costs allocated, 4/9 and 5/9		(4,500)	2,000	2,500
Totals			$8,500	$56,000

    b. step-down method

	Dept. 1	Dept. 2	Dept. X	Others
Overhead costs before allocation	$ 4,000	$ 4,500	$5,000	$51,000
Dept. 2 costs allocated, 10%, 40%, 50%	450	(4,500)	1,800	2,250
Dept. 1 costs allocated, 3/8 and 5/8	(4,450)		1,669	2,781
Totals			$8,469	$56,031

3. Lewis Company
   a. Physical units

Product	Units	Weighting	Allocation of Joint Cost	Separable Costs	Cost per Unit
X	500	5/12 x $5,000 =	$2083	$1,000	(2083 +1000) 500 = $6.17
Y	700	7/12 x $5,000 =	2917	3,000	(2917 + 3000) 700 = $8.45
Z*	-				
Total	1200		$5,000		

   b. Relative sales value

Product	Revenue	Relative sales value less Separable Costs	Weighting	Allocation of Joint Cost	Cost per Unit
X	500 x $12 = $6,000	$6,000 - $1,000 = $5,000	$5,000÷$5,500	$4,545	($1,000+$4,545)÷500= $1
Y	700 x $5 = $3,500	$3,500 - $3,000 = $500	$5,000÷$500	$455	($3,000 + $455) ÷ 700 = $
Z*	50 x $1 = $50				
totals			$5,500		

*Z should be treated as a byproduct.

4. TunnelView Industries
   a. Using 150% of direct design cost:

	Alpha	Beta	Gamma
Direct design cost	$900	$2,000	$1,000
Overhead @ 150%	$1,350	$3,000	$1,500
Total cost	$2,250	$5,000	$3,500

   b. Using new overhead rates:

	Alpha	Beta	Gamma	New overhea
Direct design cost	$900	$2,000	$1,000	
Design cost overhead	180	400	200	@20% of desi
Computer time overhead	8x$65 = $520	14x$65 = $910	3x$65 = $195	@ $65 per
Systems integration	10x$110=$1,100	26x$110=$2,860	5x$110 = $550	@ $110 per
Total cost	$2,700	$6,170	$1,945	

   c. All of the costs differ somewhat, several dramatically. The cost of Alpha is 20% higher using the new overhead rates. The cost of Beta is 23% higher, but the cost of Gamma is 44% lower using the new rates. The reason for these differences in costs is that each service uses relatively different amounts of the three cost drivers. The new overhead rates charge services for their usage of the activities that drive costs. Direct design cost was shown to drive much less overhead cost than previously believed. The old, single rate penalized relatively high design-cost products but did not consider that these services may use relatively less computer time or systems integration. Conversely, the old rate unfairly shielded services with low direct design time but high levels of computer and systems integration time. If the activity analysis is valid, the new service costs are more accurate. These new service costs should lead to improved decision making (e.g., pricing, service mix, and so on).

Review pg 486 Textbook: Job Cost Sheet Exhibit 14-1

CHAPTER **14**

Job-Costing Systems, Overhead Application, Service Industries

> **MAIN FOCUS AND OBJECTIVES**
>
> This chapter examines the job-costing system and the application of overhead costs to products and services. Note that this chapter utilizes *journal entries* to describe cost flows. *If you are unfamiliar with journal entries or need a refresher, turn to the Appendix at the end of this study guide.* Your main objectives are to clearly understand:
>
> - Differences between job-order and process costing
> - Journal entries for typical job-order transactions
> - Budgeted overhead rates and overhead application
> - Use of appropriate cost drivers for overhead application
> - Normal overhead rates
> - Use of two alternative methods for disposing of under- or overapplied overhead
> - Use of job-order costing in service organizations

REVIEW OF KEY CONCEPTS

A. Two product costing sytems are widely used:

1. **Job-order costing** is suitable for controlling the costs of custom-made products or services that are readily identified by individual units or batches, each of which receives varying degrees of attention and skill.
    a. The *cost object* is the individual product, a batch of like products, or a job or order for a particular customer or client.
    b. For example, products such as furniture, machinery, highway bridges, and drilling platforms for off-shore oil exploration; or services such as systems installations, management consulting, auditing, legal consultation.

2. In contrast, **process costing** is appropriate for the mass production of uniform units, which usually flow continuously through a series of standard production

steps called operations or processes, for example: textiles, chemicals, petroleum products, cement, bricks, newsprint, ice cream, and breakfast foods. Process costing is presented in Chapter 15.

B. **Job-order costing essentially involves cost application,** which is the identification of accumulated costs with specific jobs or orders of products or services.

1. Job-order costing was first designed for manufacturing, but it can be used equally well by service companies. The first examples in the chapter are manufacturing, but later examples are costing for services.

> See textbook Exhibit 14-1

2. The primary record of the job-cost system is the **job-cost record,** which contains accumulated costs for *each* product, batch, or a job according to the definition of the cost object according to these supporting documents:
    a. Material requisitions, used to apply *direct-material costs.*
    b. Time tickets, used to apply *direct-labor costs.*
    c. Budgeted rates, used to apply *factory-overhead costs.*

3. The typical transactions for manufacturing activities describe the flow of resources and costs to the cost object, during its manufacture or development, and after completion.
    a. Note carefully the formal *journal entries* and the accompanying detailed transaction analyses in the textbook.

> See textbook Exhibit 14-2

   b. Observe the *cost flows* through the general ledger accounts.

4. Factory overhead is usually applied by a budgeted rate.
    a. Many factory costs are indirect manufacturing costs and thus cannot be identified with specific jobs.
    b. Therefore the amounts of factory overhead cost applicable to specific jobs must be allocated by a reasonable procedure that measures consumption of basic resources and activities, as discussed in Chapter 13.
    c. A budgeted rate is preferred to an actual rate because:
        - budgeted rates are more timely, if less accurate, than actual rates
        - budgeted rates promote efficiency
    d. Separate fixed cost and variable cost allocations are preferable, as discussed in Chapter 13, but more traditional practice is to use a single overhead rate to cover total overhead.
    e. Organizations usually budget a rate on an annual basis by dividing budgeted factory overhead by the budgeted activity base (that is, the budgeted cost driver level or cost allocation base). Such predetermined overhead rates are typically used on an annualized basis rather than a monthly basis in order to avoid month-to-month fluctuations in overhead cost rates.
    f. Ideally, the cost allocation base used in a particular production process should be the principal cost driver, that is, the activity that causes the cost.
    g. *Applied overhead* is the budgeted rate times the *actual* usage of cost driver activity.

- h. The *excess* of the applied overhead over the actual overhead incurred is called *overapplied overhead* or overabsorbed overhead.
- i. If the actual amount of overhead incurred *exceeds* the applied amount, the difference is called *underapplied* or underabsorbed overhead.

5. The amount of underapplied or overapplied overhead is disposed of in two alternative ways: at the end of the year write-off to the period or *proration* over inventories.
    - a. **Immediate write-off:** If the underapplied or overapplied amount is relatively small, as it typically is, the entire amount is treated as an adjustment of the year's net income.
        - This means that it is simply written off directly to cost of goods sold (an addition if factory overhead is underapplied, a subtraction if overapplied).
        - Such an immediate write-off is largely justified because most of the manufactured products have usually been sold by the end of the year.
        - Another justification for such treatment is that when there is underapplied overhead, it is due mostly to *inefficiencies* or to the *underutilization of available facilities* (which would not be appropriate costs of the inventory assets).

        See textbook Exhibit 14-3

    - b. **Proration:** If there is a *relatively large* amount of underapplied or overapplied overhead, it may be **prorated.**
        - This means that the amount is allocated to the three balances that were affected by the use of budgeted overhead rates: work-in-process inventory, finished-goods inventory, and cost of goods sold.
        - This method tends to adjust applied costs to an actual basis and is therefore conceptually appealing if the difference is due to forecasting errors.

6. The cost system we are describing is sometimes called an *actual cost system*.
    - a. However, it is more accurately called a **normal cost system** because the factory overhead included in product costs is not the actual amount incurred but is the amount applied by means of *budgeted* overhead rates.
    - b. Typically, the normal system is used to cost products during the year, and the year-end procedures described above are used to reconcile total results to an approximate actual-cost basis.

> Before going on to the next section, review this long section and be sure that you understand how costs are applied to products, batches, and jobs using job-order costing. Do you understand the calculation, meaning and disposition of under- or over-applied overhead?

C. The job costing approach described for manufacturing companies is also used in service and nonprofit organizations.

1. Costs are allocated to projects or programs, which are identifiable groups of activities that produce *services*.

> See the textbook example of costing for audit engagements

2. Service organizations are just as concerned with identifying appropriate cost drivers for their delivered services as manufacturers are.
   a. In service organizations, which are typically labor intensive, one of the primary cost drivers is *time*.
   b. Understanding how employees spend their time is important for several reasons:
      - If time spent drives costs, then knowing time allocations is prerequisite to knowing cost allocations (for all its purposes, as discussed above).
      - Identifying how and where employees spend time is an important step in eliminating non-value-added activities in delivering service.
      - If certain activities can be identified as redundant or non-value added, the human resources spent on those activities can be redeployed to value-added activities.
      - Some managers of large companies believe that their most significant improvements in efficiency will come from eliminating non-value added service activities and enhancing value-added ones.

PRACTICE TEST QUESTIONS AND PROBLEMS WITH SOLUTIONS

True or False Statements

Determine whether each of the following statements is True (T) or False (F) and enter your answer in the space provided.

__T__ 1. Examples of products or services for which a job-order costing system would probably be suitable include custom machinery and consulting.

__T__ 2. Examples of products for which a process cost system would probably be suitable include chemicals and textiles.

__F__ 3. Actual factory overhead incurred should be charged to Work in Process. *applied*

__T__ 4. A cost driver in a job-cost system is the same as an indirect cost application base.

__T__ 5. Compared with the use of actual factory overhead rates, the use of budgeted rates would provide the accumulation of cost data that are less accurate and less timely, and with adverse motivational implications.

__T__ 6. If underapplied overhead is caused largely by forecasting errors, the year-end treatment that would more likely be justified is the proration method. (MAGNITUDE)

__F__ 7. Within a normal costing system, the costs charged to job-cost records would include normal applied factory overhead and normal direct material.

__F__ 8. If direct-labor factory workers are paid unequal hourly wage rates, direct-labor dollars would most likely be a better base for applying overhead to labor-intensive jobs than direct labor hours.

_____ 9. The related general ledger account for the subsidiary ledger of job-cost records is Work-in-Process Inventory.

__F__ 10. Job-order costing, with its emphasis on direct-labor-based allocations, cannot be used with activity-based costing.

__T__ 11. Job-order costing can separately allocate of fixed and variable overhead to jobs or products.

__T__ 12. Individual products are the cost objects in job-order costing.

__T__ 13. There is no fundamental difference between job-order costing in manufacturing and service companies.

__F__ 14. At the end of a particular period, the factory overhead account was closed with a debit to Cost of goods sold. Therefore, factory overhead was overapplied.

__T__ 15. During a particular period, factory overhead was overapplied by $10,000, and total credits to factory overhead were $150,000. Therefore, total debits to factory overhead for the period were $140,000.

Multiple Choice Questions

For each of the following multiple-choice questions, select the best answer(s) and enter the identification letter(s) in the space provided.

__D__ 1. In job-order cost systems, the issuance of direct materials to production requires a debit to: (a) Materials Used, (b) Direct Materials, (c) Finished Goods, (d) Work in Process.

__C__ 2. See the preceding item. The credit should be to: (a) Accounts Payable, (b) Work in Process, (c) Direct Materials Inventory, (d) Materials Used.

__A__ 3. Cost of goods manufactured should be: (a) debited to Finished Goods, (b) debited to Cost of Goods Sold, (c) credited to Direct-Materials Inventory, (d) debited to Work in Process.

__D__ 4. Factory overhead applied should be: (a) debited to Finished Goods, (b) debited to Cost of Goods Sold, (c) credited to Cost of Goods Manufactured, (d) debited to Work in Process.

__C__ 5. A labor-intensive service company budgeted for 19X3 a total of 40,000 direct labor hours and $220,000 of overhead costs. However, the actual 19X3 amounts

208 Chapter 14

APPLIED = 220,000 / 44,000 = $5.50

were 44,000 hours and $240,000 cost, respectively. Compute the proper rate for applying overhead to programs: (a) $5.00, (b) $5.45, (c) $5.50, (d) $6.00.

__C__ 6. See the preceding test item. The applied overhead should be: (a) $220,000, (b) $240,000, (c) $242,000, (d) $264,000.   5.50 × 44,000 = $242,000

__A__ 7. See items 5 and 6 above. Overhead in 19X3 was (a) $2,000 overapplied, (b) $2,000 underapplied, (c) $20,000 overapplied, (d) $20,000 underapplied.

__C__ 8. A company reported for 19X4 sales of $790,000, cost of goods sold $500,000 (including $190,000 of applied overhead), and overapplied overhead amounting to $10,000. The actual factory overhead incurred was: (a) $190,000, (b) $200,000, (c) $180,000, (d) $515,000.   OH Applied = 190,000   OVER APP. OH = 10,000 ⇒ 180,000.

__A__ 9. See the preceding test item. If the year-end overhead difference was not prorated, the gross profit would be (a) $300,000, (b) $265,000, (c) $275,000, (d) $288,000.

790,000
− 490,000
300,000

__B__ 10. See test item 8. If the year-end difference was prorated across Cost of Goods Sold and Finished Goods of $300,000, the gross profit would be (a) $306,250, (b) $296,250, (c) $286,250, (d) $276,250.

Completion

Complete each of the following statements by filling in the blanks.

1. __job order__ costing is appropriate when the __cost object__ are individual products or batches, but __process__ is appropriate when the __cost objects__ are __process over per. of time__.

2. Budgeted factory-overhead rates can be computed by dividing __Budgeted OH__ cost by __cost driver activity__.

3. Costs of materials used in production are carried through three accounts:
    (a) __work in process__
    (b) __finished goods__
    (c) __CGS__

4. At the end of the year, if the underapplied or overapplied factory-overhead cost is to be treated in a theoretically correct and precise manner, it should be prorated over three accounts:
    (a) __work in process__
    (b) __finished goods__
    (c) __CGS__

5. The fundamental record in a job-order cost system is the __job cost record__.

6. Application of manufacturing overhead to a job requires a __debit__ journal entry to the __work in process__ account.

7. Overapplied overhead is disposed of with a debit entry to the __FOH__ account.

8. Overhead is applied to jobs using a __budgeted__ overhead rate multiplied by __cost driver usage__.

Job-Costing Systems, Overhead Application, Service Industries 209

9. One effect of using activity-based costing is to shift the classification of some indirect costs to ___direct costs___.

10. For product/service costing purposes, the difference between an auto repair shop and a custom-home builder _____. The similarity between them is _____.

Problems

1. For each of these transaction types of Aaron Company, make a journal entry (without explanation or dollar amounts) to fit the following data (all beginning inventories are zero):

Material purchases on credit	$14,000
Direct labor used and paid:	$8,000
Factory utilities paid	$2,000
Supervisory salaries on account	$4,000
Indirect labor paid	$3,000
Supplies used	$1,000
Materials issued	$10,000
Factory overhead applied @ 150% of direct labor	
Ending Work in Process	$2,000
Ending Finished Goods	$3,000
Sales	$45,000

	Accounts:	Debit:	Credit:
a. Direct-materials purchased:	MATERIAL	14,000	
	ACCOUNTS PAYABLE		14,000
b. Direct labor incurred:	WORK IN PROCESS	8,000	
	CASH		8,000
c. Factory overhead incurred:	FOH	10,000	
	CASH		6,000
	SALARIES PAYABLE		4,000
d. Factory overhead applied: 8 × 1.5 = 12	WORK IN PROCESS	12,000	
	FOH		12,000
e. Direct materials used:	WORK IN PROCESS	10,000	
	MATERIALS		10,000
f. Work in process completed:	FINISHED GOODS	28,000	
	WORK IN PROCESS		28,000
g. Cost of goods sold: 28,000 − 3,000 (END INV.)	CGS	25,000	
	FINISHED GOODS		25,000
h. Product sales on account:	A/R	45,000	
	SALES		45,000
i. Close overhead account			

210 Chapter 14

2. Burr Products Company has the following data for 19X4 (in millions):
Beginning inventories:
> Direct material $30
> Work in process 42
> Finished goods 40

Transactions for the year:
> Direct-material purchases on account $160
> Direct labor incurred 190
> Factory overhead incurred 153
> Factory overhead applied 148
> Direct materials used 150
> Work in process completed 498
> Normal cost of goods sold 496
> Sales on account 750

Compute the following, assuming that the year-end overhead differences are not prorated:

a. Ending inventories:
   Direct material 30

   Work in process

   Finished goods

b. Adjusted cost of goods sold

c. Gross profit on sales

3. Given for Hancock Products, Inc. (in millions):

> Budged factory overhead cost $280
> Budgeted machine-hours 70 hrs.
> Actual factory-overhead cost incurred $293
> Actual machine-hours used 72 hrs.

a. Compute:
   Budgeted overhead rate:

   Applied factory-overhead cost:

   Amount of overhead underapplied or overapplied:

b. Prepare the journal entry to write off the overhead difference at year-end (without proration):

Handwritten annotations:
DIRECT MTL = 30 + 160 − 150 = $40
WIP = 42 + 150 + 190 + 148 − 498 = $32
FG = 40 + 498 − 496 = $42
CGS + (153 − 148) = 501

Job-Costing Systems, Overhead Application, Service Industries 211

4. Given for Harrison Company (in millions):

Sales	$540
Cost of goods sold at normal cost	325
Overapplied factory overhead	12

Compute the gross profit for the year, assuming that the overapplied factory overhead is written off in one lump-sum without proration.

CHAPTER 14 SOLUTIONS TO PRACTICE TEST QUESTIONS AND PROBLEMS

True or False Statements

1. True — Job-order costing is best suited when costing individual products or services is economically desirable. Both custom machinery and consulting services are probably designed for specific customers, and the costs are probably relatively high. If the jobs were awarded by bid or reimbursement, it is important for managers to learn how accurately they predicted costs and to learn whether faulty implementation caused excess costs. Likewise, it is important to know how profitable each job is, for evaluation and feedback for planning.

2. True — These are examples of products that are undifferentiated (e.g., one yard of fabric is just like any other of its type -- hopefully) and result from a continuous process. The most feasible cost object here is the process during some time period -- using process costing, the topic of Chapter 15.

3. False — Actual factory overhead is charged to a factory overhead account, which is a temporary asset account that records a period's overhead costs. *Applied factory overhead* is charged to work in process.

4. True — Or at least it should be. Many companies still use direct labor hours or cost as the only cost driver and allocation base for indirect costs, when it is likely that other cost drivers would be more appropriate allocation bases.

5. False — Though using budgeted rates may give less accurate cost information than actual rates, this need not be a major issue if costs and activities are budgeted accurately. The information will be more timely and should promote cost efficiency, whereas actual cost information must wait until the end of a period and does not give the same cost-control incentives.

6. False — The source of the error is less important than the magnitude of the error. If the error is large enough that inventory balances would be seriously misstated by writing-off the error, the underapplied overhead should be prorated. Otherwise, the error should be charged to the period and written-off.

7. False — A normal costing system charges factory overhead at budgeted rates and actual direct labor. A system that charged normal direct labor sounds like a standard cost system.

8. False — The issue is which is the better cost driver -- direct labor hours or direct labor cost. This could be established by statistical analyses of the type recommended in Chapter 3.

9. True — Work in process inventory accumulates all the costs applied to all jobs as they are recorded in job-cost records.

10. False — It is true that job-order costing has historically and traditionally applied overhead on the basis of direct labor, but there is no rule that says this must be so. Job-order costing can and should use the most appropriate cost drivers to apply overhead to jobs.

11. True — Again traditionally, job-order costing has used a single rate to apply both fixed and variable overhead. This remains the most common practice today, despite our recommendations in Chapter 13 to allocate variable overhead on a per unit of activity basis and fixed overhead on a lump sum basis. Our advice is not being followed probably because it is just easier to use one rate and errors are likely to be small if budgeting has been accurate.

12. True — But sometimes batches of product or specific orders are cost objects. It depends on the feasibility of tracing costs and on the nature of the business.

13. True — The only differences are slightly different terminologies and probably different cost drivers. Service industry cost drivers are most likely related to time spent by employees, whereas in manufacturing industries cost drivers are probably related to product complexity and cycle time.

14. False — If factory overhead is closed with a debit to CGS, the credit would be to factory overhead, to close a debit balance there. A debit balance in factory overhead that must be disposed of means that more overhead was incurred than was applied. Therefore, factory overhead was underapplied.

15. True — An overapplied factory overhead balance means that credits (overhead applied) exceed the debits (overhead incurred). Therefore, if total factory overhead applied was $150,000 and $10,000 overapplied, the factory overhead incurred must have been $140,000.

Multiple Choice Questions

1. d — Issuance of direct materials requires a credit to Materials and a debit to Work in Process.

2. c — credit Materials

3. a   Cost of goods manufactured represents the costs of products completed, and therefore transferred from work in process to finished goods. The complete entry would debit finished goods and credit work in process.

4. d   Factory overhead applied is the amount of overhead cost added to jobs. This addition requires a debit to work in process and a credit to factory overhead.

5. c   The proper rate should be the budgeted rate: $220,000 ÷ 40,000 hours = $5.50 per hour.

6. c   The amount applied is the budgeted rate multiplied by the actual cost-driver activity: $5.50 x 44,000 = $242,000.

7. a   Actual overhead was $240,000, and applied overhead was $242,000. Thus overhead was $2,000 overapplied.

8. c   Overhead applied was $190,000 and it was overapplied by $10,000. Therefore actual overhead was $180,000.

9. a   Cost of goods sold would be reduced by the amount of overapplied overhead from $500,000 to $490,000. Thus gross profit would be $10,000 greater, or $300,000.

10. b   The difference would be prorated on the basis of account balances: 3/8 to finished goods, and 5/8 to cost of goods sold. The portion to subtract from cost of goods sold is 5/8 x $10,000 = $6,250. Therefore gross profit would be $6,250 higher or $290,000 + $6,250 = $296,250.

Completion

1. Job-order, cost objects, process costing, cost objects, processes during a period of time
2. budgeted factory overhead cost, budgeted cost driver activity
3. work in process, finished goods, cost of goods sold
4. work in process, finished goods, cost of goods sold
5. job-cost record
6. debit, work in process or credit, factory overhead
7. factory overhead
8. budgeted, actual cost driver usage
9. direct cost classification because the cost can be traced by cost driver usage
10. terminology and the nature of the product, both produce something of value to a particular customer requiring cost accounting by customer

Problems

1. Aaron Company, journal entries:

	Accounts:	Debit:	Credit:
a. Direct-materials purchased:	Materials Accounts payable	$14,000	$14,000
b. Direct labor incurred:	Work in process Cash	8,000	8,000

c. Factory overhead incurred:	Factory overhead
	  Cash
	  Salaries payable
		10,000	6,000
			4,000

d. Factory overhead applied:	Work in process Factory overhead	12,000	12,000
e. Direct materials used:	Work in process Materials	10,000	10,000
f. Work in process completed:	Finished goods Work in process	28,000	28,000
g. Cost of goods sold:	Cost of goods sold Finished goods	25,000	25,000
h. Product sales on account:	Accounts receivable Sales	45,000	45,000
i. Close overhead account	Factory overhead Cost of goods sold	2,000	2,000

2. Burr Products Company (in millions)

   a.
       Direct material: 30 + 160 - 150 = $40
       Work in process: 42 + 150 + 190 + 148 - 498 = $32
       Finished goods: 40 + 498 - 496 = $42

   b.   496 + (153 - 148)   496 + 5 = $501

   c.   750 - 501 = $249

3. Hancock Products, Inc. (in millions)
   a. Compute:

   Budgeted overhead rate: Divide budgeted factory overhead cost by budgeted machine hours: $280÷70 hrs = $4 per hour.

   Applied factory overhead cost: Multiply the actual machine-hours used by the budgeted overhead rate; 72 hrs x $4 = $288

   Underapplied overhead: Subtract the applied factory-overhead cost incurred from the actual factory-overhead cost: $293 - $288 = $5 underapplied overhead.

   b. Cost of goods sold   5
       Factory department overhead   5

4. Harrison Company (in millions):

Sales	$540
Cost of goods sold at normal cost	$325
Less overapplied overhead	12
Cost of goods sold at actual cost	$313
Gross profit	$227

CHAPTER 15

Process-Costing Systems

MAIN FOCUS AND OBJECTIVES

The preceding chapter described manufacturing costs in general and the *job-cost system* in particular. This chapter deals with the other basic system for costing products - *process costing*. The key concept to learn in this chapter is *equivalent units produced,* the measure of the amount of work done in a process in a given period. Your learning objectives are to be able to

- Understand how process costing differs from job-order costing

- Compute output as equivalent units

- Compute costs and prepare journal entries for process-costing transactions

- Incorporate beginning inventories into process costing using the weighted average and the FIFO methods

- Use backflush costing

- Describe operation costing

The only sure path to the attainment of these objectives is conscientious pencil pushing in solving practice problems. Most students find this material a bit more difficult than other cost accounting topics.

REVIEW OF KEY CONCEPTS

A. The two basic systems of product costing are:
1. **Job-order costing** is appropriate when different products are manufactured in identifiable batches called *jobs*.
   a. Job-order costing is used when it is economically feasible to trace direct costs to identifiable products.
   b. Indirect costs are allocated to products as described in Chapters 13 and 14.
   c. The cost object is the *product*.
2. **Process costing** is appropriate when uniform product units are manufactured in a continuous flow through a series of standard operations called *processes*.

- a. Process costing is used when it is not feasible to trace direct costs to individual products or batches of products -- the product is uniform and the process is more or less continuous.
- b. The initial cost object is the *work done in some time period.*
- c. In essence, all product costs in process costing are treated as costs of the period and then costs of the products -- it is not feasible to trace costs directly to individual products -- costs of products are averages for the period.

3. The flow of costs through each process differs somewhat, though the general progression follows the production process:
    - a. Resources are applied to the process from direct material, direct labor, and manufacturing overhead.
    - b. The costs of resources when combined in the process become work-in-process.
    - c. When products are completed, the costs become finished goods.
    - d. When products are sold, the costs become cost of goods sold.

> See textbook Exhibit 15-1

4. Both cost systems follow the application of costs through work-in-process, finished goods (or goods transferred out), and cost of goods sold. The primary difference between the two systems is the method of measuring unit costs.
    - a. Job-order costing traces the costs to identifiable units, batches, or jobs of products.
    - b. Process costing traces the costs to the process or parts of the process during a specified time period and divides the costs by units produced to get unit costs.

> Before going on to the next section, be sure that you understand the basic rationales of and the difference between job-order costing and process costing.

B. The key to understanding how process costing assigns costs to units of product is understanding the concept of *equivalent units produced.*

1. **Equivalent units produced** measures the amount of resources applied during a time period that could have *fully processed* units of product.
    - a. Process costing computes equivalent units produced for each category of assigned cost.
    - b. The usual cost categories are direct material and conversion costs (direct labor and manufacturing overhead), but there are many variations in practice. For example, different materials may be traced separately to the process.
    - c. By computing equivalent units produced, process costing answers the question: "If I had applied all the materials (or conversion) used during the period toward the completion of products, how many could I have fully completed?"
    - d. For example, a product takes 2 hours of direct labor to fully complete. The process used 2,000 direct labor hours. How many units could have been fully processed by labor effort? Enough labor effort was applied to fully complete the equivalent of:

2,000 hours ÷ 2 hours per unit = 1,000 *equivalent units*.
- e. This is the essence of computing equivalent units produced: divide the resources applied during a period by the expected (or standard) resource necessary to fully complete a single unit of product.

2. In contrast, the number of *physical units* worked on during a period is usually greater than the equivalent units because not all units worked on are actually fully processed during a time period.
    - a. In the previous simple example, 2,000 physical units may have been started during the period.
    - b. What if not a single unit had been transferred out of the process (as finished goods or to the next process stage)? What would you infer about the status of completion of those 2,000 units begun during the period but still counted as work-in-process?
    - c. 2,000 physical units have received 1,000 equivalent units of labor, so on average, they should be 50% complete.
    - d. In practice, we try to obtain better information about the degree of completion of work-in-process.

3. Process costing keeps track of the number of physical units worked on, accumulates costs of resources used during a time period, and assigns these costs to *equivalent units produced*, not physical units.
    - a. The calculation of cost per equivalent unit is simple: divide the costs of the period by the equivalent units produced.
    - b. Continuing the simple example, suppose total direct labor cost of the period was $10,000. The direct labor cost per equivalent unit was $10,000 ÷ 1,000 equivalent units = $10 direct labor cost per equivalent unit.
    - c. The meaning of this *cost per equivalent unit* is that every unit that was fully completed cost $10 in direct labor to do so. Any unit that was 50% completed now has $5 of direct labor cost attached to it, and so on.

4. A systematic approach to process-costing involves five steps:
    - a. Account for the physical units of production into the process and out of the process:
        - (1) Units in process in the beginning of the period*
            + <u>Units started during the period</u>
            = <u>Total units worked on during the period</u>

        - (2) Units completed during the period
            + <u>Units still in process at the end of the period</u>
            = <u>Total units worked on during the period</u>
        * Note at first we assume that there are no units in process at the beginning of the period, so only the second calculation is required to account for units.
    - b. Compute equivalent units of production applied *in each category of cost*: usually direct materials and conversion cost, *separately*.

> See textbook Exhibit 15-2

c. Summarize the total costs to be accounted for in each cost category.
d. Compute the costs per equivalent unit in each cost category.
e. Use these unit costs to allocate and reconcile the total costs of goods completed and ending work in process.

> See textbook Exhibit 15-3

> Before going on, review this important section, review Exhibits 15-2 and 15-3. Most importantly, carefully work through Summary Problem One in the text. Be sure that you understand each calculation and how each calculation flows into the next one. Learn to set these analyses up systematically and the entire process will be easier and more intuitive. Please do not go on until you are ready.

C. If the process begins a period with partially completed units from the preceding period (this is typically the case), process costing becomes only a little more complicated.

1. The problem is that since the cost object is the *process during a specific time period*, costs may be different in different periods.

2. Process costing has two common approaches to accounting for the costs of separate periods: the *weighted average* costing method and the *first-in, first-out* (FIFO) method.

3. **The weighted-average method** treats the beginning inventory of work in process as though it were begun and finished during the current period.
   a. Beginning-inventory costs for each type of cost are mingled with the respective current period costs.
   b. These costs include **transferred-in costs** (or *previous-department costs*), as well as the present department's currently added costs of material, labor, and overhead.

   > See textbook Exhibit 15-4

   c. Therefore, the divisor for computing per equivalent unit costs is the *total equivalent units*, that is, the equivalent units from the previous work on the beginning inventory as well as the current work.
   d. Thus, monthly unit costs actually represent *weighted averages* of beginning-inventory costs and currently added costs.

   > See textbook Exhibit 15-5

4. In contrast, the **first-in, first-out method (FIFO)** treats the beginning inventory of work in process as though it were a batch of goods separate and distinct from goods started and finished by a process within the same period.
   a. Beginning-inventory costs are *not* mingled with current costs.
   b. Therefore, the divisor for computing equivalent unit costs of the period includes *only the equivalent units for work done during the current period* and *not* the equivalent units of work done on the beginning inventory during previous periods.

   > See textbook Exhibit 15-6

        c.   As a result, monthly equivalent unit costs represent only the work that was actually done *during the current period.*

> See textbook Exhibit 15-7

        d.   Costs that are transferred out of one process to the next process or to finished-goods inventory, include costs from both beginning work in process and the current costs to complete them plus units started and completed are transferred out at the current costs.

5. Unless prices of inputs fluctuate greatly, the weighted-average and FIFO methods arrive at about the same product costs.

   a. Because of its ease of use, the weighted-average approach is commonly used in practice.

   b. Because FIFO identifies current productive activity, it may be more useful for cost variance analysis and when costs and inventories fluctuate.

   c. Budget analysts usually prepare flexible budgets based on current equivalent units so as not to confuse current work with prior work.

> Before going on to the next section, be sure that you understand the difference between the weighted-average and the FIFO methods. Work through every step of Summary Problem Two in the text, noting how equivalent units and costs per equivalent units are calculated using each method.

D. Just-in-Time manufacturing companies can simplify their process costing method because inventories are minimal.

    1.   If there are zero inventories, **backflush costing** applies all costs of production directly to cost of goods sold.

    2.   In practice, many JIT firms in the U.S. maintain some inventories, so some inventory accounting is required for financial control.

> See textbook Summary Problem Three

E. Appendix 15A demonstrates how to account for process costs in a subsequent process.

    1.   Essentially, another cost category is created in the subsequent process: **transferred-in costs**.

    2.   Transferred-in cost is in addition to the subsequent department's own direct materials and conversion costs.

    3.   The subsequent process computes physical units, equivalent units, and costs per equivalent unit in the three cost categories, just as described earlier.

    4.   Subsequent processes may account for costs using the weighted-average method.

> See textbook Exhibits 15-8 and 15-9

    5.   FIFO methods may also be used.

> See textbook Exhibits 15-10 and 15-11

    6.   You should review Summary Problems Four, Five, and Six

F. Appendix 15B reviews *operation costing*, which is one of the many hybrid costing systems that blend features of job-order costing and process costing.

  1. Operation costing traces costs by job or work order through standardized operations. Thus, operation costing applies costs to a specific job as it passes through a series of processes.

  2. Different operations may have different cost drivers on which equivalent units are based.

  3. Typically, direct materials are applied to the job, and conversion costs are applied to the separate operations (and then to the jobs as they pass through).

> Before going on to the practice test, review the fundamentals of process costing: the computation of equivalent units and cost per equivalent unit.

PRACTICE TEST QUESTIONS AND PROBLEMS WITH SOLUTIONS

True or False Statements

Determine whether each of the following statements is True (T) or False (F) and enter your answer in the space provided.

____1. The primary purpose for computing equivalent units produced is to compare the volume of production across individual manufacturing processes.

____2. Equivalent units of production are computed as the physical units worked on multiplied by the expected cost per unit in each cost category.

____3. In process cost calculations, the completion percentages of work-in-process inventories typically pertain to the conversion costs of the present department.

____4. The costs of the beginning inventory of work in process are mingled with current costs in making cost per equivalent unit calculations by the weighted-average method.

____5. In comparison with the FIFO method of computing equivalent units produced, the weighted-average method would never result in a lower quantity.

____6. Conceptually, the FIFO method of process costing is closer to job-order costing than the weighted-average method.

____7. The unit costs developed by the FIFO process costing method would be more sensitive to current operating influences than the unit costs developed by the weighted-average method.

____8. When the FIFO process-cost method is used, the divisor for computing unit costs for a period should *exclude* the equivalent units for work done on the beginning inventory of work in process during previous periods.

____9. The process-cost method that treats the beginning inventory of work in process as though it were begun and finished during the current period is first-in, first-out.

____10.	When the FIFO process costing method is used on a monthly basis, the Finished Goods account would be charged at a different unit cost for each batch of product completed within each month.

____11.	The primary difference between job-order costing and process costing is the specification of the appropriate cost object.

____12.	FIFO process costing is preferred to the weighted-average method because of its ease of use.

____13.	Backflush costing works best when physical inventories are negligible.

____14.	Accounting for the costs of subsequent processes is identical to accounting for the costs of the initial process.

____15.	In an operation costing system, direct material costs are identified with specific product batches, and conversion costs are identified with specific jobs.

Multiple Choice Questions

For each of the following multiple-choice questions, select the best answer(s) and enter the identification letter(s) in the space provided:

____1.	The current period's equivalent units are (a) the number of units worked on, (b) the number of units transferred out, (c) the number of units started multiplied by their weighted average ending degree of completion, (d) the number of units started and completed plus the number of units in process multiplied by their average degree of completion.

____2.	The cost per equivalent unit in a particular period is (a) the unit cost of input multiplied by the expected usage of input per unit of output, (b) total cost applied or transferred-in divided by total equivalent units, (c) current cost applied or transferred-in divided by current equivalent units, (d) current cost applied or transferred-in divided by total equivalent units.

____3.	(Hint: set up a worksheet) A certain process that adds all material at the beginning of the process had a beginning inventory of 5,000 units that were 40% completed as to conversion costs and an ending inventory of 1,000 units that were 50% completed. Units started were 20,000, and units completed were 24,000. The equivalent units of conversion produced using the weighted-average method were: (a) 24,500, (b) 22,000, (c) 22,500, (d) 20,000

____4.	See the preceding item. Using the FIFO method, the equivalent units of conversion produced were: (a) 24,500, (b) 22,000, (c) 22,500, (d) 20,000.

____5.	See item 3 above. The equivalent units produced for materials, using the FIFO method, were: (a) 24,500, (b) 25,000, (c) 22,500, (d) 20,000,

____6.	See the preceding item. The equivalent units produced for materials, using the weighted-average method, were: (a) 24,500, (b) 25,000, (c) 22,500, (d) 20,000,

____7.	See the preceding item. Beginning work-in-process material costs were $50,000 and current material costs were $220,000. The FIFO cost of material per equivalent unit was: (a) $10.80, (b) $11.00, (c) $10.00, (d) $8.80.

____8.   Bonzo Company uses backflush costing. Resources applied to production during the past week were $5,000 direct materials plus $20,000 conversion cost. All production was sold as completed. Finished goods and cost of goods sold for the month respectively were: (a) $25,000 and $25,000, (b) zero and $25,000, (c) $25,000 and zero, (d) cannot determine because beginning inventories are not known.

____9.   (Appendix) When direct materials are added to the *second* process in a series of three manufacturing processes, the journal entry would include: (a) a credit to the second process, (b) a credit to the first process, (c) a debit to the first process, (d) a debit to material inventory.

____10. (Appendix) No new materials are applied in Process Two. The ending inventory of work in process consists of 50 units that are 60 percent completed in Process Two. Compute the total cost of this inventory if unit costs for the month are $8.00 for conversion costs and $10.00 for transferred-in costs: (a) $900, (b) $540, (c) $700, (d) $740.

Completion

1. The cost object of _____ is the product or batch of product, whereas the cost object of _____ is the _____ during a specific time period.

2. When there are no beginning _____ inventories, equivalent units produced are the same as _____.

3. When there are beginning work-in-process inventories, total equivalent units produced using the weighted-average method are computed by _____ _____.

4. The first-in, first-out process-costing method differs from the weighted-average method because _____ are kept separate.

5. The five steps in the analysis of process costing are:
   (a)_____
   (b)_____
   (c)_____
   (d)_____
   (e)_____

6. The FIFO _____ is the current costs applied divided by the current equivalent units.

7. The total costs to account for are the sum of _____ and _____.

8. Many companies with _____ manufacturing methods use _____ costing because they have virtually no inventories.

9. Companies with multiple, linked processes generally have three categories of costs: _____, _____, and _____.

10. Operation costing is a hybrid costing system that blends elements of _____ and _____.

Problems

1. Given for the Bleaching Process for July:

	Units
Inventory in process, November 1, 70% completed for conversion costs	300
Transferred into process in November	600
Completed and transferred out of process in November	700
Inventory in process, November 30, 60% completed for conversion costs	200

a. Find the equivalent units produced for computing unit costs by the *weighted-average* method:

        Material Costs   Conversion Costs

b. Find the equivalent units produced for computing unit costs by the *first-in, first-out* method:

        Material Costs   Conversion Costs

2. Given for the Milling Process for March:

Inventory in process, January 1, 40% completed for conversion costs	300 units
Started in January	600 units
Completed and transferred out of process in January.	700 units
Inventory in process, January 31, 50% completed for conversion costs.	200 units
January 1 inventory costs:	
Direct materials costs	$3,900
Conversion costs	$2,800
Costs added in January:	
Direct materials	$5,100
Conversion costs	$3,600

Direct materials are added at the beginning of this process.

Using the *weighted-average* method, calculate the cost of work transferred out in March and the cost of the March 31 inventory of work in process:

Step 1-Summarize physical units:

Step 2-Compute output in equivalent units:
                        Direct Materials   Conversion

Step 3-Summarize total costs to account for:
                        Direct Materials Costs   Conversion Costs   Total Costs

Step 4-Compute unit costs:
                        Direct Materials Cost   Conversion Cost   Total Unit Cost

Step 5-Compute total costs of work completed and in process:

3. Given for the Cutting Process for February:

Inventory in process, February 1, 75% completed for conversion costs	200 units
Transferred into process in February	600 units
Completed and transferred out of process in February	500 units
Inventory in process, February 28, 50% completed for conversion costs	300 units

February 1 inventory costs:
  Transferred-in costs $2,200
  Conversion costs $1,300
Costs added in February:
  Transferred-in costs: $6,000
  Conversion costs $4,000
No direct materials are added in this process.

Using the *first-in, first-out* method, calculate the cost of work transferred out in February and the cost of the February 28 inventory of work in process:

Step 1-Summarize physical units:

Step 2-Compute output in equivalent units:
                                        Transferred-in Costs   **Conversion Costs**

Step 3-Summarize total costs to account for:
                                        Transferred in Costs   **Conversion Costs**   **Total Costs**

Step 4-Compute unit costs:
                                          Transferred in Costs   **Conversion Costs**   **Total Costs**

Step 5-Compute total costs of work completed and in process

CHAPTER 15 SOLUTIONS TO PRACTICE TEST QUESTIONS AND PROBLEMS

True or False Statements

1. False   The primary purpose of equivalent units is to measure the output of a production process in a standardized manner.

2. False   Equivalent units of production are the number of units that could have been fully completed from the resources applied. Equivalent units could be computed by the amount of the resource applied divided by the standard or expected resource required per completed unit.

3. False   Equivalent units of transferred-in costs are almost always equal to physical units. Equivalent units of material at any point in the process depend on when materials are added. In all the examples in the text and study guide, materials are always added at the beginning of a process, but that is not always the case. Thus, work-in-process inventories may be partially complete with regard to materials as well as conversion. It depends on the process.

4. True   The weighted-average method does not distinguish current period costs from prior period costs carried over as beginning work-in-process, but averages them together. It is simpler to do so than to maintain separate period cost identities.

5. True   At a minimum, weighted-average equivalent units would equal FIFO equivalent units. When there are beginning work-in-process inventories, weighted-average equivalent units are greater than FIFO because of the combining of both beginning work-in-process and current work.

6. True   But only because they are both concerned with identifying costs more precisely than the weighted-average method. FIFO maintains separate time period cost identities, and job-order costing maintains separate job or batch identities. But they really are not very close because job identity may have little to do with time period identity.

7. True   Because current period costs are applied only to the work of the current period, FIFO process costing would identify certain units of products as having different unit costs than prior period's work if current costs deviate from past costs. Weighted average costing would blur the line between the past periods' costs.

8. True   FIFO costing is concerned with identifying the current cost per equivalent unit; thus it divides current costs by current equivalent units, which is total equivalent units less beginning work-in-process equivalent units.

9. False   Weighted-average process costing is the method that blurs the distinction between the prior period's work and the current period's work. FIFO costing assumes that beginning work-in-process was begun in a prior period and partially completed at the prior period's unit cost.

10. False   This is true only if current period cost per equivalent unit differs from the prior period cost per equivalent unit. If the costs per equivalent unit are the same over time, then the cost per unit charged to finished goods will not change either.

11. True   Job-order costing applies costs to individual products or batches of product. Process costing applies costs to the process operating for a specific period of time and then to products by dividing the period's costs by equivalent units..

12. False   Weighted-average costing is easier to use. FIFO costing might be preferred if prices are volatile and for preparing flexible budgets for the current period.

13. True   Backflush costing requires negligible inventories because it charges all manufacturing costs of the period to finished goods or preferably to cost of goods sold directly. Backflush costing makes JIT manufacturing firms look much like service firms, which cannot inventory their product.

14. True   In concept, the accounting for subsequent processes is identical to accounting for the first process. The only difference is that subsequent processes must also account for the costs transferred in from preceding processes.

15. False   Though there are many hybrid variations, a common version of operation costing identifies materials with specific jobs or batches and identifies conversion costs with specific operations or processes.

Multiple Choice Questions

1. c, d   Though the second definition (d) is the more usual one, the first one (c) is also true. For example, assume 100 units were started. At the end of the period 80 of these were completed, and 20 were 40% completed. Current equivalent units are by (d) equal to 80 + 20 x .4 = 88. Likewise the average degree of completion is (80 x 100% + 20 x 40%) ÷ 100 = 88%, which multiplied by 100 units is 88 units.

2. c   The cost per equivalent unit in a particular period is the current cost applied or transferred-in divided by current equivalent units. The expected or standard cost per equivalent unit is the unit cost of input multiplied by the expected usage of input per unit of output.

3. - 7. computations:

Beginning work-in-process (40% complete)	5,000 units
Started	20,000 units
total units to account for	25,000 units
Units completed	24,000 units
Ending work-in-process	1,000 units
total units accounted for	25,000 units

	Physical units	Equivalent units Materials	Conversion
Completed	24,000	24,000	24,000
Ending work-in-process	1,000	1,000	500
Weighted average total equivalent units	25,000	25,000	24,500
Less beginning work-in-process	5,000	5,000	2,000
FIFO total equivalent units	20,000	20,000	22,500

3. b

4. c

5. d

6. b

7. b,c   The FIFO cost of material per equivalent unit in the current period was $220,000 ÷ 20,000 = $11 per unit. The FIFO cost of material per equivalent unit in the preceding period was $50,000 ÷ 5,000 = $10 per unit.

8. b   Under backflush costing and the conditions described, it is most likely that costs of production would be directly applied to cost of goods sold.

9. b   The journal entry would debit the second process to record the costs transferred in and credit the first process to record the costs transferred out.

10. d   The cost of ending work in process is $10 x 50 + $8 x 50 x .6 = $740

Completion

1.   job-order costing, process costing, process

2.   work-in-process, the current equivalent units

3.   the sum of equivalent units started and completed plus equivalent units in ending work in process

4.   costs of different periods

5.   (a) summarize the flow of physical units
      (b) calculate output in terms of equivalent units
      (c) summarize total costs to account for
      (d) calculate unit costs
      (e) apply costs to units completed and ending work in process

6.   cost per equivalent unit

7.   costs of beginning work in process, current costs
8.   JIT, backflush
9.   transferred-in cost, direct materials cost, conversion cost
10. job-order costing, process costing

Problems

1. **Bleaching Process**

   a. Transferred out   700   700
      Ending inventory: 200 x 100%   200
                       200 x 60%   -   120
      Equivalent units produced   <u>900</u>   <u>820</u>

   b. Computed above   900   820
      Less beginning inventory work
         done previously: 300 x 100%   300
                          300 x 70%   -   210
      Equivalent units produced   <u>600</u>   <u>610</u>

2. **Milling Process**

Step 1: Units of physical flow

Work in process, beginning	300 (40%)	Units completed.....	700
Units started	600	Work in process, end	200 (50%)
Units to account for	900	Units accounted for	900

Step 2: Equivalent units

	Direct Materials	Conversion Costs
Completed and transferred out	700	700
Ending work in process: 200 x 100%	200	
200 x 50%		100
Work done to date (equivalent units produced for weighted-average method)	<u>900</u>	<u>800</u>

Step 3: Summary of total costs to account for

	Direct Materials	Conversion Costs	Total Costs
Work-in-process, beginning	$ 3,900	$ 2,800	$ 6,700
Costs added currently	<u>5,100</u>	<u>3,600</u>	<u>8,700</u>
Total costs to account for.	<u>$ 9,000</u>	<u>$6,400</u>	<u>$15,400</u>

Step 4: Unit costs

	Direct Material	Conversion Costs	Total Unit Cost
Total costs to account for (Step 3)	$ 9,000	$ 6,400	
Divide by equivalent units (Step 2)	900	800	
Unit costs	<u>$ 10.00</u>	<u>$ 8.00</u>	<u>$18.00</u>

Step 5: Total costs of work completed and in process
Units completed: (700)($18) $12,600
Work-in-process, end:
Direct Materials costs: (200)($10) $2,000
Conversion costs: (200)(50%)($8) 800 2,800
Total costs accounted for $15,400

3. Cutting Process:
Step 1: Units of physical flow
Work-in-process, beginning 200 (75%)
Units transferred in 600
Units to account for 800
Units completed and transferred out during February 500
Work in process, end 300 (50%)
Units accounted for 800

Step 2: Equivalent units

	Transferred-in Costs	Conversion Costs
Completed and transferred out	500	500
Ending inventory in process: 100% x 300	300	
50% x 300	-	150
Total work done to date	800	650
Less beginning inventory in process:		
100% x 200	200	
75% x 200	-	150
Work done in current period only (equivalent units produced for FIFO method)	600	500

Step 3: Summary of total costs to account for

	Transferred-in Costs	Conversion Costs	Total Costs
Work in process, beginning	$ 2,200	$ 1,300	$3,500
Costs added currently	6,000	4,000	10,000
Total costs to account for.	$ 8,200	$5,300	$13,500

Step 4: Unit costs

	Transferred-in Costs	Conversion Costs	Total Unit Cost
Costs added currently	$ 6,000	$ 4,000	
Divide by equivalent units (Step 2)	600	500	
Unit costs	$ 10.00	$ 8.00	$18.00

Step 5: Total costs of work completed and in process
Work-in-process, end:
Transferred-in costs: (300)($10) $3,000
Conversion costs: (300)(50%)($8) 1,200 $4,200
 Completed and transferred out:
  $13,500 - $4,200 9,300
Total costs accounted for $13,500

CHAPTER 16

Overhead Application: Variable and Absorption Costing

MAIN FOCUS AND OBJECTIVES

Much of this chapter discusses the difference between two approaches to income measurement: *variable costing and absorption costing*. The difference between them is the treatment of *fixed factory-overhead* costs as either noninventoriable (period) costs by variable costing or inventoriable (product) costs by absorption costing. In addition, the chapter gives emphasis to the nature and effects of alternative ways of allocating fixed overhead to production. The different ways affect the *production-volume variance* for fixed overhead costs. Specific learning objectives are to:

- Identify the basic difference between variable costing and absorption costing
- Construct income statements using variable and absorption costing
- Identify the production volume variance
- Identify the differences between actual, normal, and standard absorption costing
- Identify the relative merits of variable costing
- Use two alternative methods for disposing of standard cost variances
- Analyze major variances in a standard absorption costing system

---

REVIEW OF KEY CONCEPTS

A. There are two major approaches in the application of costs to products for measuring net income:

1. The full-costing, functional, or traditional approach uses **absorption costing.**
    a. Recall that in absorption costing, *fixed manufacturing overhead costs* are treated initially as *product costs* and therefore are *included in product inventories* and cost of goods manufactured and sold, along with direct material, direct labor, and *variable* manufacturing overhead costs.

b. Absorption costing must be used for income tax purposes and is generally accepted for making financial reports to stockholders and other external parties.

2. The contribution approach to income measurement uses **variable costing,** less accurately called **variable costing.**
   a. Recall that in variable costing, *fixed manufacturing overhead costs* are treated immediately as *expense* and therefore are *excluded from product inventories,* which include *only* direct material, direct labor, and *variable* factory-overhead costs.
   b. Variable costing is growing in use for internal performance reports to management, but it is not acceptable for income tax purposes or external reporting.

3. The essential difference between these two costing methods is *timing* of the recognition of the expense of fixed manufacturing overhead costs.

   > See textbook Exhibit 16-1

   a. In absorption costing, fixed manufacturing overhead is *first included in inventory* and therefore is treated as an *unexpired cost* (an *asset*) until the period in which the inventory is sold and included in cost of goods sold (an *expense*).
   b. However, in variable costing, fixed manufacturing overhead is regarded as an *expired cost* and is *charged against sales immediately,* only *variable* manufacturing costs being included in product inventories.

4. These two approaches can produce different reported figures for net income.

   > See textbook Exhibits 16-2 and 16-3

   a. Notice that when the *quantity of inventory increases* during a period (19X1), *absorption costing* will generally report *more net income* than *variable costing.* This is because a portion of the period's fixed manufacturing overhead cost was assigned to products that *remain* in inventory, whereas in variable costing all the period's fixed manufacturing overhead was recognized as expense.
   b. However, when the *quantity of inventory decreases* during a period (19X2), *absorption costing* will generally report *less net income* than variable costing. Each unit was assigned a portion of fixed manufacturing overhead, and some units had been produced in a prior period. Because more units were sold than were produced, the total fixed manufacturing overhead included in cost of goods sold was greater than the *current* period's fixed manufacturing overhead *cost*. In variable costing, only the current period's fixed manufacturing overhead cost was expensed, none from a previous period.
   c. You should also note that the absorption-costing approach includes a plus or minus adjustment to gross profit for the *production-volume variance* in fixed factory overhead (this will be covered below).

   > Before going on be sure that you understand how changing inventories can affect net income under absorption costing but not under variable costing.

B. Two principal purposes of a cost accounting system are for planning and control and for product costing. As mentioned in earlier chapters, some firms use multiple cost systems to accomplish these separate purposes.

1. If the proper cost drivers are identified, virtually any cost system can assist in planning, controlling, and applying *variable* costs to products and services.
    a. This is because, as activity levels increase, the total variable costs rise proportionately.
    b. Difficulties in working with variable costs arise when appropriate cost drivers are not known or it is too costly to use them for accounting purposes.

> See the first two graphs in the text

2. On the other hand, planning, controlling, and applying fixed costs for product-costing purposes can be more confusing.
    a. For planning and control purposes, total fixed costs may be predicted and evaluated as constant levels of expenditure within a specific relevant range.
    b. If variable costing is used, the role of fixed costs in product costing is also simple -- it is expensed as a cost of the period.
    c. However, for financial reporting using absorption-costing, fixed costs are applied on a *per-unit* basis, and the method of allocating fixed costs to units of product or service will affect product costs and reported, absorption-cost-based income.
    d. Fixed cost applied to products under absorption costing is a function of the fixed overhead rate:

    Fixed cost applied = actual activity level × fixed overhead rate

    > See the second set of graphs in the text

    e. Thus in absorption costing, fixed overhead is applied to products and services as though it were variable. Since we know this is not the case, some accounting problems result, as discussed below.

> Before going on, reinforce your understanding of the different ways that variable and absorption costing deal with fixed manufacturing overhead.

C. To obtain an absorption product cost for pricing and inventory uses, one must select an expected level of activity as the basis for applying fixed overhead.

1. A budgeted rate for applying fixed factory overhead is then predetermined for a given year:

    Fixed overhead rate = budgeted fixed overhead ÷ expected activity level.

2. Most absorption cost systems, since they are primarily for financial reporting not internal decision making, use *expected* unit production volume as the allocation base.
    a. Since the resulting rates and unit costs have limited significance for planning, pricing, and control purposes, many companies are beginning to use activity analysis and activity-based costing (Chapters 3 and 4) to

Overhead Application: Variable and Absorption Costing **235** determine more appropriate cost drivers for variable costs and for applying fixed costs.

b. The analysis that follows, however, applies conceptually to absorption costing, regardless of the nature of the fixed overhead allocation base.

c. Some accountants argue that the best fixed overhead allocation base is **practical capacity,** which is the level of production activity that would utilize facilities optimally. When expected or actual production is less than optimal, the production-volume variance is an indication of the cost of excess capacity -- excess fixed cost that is incurred because production is lower than the facility was designed for.

3. A **production-volume variance** arises whenever the actual production volume deviates from the expected or practical-capacity level (for ease of discussion, we will only use expected levels from here on).

a. When actual production volume is *less* than the expected volume, the fixed overhead production-volume variance is *unfavorable* because fixed overhead expected is greater than applied (or fixed overhead is *underapplied*).

b. When actual production volume is *greater* than the expected volume, the volume variance is *favorable* because fixed overhead applied is greater than expected (or fixed overhead is *overapplied*).

Production-volume variance = Applied fixed overhead - budgeted fixed overhead
= (actual volume x fixed overhead rate) - (expected volume x fixed overhead rate)
= (actual volume - expected volume) x fixed overhead rate

c. This variance is similar in nature to the sales activity variance discussed in Chapter 7 -- it is the result of actual activity (production volume in this case) differing from the expected level. When the two production levels are equal, there is not production-volume variance.

4. There are three basic ways for applying costs to products by the absorption-costing approach: Actual costing, normal costing, and standard costing.

a. Actual costing uses the actual production level to allocate fixed overhead. Therefore, the volume variance is always zero. Prime costs are applied as they are actually incurred.

b. Normal costing uses the expected production volume to apply overhead, so a volume variance may exist. Prime costs are applied as they are actually incurred.

c. Standard costing applies *all* costs at standard rates multiplied by the inputs allowed for actual outputs achieved. A number of variances, including a volume variance, may result (standard cost variances are discussed in Chapter 8).

> Can you explain how to determine the fixed overhead rate? Can you also explain the meaning and derivation of the production-volume variance?

D. One can reconcile the difference in the operating incomes measured by the variable-costing and absorption-costing approaches for a given year by adjusting for changes in inventory levels.

1. Recall from the discussion above that the reason the two income measures may differ is that in absorption costing fixed overhead first flows through inventory accounts before being expensed.
   a. When actual production volume equals actual sales volume then usually (inventory accounting methods can complicate this) the period's fixed overhead is expensed, just as in variable costing, so there is no difference in income measures.
   b. When actual production volume does not equal actual sales volume, the income measures can differ because the amount of fixed overhead recognized as expense by the two methods differs.
2. There are several straight-forward methods for reconciling the income differences between the two methods (the first is probably easier):
   a. *Multiply the budgeted rate of fixed manufacturing overhead by the increase or decrease in inventory units for the year.*

   > See textbook Exhibit 16-4

   - Note in this exhibit there was a decrease of 20,000 inventory units in 19X2.
   - At $1 per unit, this accounts for the $20,000 lower operating income under the absorption-costing approach in 19X2.
   - If inventory decreased, absorption-cost-based income is lower than variable-cost-based income because more fixed cost is expensed than expected.
   - If inventory increased, absorption-cost-based income is higher than variable-cost-based income because less fixed cost is expensed than expected.

   b. *Compute the difference between the total amount of fixed manufacturing overhead expensed by the two approaches for the year.*

   > See textbook Exhibit 16-5

   - In 19X2 the difference in expense charged to income is: $170,000 - $150,000 = $20,000.

   > Before going on to the next section, be sure that you understand how to reconcile income reported under both variable and absorption costing under conditions of: no change in inventory, increase in inventory, decrease in inventory.

E. Many companies use the variable-costing approach for their internal income statements.
   1. One reason is that an increase in the quantity of product manufactured would, of course, not affect reported operating income because there would be no effect on the amount of fixed overhead expensed in the period.
      a. On the other hand, if the absorption-costing approach is used, an increase in the quantity of goods manufactured would reduce an unfavorable production-volume variance (an expense).
      b. Thus, there would be an increase in reported operating income, which might be falsely interpreted as an improvement in operating performance.

Overhead Application: Variable and Absorption Costing **237**

2. Another reason, as mentioned in earlier chapters, is that variable costing is consistent with CVP planning models, and evaluating performance by comparing plans with actual results is easier.

F. In addition to the production-volume variance, there can, of course, be other variances of actual costs from standard costs, as discussed in Chapter 8.

1. These typically include *price* and *usage* variances for direct material, direct labor, and variable manufacturing overhead, plus a *spending* variance for fixed overhead.

> See textbook Exhibit 16-7

2. These variances are usually treated as expired costs of the period and charged to current income.

> See textbook Exhibit 16-8

a. In some cases when the variances are unusually large, these variances would be prorated over inventories and costs of goods sold, thus resulting in inventory valuations that are more representative of the "actual" costs of obtaining the products.

> Before going on to the practice test, review the accounting treatment of cost variances at the end of a reporting period.

PRACTICE TEST QUESTIONS AND PROBLEMS WITH SOLUTIONS

True or False Statements

Determine whether each of the following statements is True (T) or False (F) and enter your answer in the space provided.

_____1. In the U.S. the variable-costing approach is acceptable for internal reporting, income tax reporting, and external reporting.

_____2. Variable selling expenses are not included in product inventories by either the absorption-costing method or the variable-costing method.

_____3. Variable factory-overhead costs are included in product inventories under both the absorption-costing and variable-costing methods.

_____4. Manufacturing overhead costs are treated as expenses of the period by both the absorption-costing and the variable-costing methods.

_____5. Under absorption costing all product costs are initially treated as unexpired product costs.

_____6. Unfavorable production-volume variances in fixed factory-overhead costs that occur in the absorption-costing approach should be reported as expenses.

_____7. Production-volume variances are analogous to flexible budget variances.

_____8. Actual costing and normal costing differ in the way manufacturing overhead is applied to products.

____9.   Normal costing and standard costing differ in the way manufacturing overhead is applied to products.

____10. Actual costing and standard costing differ in the way prime costs are applied to products.

____11. Actual costing and standard costing differ in the way cost variances are disposed of.

____12. Variable costing and absorption costing differ in the way variances are disposed of.

____13. When inventories increase, variable-cost-based income is greater than absorption-cost-based income.

____14. The fixed overhead spending variance occurs only in absorption costing.

____15. Price and usage variances for direct material, direct labor, and variable factory overhead are prorated among inventory accounts unless they are unusually large.

Multiple Choice Questions

For each of the following multiple choice questions, determine the best answer(s) and enter the identification letter(s) in the space provided.

Use these selected data (in millions) for the first four test items:

Fixed selling expenses	$ 10
Variable selling expenses	$ 30
Fixed factory overhead	$ 50
Variable factory overhead	$ 15

____1.   In a variable-costing income statement, the total of the above amounts to be included as part of the contribution margin is: (a) $30, (b) $40, (c) $45, (d) $60.

____2.   In a variable-costing income statement, the total of the above amounts to be excluded from the contribution margin is: (a) $40, (b) $45, (c) $60, (d) $65.

____3.   In an absorption-costing income statement, the total of the above amounts to be included in gross-profit is: (a) $40, (b) $45, (c) $60, (d) $65.

____4.   In an absorption-costing income statement, the total of the above amounts to be excluded from gross-profit is: (a) $40, (b) $45, (c) $55, (d) $60.

____5.   In its first year of operations, a company produced 20,000 units of a uniform product and sold 18,000 units. Selected data include: direct materials used $80,000, direct labor $150,000, and manufacturing overhead $100,000 (half fixed, half variable). There is no ending inventory of work in process. Compute the ending inventory of finished goods if the absorption-costing method is used: (a) $33,000, (b) $66,000, (c) $23,000, (d) $28,000

____6.   See the preceding test item. Compute the ending inventory of finished goods if the variable-costing method is used: (a) $33,000, (b) $66,000, (c) $23,000, (d) $28,000.

____7.   See item 5 above. Compared with the absorption-costing method, the variable-costing method would measure an operating income that is: (a) $10,000 higher, (b) $5,000 lower, (c) $5,000 higher, (d) $10,000 lower.

_____8.   See item 5 above. Under absorption costing, the production-volume variance would be (a) $5,000 favorable, (b) $5,000 unfavorable, (c) zero, (d) cannot determine.

_____9.   Amerada Co. manufactured and sold 5,000 units of a uniform product in its first year of operations when it expected to manufacture 6,000 of these units. Variable manufacturing costs were $240,000 and fixed factory overhead was $120,000. Selling and administrative expenses were $100,000 fixed and $60,000 variable. The production volume variance was: (a) $40,000 unfavorable, (b) $20,000 favorable, (c) $20,000 unfavorable, (d) $40,000 favorable.

_____10. When a normal costing system is used, budgeted rates would be used for applying costs by the absorption-costing method for: (a) direct labor and variable factory overhead, (b) variable factory overhead and fixed factory overhead, (c) fixed factory overhead and direct materials, (d) direct materials and direct labor.

Completion

Complete each of the following statements by filling in the blanks.

1. The predicted activity level for determining the fixed-overhead rate is the _____.

2. The absorption-costing method would tend to report greater profits than would the variable-costing method when the quantity of inventory during a period _____.

3. Absorption costing and variable costing differ because _____.

4. The difference in income measured by absorption costing or variable costing may be calculated by _____ or by _____.

5. When the actual production level is less than the predicted level, the fixed overhead _____ variance is _____.

6. In practice, variances for direct material, direct labor, and variable factory overhead are usually treated as _____.

7. Allocating standard-cost variances to inventories is called _____ and is usually done _____.

8. Practical capacity differs from expected volume by _____.

9. There are two fixed manufacturing overhead variances; the _____ variance occurs only in _____ costing but the _____ variance occurs in both _____ and _____.

10. When _____ increase _____-cost-based income is greater than _____-cost-based income.

240 Chapter 16

Problems

1. Given for the first year of operations of Random Products, a manufacturer of a uniform product:

	Fixed	Variable
Direct labor cost	$ -	$140,000
Selling and administrative expenses	10,000	70,000
Direct materials used	-	100,000
Factory overhead	72,000	36,000

The company manufactured 12,000 units and sold 9,000 of these units for $380,000. There was no ending inventory of work in process. Compute these amounts:

    a. Ending inventory of finished goods:
        Absorption-costing method

        Variable-costing method

    b. Gross profit on sales

    c. Contribution margin

    d. Operating income:
        Absorption-costing method

        Variable-costing method

2. Given for Martingale Corporation for 19X7:

Beginning inventory	none
Production	10,000 units
Sales at $40 each	8,000 units
Ending inventory	2,000 units
Standard manufacturing costs per unit:	
Variable manufacturing costs	$12
Fixed factory overhead	4
Total	$16
Selling and administrative expenses:	
Variable	$95,000
Fixed	45,000
Total	$140,000

a. Prepare an income statement, using absorption costing, ignoring income taxes, and assuming no production-volume variance:

b. Prepare an income statement, using variable costing and ignoring income taxes:

c. Reconcile the difference in net income shown by these two methods:

3. The following information pertains to the operations of Deterministic Corporation:

Budgeted fixed overhead cost	$1,500,000
Expected volume of activity	500,000 hrs.

242 Chapter 16

a. Compute the standard rate for applying fixed overhead:

b. Compute the fixed-overhead production-volume variance if the actual activity level is 498,000 hours:

c. State how this production-volume variance would be shown in an absorption-costing income statement:

d. Compute the fixed-overhead production-volume variance if the actual activity level is 506,000 hours:

e. State how this production-volume variance would be shown in an absorption-costing income statement:

CHAPTER 16 SOLUTIONS TO PRACTICE TEST QUESTIONS AND PROBLEMS

True or False Statements

1. False — In the U.S. the variable costing approach is not "generally accepted accounting practice" and is therefore not allowed for either tax or financial reporting. Any method, including variable costing, is acceptable for internal reporting.

2. True — Variable selling expenses are not considered an inventoriable product cost by either absorption costing or variable costing.

3. True — Variable factory overhead costs are inventoriable product costs under both costing systems.

4. False — Fixed manufacturing overhead is treated by variable costing as an expense of the period, but as an inventoriable product cost by absorption costing. Both costing methods regard variable manufacturing overhead as inventoriable product cost.

5. True — All product costs flow through inventory accounts under absorption costing and so are unexpired costs until the products are sold. An exception would be under backflush costing, where all product costs are charged to cost of goods sold immediately (see Chapter 15).

6. True — All production-volume variances are treated as adjustments to the period's income -- whether they are favorable or unfavorable.

7. False — Production-volume variances are more analogous to sales-activity variances because they are caused by actual activity levels that are different from expected.

8. True		Actual costing applies fixed overhead to products based on actual production levels, whereas normal costing applies fixed overhead based on expected, standard, or normal levels.
9. False		Both normal costing and standard costing apply fixed overhead based on expected, standard, or normal levels.
10. True		Actual costing applies prime costs (direct labor and direct materials) as actually incurred. Standard costing applies prime costs according to standard amounts allowed for the actual output. Variances between actual and standard costs are adjustments to current income.
11. True		Trick question. Cost variances do not arise in actual costing, only in standard and normal costing.
12. Unclear		Variable costing can use either actual or standard variable costs, so the question is not specific enough. If the variable costing uses actual costs, then there are no variances to dispose of. However, if variable costing uses standard costs, then the variances are, as is usually the case, charged to periodic income.
13. False		When inventories increase, a portion of the period's fixed manufacturing overhead remains in inventory, which increases absorption-cost income relative to variable-cost income. When inventories decrease, just the opposite effect and result occur.
14. False		The fixed overhead spending variance occurs whenever actual fixed overhead exceeds budgeted fixed overhead, regardless of the costing system.
15. False		Just the opposite is the accepted procedure. If the variances are small, it matters little where they are put, so the easiest thing to do is charge them to income. When the variances are large, there is a chance of materially misstating inventory balances, so the variances are prorated over the inventories and cost of goods sold.

Multiple Choice Questions

1. c		Variable costs of the period are counted as part of contribution margin: $30 + 15 = $45.
2. c		Fixed costs are deducted after contribution margin is computed: $10 + $50 = $60.
3. d		Gross profit includes all product costs, including: $50 + $15 = $45.
4. a		Gross profit excludes non-product costs: $10 + $30 = $40.
5. a		The absorption cost per unit = ($80 + $150 + $100) ÷ 20 = $16.50. Ending finished goods inventory is 2,000 x $16.50 = $33,000.
6. d		The variable cost per unit = ($80 + $150 + $50) ÷ 20 = $14.00. Ending finished goods inventory is 2,000 x $14 = $28,000.
7. b		The absorption-cost fixed overhead per unit is $50 ÷ 20 = $2.50. Ending inventory retains this amount under absorption costing, so variable-cost net income is $5,000 less than absorption-cost net income.

8. a or c or d   The production-volume variance is the fixed overhead rate times the difference between expected and actual production volume. If one assumes that the expected production level is 20,000 units, the production-volume variance is zero. If one assumes that the expected production level was 18,000 units, then the problem needs to be reworked because the fixed overhead rate would have been $50,000 ÷ 18,000 = $2.78. The production-volume variance would be 2,000 x $2.78 = $5,560 favorable because overhead was overapplied. If you do not care to guess, you cannot determine the production-volume variance.

9. c   The fixed factory overhead rate was $120,000 ÷ 6,000 = $20 per unit. The production-volume variance is 1,000 x $20 = $20,000 unfavorable, because overhead was underapplied.

10. b   Normal costing charges production for the actual prime costs, but budgeted costs for variable and fixed factory overhead.

Completion

1. expected, normal, or practical capacity level.
2. decreases
3. of the way that fixed factory overhead is treated.
4. multiplying the fixed overhead rate by the increase or decrease in inventories, comparing the amount of fixed overhead charged to income during the period.
5. volume, unfavorable
6. expenses of the period or adjustments to income
7. pro-rating, at the end of a period if variances are unusually large
8. the amount of excess capacity
9. volume, absorption, spending, absorption, variable
10. inventories, absorption, variable

Problems

1. Random Products

    a. The ending inventory is 12,000 - 9,000 = 3,000 units.

    Absorption costing:
      The cost per unit = ($72 + $140 + $100 + 36) ÷ 12 = $29
      Ending finished goods inventory = 3,000 x $29 = $87,000.

    Varible costing:
      The cost per unit = (140 + 100 + 36) ÷ 12 = $23
      Ending finished goods inventory = 3,000 x $23 = $69,000

    b. Cost of goods sold is 348,000 - 87,000 = $261,000. Gross profit is 380,000 - 261,000 = $119,000.

c. Variable cost of goods sold is 276,000 - 69,000 = $207,000. Total variable expenses are 207,000 + 70,000 = $277,000. Contribution margin is 380,000 - 277,000 = $103,000.

d. Operating income:
   Absorption-cost costing:
   Operating income = 119,000 - (10,000 + 70,000) = 119,000 - 80,000 = $39,000
   Variable-cost income:
   Operating income = 103,000 - (10,000 + 72,000) = 103,000 - 82,000 = $21,000
   Proof: Profit difference 39,000 - 21,000 = $18,000
   Fixed overhead rate = $72,000 ÷ 12,000 = $6 per unit
   $18,000 = $6 x 3,000 units increase in inventory

2. Martingale Corporation
   a. Absorption-costing income statement:

Sales: 8,000 units @ $40		$320,000
Less standard cost of goods sold:		
Cost of goods manufactured at standard:		
10,000 units @ $16	$160,000	
Less ending inventory: 2,000 units @ $16	32,000	128,000
Gross profit at standard		$192,000
Less selling and administrative expenses:		
Variable expenses	$ 95,000	
Fixed expenses	45,000	140,000
Operating income		$ 52,000

   b. Variable-costing income statement:

Sales: 8,000 units @ $25		$320,000
Variable manufacturing cost of goods produced:		
10,000 units @ $12	$120,000	
Less ending inventory: 2,000 units @ $12	24,000	
Variable manufacturing cost of goods sold:		
8,000 units @ $12	$ 96,000	
Variable selling and administrative expenses	95,000	
Total variable expenses		191,000
Contribution margin		$129,000
Less fixed costs:		
Factory overhead: 10,000 units @ $4	$ 40,000	
Selling and administrative expenses	45,000	85,000
Operating income		$44,000

   c. Reconciliation of difference in operating income:
   Operating income difference: $52,000 - $44,000 = $8,000
   Ending inventory difference: 2,000 units x ($16 - $12) = 2,000 x $4 fixed overhead cost per unit = $8,000

3. Deterministic Corporation

   a. The standard rate is $1,500,000 divided by 500,000 hours = $3 per hour.

   b. Production-volume variance is: (500,000 - 498,000) x $3 = $6,000 U, because fixed overhead is underapplied.

   c. It would be shown in the income statement as a *deduction* from gross profit at standard.

   d. Production-volume variance is (506,000 - 500,000) x $3 = $18,000 F, because fixed overhead is overapplied.

   e. It would be shown in the income statement as an *addition* to gross profit at standard.

CHAPTER 17

Quantitative Techniques Used in Management Accounting

MAIN FOCUS AND OBJECTIVES

This chapter introduces some important mathematical approaches for use in management planning and control. At the minimum, managers and accountants must be able to recognize appropriate situations for using these approaches. In particular, managerial accountants should be able to:

- Understand a decision-theory approach to decision making

- Recognize the effects of uncertainty on decision making

- Compare projects based on their expected values and standard deviations

- Compute the expected value of perfect information

- Apply decision theory to decide whether to investigate a process

- Set up and use basic models for inventory planning and control

- Develop basic linear-programming models and interpret the optimal solution

---

REVIEW OF KEY CONCEPTS

A. **Decision theory** refers to a systematic approach to making all kinds of decisions.

1. Such an approach often involves the fields of statistics, mathematics, economics, and psychology, but *accountants* usually provide much of the quantitative data needed in making decisions within organizations.

2. The key device used is called a **model**, which describes the principal relationships among the critical factors in a real situation.
    a. Such decision models are typically expressed in mathematical forms.
    b. These models range in complexity from simple auditing check lists to extremely complex, *artificial intelligence* models of medical diagnoses.
    c. Another name for these decision models is *decision aids*.

d. Mathematical models may not provide perfect answers, but such models nevertheless often help in making better decisions.

e. Decision models may help decision makers the most by requiring them to put their assumptions down in writing and to think of constraints and opportunities that they might not have done otherwise.

f. The decisions recommended by decision models are rarely accepted as truth, but these recommended solutions are objective starting points given the assumptions are relationships built into the models.

g. If the recommended decision seems counter-intuitive, then maybe the decision-maker's assumptions are faulty or the relationships are not what were expected.

3. The basic approach to decision theory has five characteristics:

   a. A **choice criterion,** or **objective function,** which is a maximization (or minimization) of some form of profit (or cost) for the purpose of evaluating courses of action and thus assisting in the selection of the best alternative.

   b. A set of **alternative courses of action** that include all feasible, independent actions.

   c. A set of all relevant **events,** sometimes called **states,** that ideally cover all possible eventualities outside the control of the decision maker.

   d. A set of **probabilities** of occurrence of the various events.

   e. A set of **outcomes,** often called **payoffs,** that measure the consequences of the possible combinations of choosing particular actions when each of the relevant events occurs.

4. For illustration purposes, when there are only two possible actions that are feasible and two possible outside events, decisions can be displayed in a simple 2x2 decision table. The decision table in the text is reproduced here:

	Alternative events and outcomes	
Alternative actions	Conform	Nonconform
Accept	$12	$2
Reject	$7	$7

   a. Note that the intersection of each possible action (accept or reject) and each possible event (conform or nonconform) corresponds to an expected outcome.

   b. For example, if you *accept* a product and it does *not conform* to specifications, the outcome is reduced profit due to delays, rework, field repairs, warranty expense, or lost sales.

   c. Displaying the feasible actions, possible events, and expected outcomes is the first step in building a decision-theory model -- in this case the model will help decide when to accept or reject a unit of product.

> Before going on to the next section, be sure that you can describe the basics of decision theory and can portray a simple decision in a decision table. Make one up of your own: What are the consequences of studying or not studying for the next exam, which may be easy or difficult? Not all outcomes need to be in dollars and cents, though it makes the analysis easier to be able to compare outcomes.

B. Decisions usually are made under *uncertainty*.

  1. If decisions were made under **certainty**, for each action there would be only one event and therefore only one outcome for each action.
     a. The decision consists of choosing the action that will produce the best outcome.
     b. The role of information is strictly scorekeeping, and decision making is easy -- in the case of business-type decisions: select the most profitable alternative.
     c. The only difficulty (and it may be a serious one) is whether or not the decision model has been properly specified; that is includes all the relevant alternatives, events, and outcomes.

  2. On the other hand, most if not all situations involve **uncertainty** where for each action and event there may be *several possible outcomes*, each with its *probability of occurrence*.
     a. A probability of occurrence is like the odds of a coin toss coming up heads (1 ÷ 2 = 50%), or a card drawn from a 52-card deck being an ace (4 ÷ 52 = 7.7%).
     b. Decisions are sometimes said to be made under **risk** when these probabilities can be *determined objectively*, either by mathematical proofs or by actual experience. An example is determining the probability of drawing an ace from a deck of cards; we know objectively (unless we suspect tampering) the probability is 7.7%.
     c. Decisions are made under **uncertainty** when such probabilities can be assessed mostly on a *subjective basis*. An example is the degree of belief that a student might have about his or her probability of getting an A on the next exam.
     d. However, we use risk and uncertainty as interchangeable terms, as do most people.

  3. We use these probabilities to compare the **expected values** of alternative courses of action.
     a. In the decision-making example above, assume that the probability that a unit of product conforms to specifications is 99%, and the corresponding probability that the product does not conform is 1% (This is far short of the parts per million standards required in most industries now). The decision making table becomes:

Alternative actions	Alternative events and outcomes	
	Conform	Nonconform
Accept	$12	$2
Reject	$7	$7
Probability	.99	.01

- b. The probabilities are used to weight the possible outcomes according to their likelihood of occurrence to form the **expected value** of each alternative:
  - Expected value of "accept" = .99 x $12 + .01 x $2 = $11.90
  - Expected value of "reject" = .99 x $7 + .01 x $7 = $7.00
- c. In this example, the decision model recommends that you always accept the product as good, never reject because the expected value of "accept" is higher than "reject".
- d. This might seem a counter-intuitive result, because we know that many firms with "defective" rates of 1% or lower still spend considerable resources testing their products to weed out defective product.
- e. In this example, it might be that we have seriously understated the costs of accepting nonconforming products. You might want to reassess these costs.

> See the textbook example of statistical quality control

4. The textbook example of the pastry retailer shows how expected-value calculations are used to determine the action that expects to maximize the payoff when more than two events are possible -- the decision table just expands to accomodate additional events.

5. When decisions are to be made under risk or uncertainty, it is necessary to try to understand what it means to say that actions plus events having several possible outcomes.
   - a. We usually say that possible outcomes can be described by a **probability distribution**.

   > See textbook Exhibit 17-1

   - b. The *expected value* of an action is the **mean** or *average* of the distribution of possible outcomes, which anchors the "middle" of the possible outcomes: 50% of possible outcomes are greater than the mean, 50% less.
   - c. The **standard deviation** of the distribution is the measure of the *dispersion* or of the probability distribution or how "spread-out" the distribution is (computed as the square root of the mean of the squared deviations from the expected value -- most people use calculators or spreadsheets to compute standard deviation).
   - d. A measure of *relative dispersion* is the **coefficient of variation**, which is the standard deviation divided by the mean. Actions with *higher* coefficients of variation have *relatively more dispersion*, so they are relatively *riskier*.

Quantitative Techniques Used in Management Accounting 251

e. As discussed in Chapters 7 and 11 regarding sensitivity analysis, a decision maker might choose to tradeoff less return for less risk; that is, choose an action with a lower expected value because its outcomes have relatively less dispersion.

6. It is sometimes feasible to compute the (marginal) **expected value of perfect information** that may be available to the decision maker at some cost, as illustrated for the pastry retailer.
   a. The first step is to prepare a decision table for arriving at the expected value *with perfect information* (the total expected value of actions selected on the assumption of perfect prediction of events).

   > See textbook Exhibit 17-2

   b. Second, compute the expected value *with existing information* (the expected value of the action that would maximize payoff under conditions of uncertainty).
   c. Third, subtract (b) from (a) to arrive at the **expected value of perfect information** (the maximum amount that should be paid for perfect advance information).
   d. Obviously, perfect information is not available at any price, but this is an upper bound on what one would be willing to pay for any imperfect information (e.g., market research, sales forecasting).

   > Before going on, be sure that you understand how to incorporate probabilities into a decision table. Can you revise your exam-studying decision table to include probabilities? Can you express the risk of an action in statistical terms? Could you calculate the expected value of perfect information in your exam-studying decision? Let's not press the ethical implications of that.

C. Inventory planning and control models have as their main objective the determination and maintenance of the optimum amount of investment in inventory.
   1. Too much inventory produces large carrying costs, obsolescence risks, reliance on inventories to cover quality problems, and lower rates of return on investment.
      a. JIT companies recognize the very high costs of carrying excessive inventories, both in terms of obvious carrying costs and unproductive capital, but also in terms of hiding quality problems.
      b. Production personnel may not be as worried about the quality of their inputs or their outputs if they know that they can always go to the storeroom and get another.
      c. Elimination of inventory requires smooth coordination and high quality products and processes -- the objectives of JIT and TQM.
   2. On the other hand, in many areas JIT deliveries of zero-defect inputs are not possible and if not enough inventory is carried to cover possible shortages, serious costs could result from production interruptions or lost sales.
   3. The cost of purchasing or manufacturing the inventory is usually *not relevant* to the type of inventory-control decisions we are studying, because the total annual requirements are the *same* for various alternatives.

4. There are two classes of costs that are relevant, however:
   a. Costs of *ordering* inventories, for example, purchasing, receiving, transportation.
   b. Costs of *carrying* inventories, for example, storage, taxes, insurance, decline in value of inventory.
   c. Specifically, the objective is to *minimize the total of these costs*.

   > See textbook Exhibit 17-3

5. One of the two key factors in applying inventory policy is the determination of the **economic order quantity (EOQ),** the optimum size of a normal purchase order for replenishing materials or a shop order for a production run in a non JIT shop.
   a. The economic order quantity may be estimated by computing the annual carrying cost and the annual purchase order cost (or setup cost) for each of several selected order sizes. The order size with the *least total cost* would be the approximate economic order quantity.

   > See textbook Exhibits 17-4 and 17-5

   b. The economic order quantity may be computed more quickly and more accurately by the formula in the text (which can be derived with simple calculus):

   $$E = \sqrt{(2AP/S)}$$

6. Another facet of inventory policy is the determination of the reorder point, the quantity level that automatically triggers a new order.

   > See textbook Exhibit 17-6

7. The inventory reorder point depends on several factors.
   a. The *economic order quantity* was described above.
   b. The **lead time** is the time interval between placing an order and receiving delivery.
   c. The **demand during lead time** is the expected usage during lead time.
   d. The **safety stock** is the estimated minimum inventory quantity needed as a buffer or cushion against reasonable expected maximum usage.

8. *The inventory reorder point is commonly computed as the safety stock plus expected usage during lead time.*

9. **Material requirements planning** (MRP) uses inventory models like EOQ to schedule purchase and delivery of materials so that inventory levels can be reduced while still enabling production schedules.

   > Before going on, review the costs that inventory models trade off to optimize inventory levels. How are EOQ and JIT related?

D. **Linear programming** (Appendix 17) is a mathematical search procedure for finding the optimum solution to certain types of problems.
   1. The objective of linear programming is to determine the combination of scarce resources that maximizes profits or minimizes costs. This is an extension of the

best use of scarce capacity decision discussed in Chapter 6; here we include more than one constraint.

2. Practical applications include blending gasoline, routing production, and making shipping or airline staffing schedules.

3. Linear programming requires that all relationships be *linear*, but it is a decision model under conditions of assumed *certainty*. Nevertheless, it is a useful technique in practice.

4. The textbook illustration of product mix shows the three basic steps of the linear-programming approach:
   a. Formulate the model:
   - the *objective function*, which is usually the same as the contribution margin of an action and
   - the *inequalities to reflect the constraints of scarce resources*, which usually are the resources needed for each product that in total cannot exceed what is available.

   b. Use a computer to identify feasible alternatives and the optimum solution. Most linear-programming problems require computers. However, many easy-to-use programs are available for nearly every type of computer.

   c. Analyze the solution, including **shadow prices**, which are the marginal values of obtaining one more unit of capacity in each scarce resource.

   d. The textbook example also shows how a simple linear program is solvable using a graphic plot in conjunction with manual computations.

   > See textbook Exhibits 17-7 and 17-8

   e. Although the graphic approach is practicable only in the simplest of situations, it is quite useful in understanding the basic concepts of linear programming. Study it carefully to understand how the constraints describe a *feasible region* where production is possible given scarce resources.

> Before you go on, review the textbook example of linear programming. When is linear programming an appropriate decision model? Can you explain the objective function? the constraints? the solution, including shadow prices?

PRACTICE TEST QUESTIONS AND PROBLEMS WITH SOLUTIONS

True or False Statements

Determine whether each of the following statements is True (T) or False (F) and enter your answer in the space provided.

____1. If decisions are made under certainty, there is only one outcome for each action.

____2. When decisions are determined under risk, the relevant probabilities can be determined objectively by mathematical proofs or by personal experience.

____3. The sets of probabilities in mathematical decision models pertain to the likelihood of occurrence of outcomes and events.

____4. The probability distribution describes how "spread-out" the possible outcomes of actions are.

____5. The expected value of an action is the most likely outcome of taking the action.

____6. The coefficient of variation of an action is a measure of the risk of the action.

____7. The decision theory approach says: Take the action with the greatest coefficient of variation.

____8. The expected value *of* perfect information is the excess of the expected value with existing information over the expected value *with* perfect information.

____9. The least one would pay for sales forecasting information is the expected value of perfect sales information.

____10. Since Just-in-Time systems are only concerned with minimizing inventories, the Just-in-Time approach may be applied only in manufacturing companies.

____11. The economic order quantity is the quantity that would miminize the annual inventory carrying cost.

____12. In linear programming, the objective function is similar to a CVP model.

____13. Product A requires 4 machine hours, and Product B requires 7 machine hours. 1,000 machine hours are available. The linear programming constraint for machine hours would be: $4A + 7B \leq 1,000$.

____14. The inventory reorder point would tend to be increased by a decrease in the expected usage of material during lead time.

____15. The quantity of the safety stock plus expected usage during lead time is equal to the economic order quantity.

Multiple Choice Questions

For each of the following multiple-choice questions, select the best answer(s) and enter the identification letter(s) in the space provided.

_____1. A company developed three predictions of its sales for the next year: optimistic $700,000 with a probability of .20, most likely $500,000 with a probability of .55, and pessimistic $300,000 with a probability of .25. Expected sales would be: (a) $490,000, (b) $500,000, (c) $700,000, (d) $300,000.

_____2. See the preceding test item. The $700,000 is an example of: (a) an event, (b) a course of action, (c) a state of nature, (d) an outcome.

_____3. See item 1 above, "pessimistic" is an example of: (a) a payoff, (b) a course of action, (c) an event, (d) an outcome.

_____4. The coefficient of variation is a relative measure of: (a) efficiency, (b) profitability, (c) accuracy or reliability, (d) risk or uncertainty.

_____5. The objective of linear programming is: (a) to measure the quality of production, (b) to control the quality of production, (c) to forecast completion dates for special projects, (d) to determine the best combination of production resources.

_____6. A production process yields two products, X and Y, with contribution margins of $12 and $25, respectively. The standard input allowed of one scarce resource for X is 5, and the standard input allowed for y is 11. The total scarce resource available is 3,300. The linear programming constraint that describes the scarce resource is: (a) 12X + 25Y, (b) 11X + 5Y = 3,300, (c) 5X + 11Y ≤ 3,300, (d) 5X + 11Y = 3,300.

_____7. See the above test item. The objective function is: (a) 12X + 25Y, (b) 11X + 5Y = 3,300, (c) 5X + 11Y ≤ 3,300, (d) 5X + 11Y = 3,300.

_____8. See test item 6. If there is only the one constraint, the optimal product mix is: (a) 3,300 X and 3,300 Y, (b) zero X and 300 Y, (c) 660 X and 300 Y, (d) 660 X and zero Y.

_____9. The prime objective of inventory control is: (a) to decrease opportunities for improper use of inventory, (b) to maximize clerical accuracy in inventory documents and records, (c) to achieve the optimum level of investment in inventory, (d) to minimize carrying and ordering costs.

_____10. Total annual needs of an input are 4,000 units. Ordering costs are $1 per order. Annual carrying costs are $5. The economic order quantity is: (a) 4,000, (b) 400, (c) 40, (d) 4.

Completion

Complete each of the following statements by filling in the blanks.

1. Typically, decision models include sets of alternative _____, alternative _____, and expected _____ for each combination of _____ and _____.

2. When there are several possible payoffs of an action, the payoffs may be described with a _____.

3. Decisions are said to be made under risk or uncertainty when there are several _____ each with its own _____ of occurrence.

4. The common measure of the dispersion of a probability distribution is called the _____.

5. The expected value of a particular action is _____ multiplied by _____.

6. The coefficient of variation is a measure of _____ that is _____ divided by _____.

7. The mathematical expressions of inequalities for linear-programming problems represent _____.

8. The objective function of a process that yields three products, X, Y, and Z, with sales prices of $10, 20, and $30, respectively, and variable costs of $5, $10, and $15, respectively would be: _____.

9. The optimum level of inventory would minimize _____ and _____.

10. In general, the inventory reorder point is the sum of _____ and _____.

Problems

1. Parachute Oil, Ltd., is an oil exploration company. A well is being drilled in the Texas panhandle with the following range of expectations of production per month:

If the well is a:	probability	monthly payoff
Light producer	.15	$ 80,000
Medium producer	.20	$160,000
Heavy producer	.10	$400,000
Dry hole	.55	0

Compute the expected value of production per month:

2. Given for Beryllium Discovery Company:

Event	A	B	C	D
Probability of event	.1	.4	.3	.2
Payoffs for actions: 1	$10	$ 5	$ 0	-$10
2	15	10	5	-5
3	20	15	0	0
4	30	10	0	-15

a. What is the expected value of action 1?

b. What is the expected value of action 2?

c. What is the expected value of action 3?

d. What is the expected value of action 4?

e. What is the total expected value *with* perfect information?

f. What is the total marginal expected value *of* perfect information?

3. Boyd Sisters Roasters Co. produce two blends of gourmet coffee: Kenyan and Mauna Kea. The following data are available:

	Daily Capacity in Units		
Product	Roasting Process A	Roasting Process B	Unit Contribution Margin
Kenyan (X)	1 per unit X	.8 per unit X	$15
Mauna Kea (Y)	.4 per unit Y	1 per unit Y	$10
Maximum	200	320	

Severe bean shortages for Kenyan will limit its production to a maximum of 180 units per day. Develop appropriate equations for a linear-programming solution:

a. Maximize total contribution margin

b. Process A constraint:

c. Process B constraint:

d. Bean shortage constraint:

258 Chapter 17

e. Non-negative production constraints:

4. Given for Zanzibarium use of Mali, Inc.:
   Total annual requirements   8,000 units
   Carrying costs per unit per year $2
   Costs per purchase order $80
   Inventory level when each order arrives (no safety stock)   zero

   a. Compute the total relevant costs of ordering one, two, five, ten, and twenty times per year in the following table:

Number of orders per year	One	Two	Five	Ten	Twenty
Order size					
Average inventory in units					
Yearly ordering costs					
Yearly carrying costs					
Total relevant costs					

   b. Identify least-cost order size

   c. Use the formula for determining the least-cost order size:

5. Given for Mellifluvium usage of Beehive Corporation:

Maximum daily usage	80 units
Expected daily usage	70 units
Minimum daily usage	60 units
Lead time	22 days

   a. Compute the safety stock

   b. Determine the reorder point

CHAPTER 17 SOLUTIONS TO PRACTICE TEST QUESTIONS AND PROBLEMS

True or False Statements

1. True — Under conditions of certainty, a decision maker knows that taking a specific action will result in a specific outcome. Obviously, this is unrealistic, but in some cases (e.g., some linear programming applications) processes are understood well enough that certainty is a reasonable assumption.

2. False — First of all, most statisticians would regard probabilities determined on the basis of personal experience to be subjective, not objective, because personal experience cannot be experienced by others. Secondly, for some actions there may be no precedent, experience is not available, and the mathematical proofs are based on assumptions derived from other, related experiences.

3. True — Future events are unknown, but we may be able to estimate the probabilities of their occurrence. Likewise, we may be able to estimate the probabilities of outcomes that are the joint result of specific actions and particular future events.

4. False — The standard deviation (and variance) describe how "spread-out" the possible outcomes are.

5. True — The expected value literally means that, if the action is taken a large number of times, on average the mean outcome will occur. With "well-behaved" (symmetrical) distributions, of all the possible outcomes, it is the most likely.

6. True — But the measure is only meaningful when compared with the coefficients of variation of other possible actions.

7. False — Generally, the advice is more neutral: "here are the expected values of actions and their relative risk. You make the tradeoff." Actually, decision theory can be adapted for an individual's attitude toward risk and can give more direct advice: "given your attitude toward risk, here is the best choice."

8. False — This definition is inverted. The expected value *of* perfect information is the excess of the expected value *with* perfect information over the expected value with existing information.

9. False — This is the *most* one would pay for such information.

10. False — The only purpose of JIT is not to eliminate inventories; the primary purpose is to eliminate waste. Therefore, any organization can apply JIT approaches to streamline operations. It so happens that one major source of waste in manufacturing firms is excess inventory.

11. False — The quantity that would minimize carrying costs is "zero." The facts that the item is needed and that ordering costs might be very high at low order quantities indicates the need for positive inventory. To implement JIT inventory, firms must drastically reduce ordering costs. Efforts to do so include long-term purchase and delivery contracts, sharing of production schedules with suppliers, and computer links between producers and suppliers.

12. True — The only major difference is that the objective function typically omits fixed costs when production remains within the relevant range.

13. True — The constraint says: four hours times the quantity of A plus seven hours times the quantity of B cannot exceed the 1,000 hours available.

14. False — Just the opposite is the case. The inventory reorder point would tend to be increased by an *increase* in the expected usage of material during lead time.

15. False — The quantity of the safety stock plus expected usage during lead time is equal to the inventory reorder point.

Multiple Choice Questions

1. a — The expected value of future sales (in 000s) is: $700 x .20 + $500 x .55 + $300 x .25 = $490.

2. d — The $700,000 is the outcome of the optimistic sales level.

3. c — "Pessimistic" sales level is one of the possible future events.

4. d — The coefficient of variation measures the relative dispersion of an action that may be compared with the coefficients of variation of other actions. The action with the lowest coefficient of variation is the least risky of the set.

5. d — Linear programming seeks to find the combination of output that best utilizes productive capacity.

6. c — The constraint says that 5 times the quantity of X plus 11 times the quantity of Y cannot exceed the total resource available, 3,300.

7. a — The objective function is the unknown contribution margin of both products.

8. d — The optimal product mix maximizes the objective function or contribution margin from both products. The approach of Chapter 6 is to compute the contribution margin per unit of scarce resource and make all that you can of that product. The contribution margin per unit of scarce resource of X = $12 ÷ 5 = $2.40. The contribution margin per unit of scarce resource of Y = $25 ÷ 11 = $2.27. Thus, produce all X: 3,300 ÷ 5 = 660 units. No other combination of X and Y (e.g., 0 X and 300 Y) produces a bigger contribution margin.

9. c, d — The optimum level of inventory includes considering carrying and ordering costs.

10. c — The EOQ = $\sqrt{2 \times 4{,}000 \times 1 \div 5} = 40$.

Completion

1. actions, events, outcomes, action and event
2. probability function
3. events or outcomes, probability
4. coefficient of variation
5. the sum of each outcome, its probability of occurrence
6. relative risk, the standard deviation, the mean
7. the limits of usage of scarce resources
8. $5 X + $10 Y + $20 Z
9. ordering costs, carrying costs

10.   safety stock, expected usage during lead time

Problems

1. Parachute Oil, Ltd.
    Expected value of drilling:

.15 x	$ 80,000 =	$12,000
.20 x	$160,000 =	32,000
.10 x	$400,000 =	40,000
.55 x	0 =	0
	Expected value	$84,000

2. Beryillium Discovery Company

a.	(.1)(10) + (.4)(5) + (.3)(0) + (.2)(-10)	= 1 + 2 + 0 - 2	= $1.00
b.	(.1)(15) + (.4)(10) + (.3)(5) + (.2)(-5)	= 1.5 + 4 + 1.5 - 1	= $6.00
c.	(.1)(20) + (.4)(15) + (.3)(0) + (.2)(0)	= 2 + 6 + 0 + 0	= $8.00
d.	(.1)(30) + (.4)(10) + (.3)(0) + (.2)(-15)	= 3 + 4 +0 - 3	= $4.00
e.	(.1)(30) + (.4)(15) + (.3)(5) + (.2)(0)	= 3 + 6 + 1.5 + 0	= $10.50
f.	Item e minus item c	= $10.50 - $8.00	= $2.50

3. Boyd Sisters Roasters Co.

    a. Maximum total contribution margin: 15X + IOY
    b. Process A constraint: X + .4Y ≤ 200
    c. Process B constraint: .8X + Y ≤ 320
    d. Material shortage constraint: X ≤ 180
    e. Non-negative production constraints: X ≤ 0 and Y ≤ 0

4. Zanzibarium usage of Mali, Inc.
    a.

Number of orders per year.	One	Two	Five	Ten	Twenty
Order size (8,000 divided by number of orders per year)	8,000	4,000	1,600	800	400
Average inventory in units (order size divided by 2)	4,000	2,000	800	400	200
Yearly ordering cost (number of orders multiplied by $80)	$80	$160	$400	$800	$1,600
Yearly carrying cost (average inventory multiplied by $2)	$8,000	$4,000	$1,600	$800	$400
Total relevant costs	$8,080	$4,160	$2,000	$1,600	$2,000

    b. Least-cost order size = 10 units, $1,600

262 Chapter 17

c.
E = economic order quantity
A = annual quantity used in units   8,000
P = cost of placing an order $80
S = annual cost of carrying one unit one year $2
   Substitute in formula:
   E = $\sqrt{(2 \times 8{,}000 \times 80/2)} = \sqrt{640{,}000}$ = 800 units per order.
Optimum number of orders per year: 8,000/800 = 10 (as above).

5. Mellifluvium usage by Beehive Corporation

   a. Safety stock

Maximum daily usage	80	units
Less expected daily usage	70	units
Excess usage per day	10	units
Multiply by lead time	22	days
Safety stock.	220	units

   b. Reorder point

Safety stock	220	units
Added expected usage during lead time; 70 units for 22 days	1,540	units
Reorder point (inventory level at which additional units should be ordered	1,760	units
Or, the reorder point may be computed as the maximum usage during lead time: 80 units for 22 days	1,760	units

CHAPTER 18

Basic Accounting: Concepts, Techniques, and Conventions

MAIN FOCUS AND OBJECTIVES

This chapter focuses on the accounting equation and how making every economic transaction balance the equation is the fundamental task of an accounting system. This chapter demonstrates how balancing the accounting equation not only is a powerful control device, it also results in the generation of three of the principal financial statements used for external reporting. Note that this chapter discusses the accounting equation without the use of journal entries. An introduction to journal entries is in the study guide appendix and in textbook Appendix 18B. The learning objectives of the chapter are to:

- Understand the relationships among the major financial statements

- Analyze business transactions using the accounting equation

- Distinguish between cash- and accrual-based accounting

- Relate measurement of expenses to expiration of assets

- Prepare a balance sheet, income statement, and statement of retained income

- Explain relationship of dividends and retained income

- Differentiate between corporate stockholders' equity and partnership or proprietorship owner's equity

- Understand some basing accounting conventions

REVIEW OF KEY CONCEPTS

A. Through the financial accounting process, the accountant accumulates data on the operations of an organization for use by managers, investors, and other interested groups.

1. The focus is on the *entity* and its *transactions*.
    a. An **entity** is a specific area of accountability. The principal form of business entity is the corporation, which is owned by its stockholders.
    b. **Transactions** are events that affect the financial position of an entity and require recording by the entity.
2. Accountants summarize transactions in the form of two main financial reports:
    a. The **balance sheet**, also called the **statement of financial position**, summarizes at a given *date* the economic resources owned by a company **(assets)** and the claims against them **(equities)**.
    b. The **income statement** summarizes for a given *period* the results of the profit-seeking operations of a company in order to measure **net income:** the excess of sales **(revenues)** over the costs of obtaining them **(expenses)**.
    c. These two financial statements have a direct relation to each other, because the net income reported in the income statement for a given period increases the owners' equity, which is shown in the balance sheet at the end of the period.

B. The accounting process records the transactions and events of the **entity,** which may be a business unit, often referred to as a **segment, firm, company,** or **corporation,** depending on its organization.

1. Accounting systems are based on the fundamental **balance sheet equation:**
    Assets = Equities, or
    Assets = Liabilities + Owner's Equity
    a. **Assets** are the economic resources owned by the entity and expected to benefit its future activities, for example, money, merchandise, and machinery.
    b. **Equities** are the total claims against, or interests in, the assets of the entity.
    c. **Liabilities** are the debts owed by the entity to its creditors and other nonowners.
    d. **Owner's equity** measures the investment interest of owners and is the excess of a company's assets over its liabilities. For a corporation, this is called **stockholders' equity.**
    e. Stockholders' equity consists of **paid-in-capital** and **retained income.**
    f. Retained income is increased periodically by **net income,** the excess of **revenues** over **expenses.**
2. Every economic transaction affects some components of the balance sheet equation, and the *accounting system insures that the equation is balanced at all times*; that is, assets always equal the total of liabilities and owners' equity.

See textbook Exhibit 18-1

Before going on to the next section, be sure that you understand the working of the accounting equation and its primary elements.

Basic Accounting: Concepts, Techniques, and Conventions 265

C. Net income is generally measured on the accrual basis of accounting, that is, by matching related revenues and expenses by periods.
1. Revenues generally arise from increases in assets caused by sales of goods and services to customers.
2. Revenues are **earned** or **realized** (recognized in the accounting records and formal financial statements) when:
   a. The goods or services sold are "fully rendered" (for example, delivered to customers).
   b. An actual exchange of resources has occurred (in terms of either cash or credit).
   c. There is a reasonable assurance that credit sales will be collected.
3. Expenses are **incurred** (recognized in the accounting records and formal financial statements) as goods or services are used to obtain revenues. Expenses generally arise from used-up assets.
4. The accrual basis of accounting, which recognizes revenues as they are earned and expenses as they are incurred, should be distinguished from the **cash basis** of accounting.
   a. The cash basis does not match revenues and expenses by periods.
   b. The recognition of revenues and expenses on a cash basis would depend solely on the timing of various cash receipts and disbursements, thus omitting changes in some assets and liabilities such as increases in accounts receivable and payable due to sales or expenses.

> Can you express the difference between a cash-based and an accrual-based accounting system?

D. The finished products of the accounting process are the formal financial statements.
1. The **income statement** may show a single-step deduction of expenses from revenues in determining net income, or the statement may use a multiple-step approach in arriving at the net income figure:
   a. **Gross profit** (or **gross margin**) is the excess of sales over the cost of goods sold.
   b. **Net income** is the gross profit minus operating expenses (also minus income taxes, which are not covered in this introductory presentation).

> See textbook Exhibit 18-4

2. **The balance sheet** summarizes an entity's assets, liabilities, and owners' equity.
   a. For a corporation, the owners' equity is divided into two main elements.
   b. One of these is **contributed capital** or **paid-in capital.** This includes **capital stock,** which usually measures the investment paid into the corporation by its shareholders.
   c. The other element is **retained income, retained earnings,** or **reinvested earnings.** This is the *accumulated increase* in the stockholders' equity caused by the total net income earned since the company was formed less *all dividends* paid to stockholders during that time.

d. Retained income is part of the stockholders' equity and therefore is not cash or any kind of asset. Moreover, retained income is not a measure of any other *particular* asset; it is part of the stockholders' general claim against, or undivided interest in, the *total* assets of the corporation.

> See textbook Exhibit 18-3

3. Generally, **dividends** are distributions of cash to stockholders that decrease the company's retained income.
   a. Don't make the mistake of confusing dividends with expenses. Dividends are not a cost of producing revenues.
   b. Expenses are deducted from revenues to arrive at net income, which in turn is *added* to retained income.
   c. Dividends are deducted *directly* from retained income because they represent asset withdrawals that reduce the ownership claims against the business entity.
   d. *Dividends do not decrease net income but do reduce retained income.*

> See textbook Exhbit 18-5

4. For partnerships and sole proprietorships, the equity of each individual owner is measured, but the distinction between contributed capital and retained income is seldom reported.

> Do you understand how financial statements are derived from entries to the basic accounting equation? If not, review this section and work through Exhibit 18-2 again.

E. It is helpful to view assets as **bundles of economic services** held for future use.

1. When unexpired or stored costs, such as merchandise inventory and equipment, are used in the production of revenue, the expired cost portions are transferred from assets to expenses, which are summarized in the income statement.

2. In practice, however, some costs are not charged to assets when they are acquired but are charged immediately to expenses because they measure services that usually are too difficult to match to anything but the accounting period, for example, research and development expense, advertising expense, and interest expense.

F. At the end of an accounting period, in order to complete the implementation of the accrual method, the accountant must make **adjustments** for some implicit transactions that are mostly the result of the passing of time.

1. Formal entries for these adjustments must be made in the accounting records at the end of an accounting period before the financial statements are constructed.

2. The adjustments form an essential element of the accrual process because they increase the precision of measurements and help provide more complete and realistic reports of operations and financial position.

3. The principal adjustments are classified into four distinctive types:
   a. Expiration of unexpired costs
   b. Realization (earning) of unearned revenues

Basic Accounting: Concepts, Techniques, and Conventions

c. Accrual of unrecorded expenses
d. Accrual of unrecorded revenues

4. Examples of the first type include write-offs to expense of the expiration of such assets as *depreciation, office supplies*, and *prepaid insurance*.

5. **Realization of unearned revenues** means the earning of revenues previously collected in advance.
   a. When cash collections are made in advance by sellers for certain types of services to be rendered later to their customers, these *explicit transactions* create *liabilities* of the sellers called *unearned revenues,* for example, rent collected in advance and insurance premiums collected in advance (unearned insurance premiums).
   b. As time passes, the services are rendered to customers, and *periodic adjustments* must therefore be made to reflect the *implicit transactions:* the decreases in these liabilities and the increases in such revenues as rent earned and insurance premiums earned.

6. **Accrual of expenses** means incurring expenses and accumulating the related liabilities as time passes or as some services are continuously acquired and used.
   a. Common examples are wages, salaries, commissions, taxes, interest on money borrowed, utility services such as electricity, and other operating expenses that are ordinarily not paid in cash until *shortly after* the consumption of the services.
   b. *Periodic adjustments* are made for the *implicit transactions* to increase expenses and the corresponding liabilities for the amounts accrued and not yet entered in the accounting records.

7. **Accrual of revenues** means earning revenues and accumulating the related assets as time passes or as some services are continuously rendered to customers.
   a. Common examples are interest on money loaned, fees for services rendered, *and* other revenues that are ordinarily not collected in cash until shortly after they have been earned.
   b. *Periodic adjustments* are made for the *implicit transactions* to increase revenues and the corresponding assets for the amounts accrued and not yet earned in the accounting records.

   See textbook Exhibit 18-6

   Before going on to the next section be sure that you understand the role of implicit accounting entries or adjusting entries.

G. When independent auditors express their opinion of the presentation of a company's financial statements, they specify whether the statements conform to **generally accepted accounting principles (GAAP)**. GAAP includes certain accounting assumptions and conventions.
   1. GAAP have evolved over many years from widespread usage.
      a. This usage has been significantly influenced by the companies that report to external users and rule-making bodies such as the ABP, FASB, and SEC.

b. In essence, although the rule-making power lies with the federal government through the SEC, most of the current rulings are made by the FASB, an independent nongovernmental entity.
c. GAAP can be said to be a collection of successful accounting practices.

2. An important accounting *convention* is **realization**, the recognition of revenues when goods or services are delivered to customers.

3. A second important convention is the periodic **matching of revenues and expenses**, as represented by the accrual basis of accounting.

4. A third important convention is the assumption that we use the **monetary unit** as a **stable measure** of the financial or economic effects of transactions. This assumption is, of course, subject to serious challenge in many parts of the world in the face of continued inflation.

H. Appendix 18A presents additional generally accepted accounting conventions and assumptions:

1. The **continuity** or **going-concern assumption** views the business entity as continuing indefinitely with no intention to sell all of its assets and discontinue operations.

2. The **principle of objectivity** or **veriftability** requires accounting measurements to be unbiased, supported by convincing evidence, subject to independent check, and therefore reliable.

3. The **materiality convention** permits relatively small dollar amounts to be accounted for and reported in an expedient manner (even though some other basic GAAP might be ignored).

4. The **conservatism convention** means, in case of doubt concerning the appropriate measurement, that accountants must use the more pessimistic alternatives.

5. **Cost-benefit** means that the benefits from increased precision in accounting for and reporting business transactions must be weighed against the costs of achieving the benefits.

6. These and other GAAP are important guidelines that still permit the use of **considerable judgment** in measuring financial data.

Can you explain each of the accounting conventions discussed above?

I. Appendix 18B looks at a more technical side of the accounting process. More detail is in the Appendix to this study guide.

1. **Accounts** are used to accumulate the effects of transactions on the **individual items** that are summarized by the terms in the balance sheet equation.
a. Increases in **asset** accounts are recorded on the left (debit) side, decreases on the right (credit).
b. Increases in **liability and stockholders' equity** accounts are recorded on the right side (credit), decreases on the left (debit).

c. The **balance** of an account is the excess of the sum of the dollar entries on one side of the account over the sum of the dollar entries on the other side.

2. To understand the use of the debit-credit rules in analyzing the effects of transactions on the accounts and financial statements, carefully follow through the example in Appendix 18B or turn to the appendix to this study guide.

> If understanding journal entries is important to your study of accounting do not go on unless you are comfortable with the basics of recording accounting transactions.

PRACTICE TEST QUESTIONS AND PROBLEMS WITH SOLUTIONS

True or False Statements

Determine whether each of the following statements is True (T) or False (F) and enter your answer in the space provided.

__T__ 1. A company could operate during a given period, earn a net income, and yet suffer a decrease in its cash balance during that period.

__F__ 2. A company could not operate at a net loss during a given period and yet increase its cash balance during that period.

__T__ 3. A company can increase its total assets without earning a net income.

__F__ 4. The stockholders' equity shown in the balance sheet of a corporation is a measure of items of property owned by the corporation.

__T__ 5. Unexpired costs are called assets.

__T__ 6. Expired costs are called expenses.

__T__ 7. Retained income is neither an asset nor a measurement of a particular asset.

__T__ ?. Items typically reported in a statement of retained income include net income and dividends to stockholders.

__F__ 9. Camera News Corp. purchased a printing press for $600,000, paying $100,000 cash and signing a four-year note payable for $500,000. As a result, the total amount of the company's assets was decreased by $100,000.

__T__ 10. Generally accepted accounting principles are the result of careful logical analysis by rule-making bodies such as the FASB and the SEC.

__F__ 11. The realization convention means that costs are not expired until revenues are earned.

__F__ 12. The accounting convention of relying on a stable monetary unit is violated in practice in the U.S. which means that accounting financial statements are invalid.

__F__ 13. The materiality convention means that as long as management does not think the item should be disclosed, it needn't be.

__F__ 14. Credit entries are used to record increases in revenue accounts.

__F__ 15. An entry on the left side of any account may be called a debit or a charge.

Multiple Choice Questions

For each of the following multiple-choice questions, select the best answer(s) and enter the identification letter(s) in the space provided. (Hint: use the accounting equation.)

__c,d__ 1. Korsikov Corp. purchased merchandise on account for $85,000. As a result, there was: (a) no change in the total amount of its assets, (b) no change in its total liabilities, (c) an increase in the total amount of its assets, (d) an increase in its liabilities.

__A__ 2. Ravel Co. purchased merchandise with $200,000 of its cash. As a result, there was: (a) no change in the total amount of its assets, (b) an increase in its stockholders' equity, (c) an increase in the total amount of its assets, (d) a decrease in its stockholders' equity.

__A__ 3. VonWilliams Co. has total assets of $420,000 and stockholders' equity of $280,000. It purchased $60,000 of merchandise on account and collected $20,000 on account from its customers. As a result, the company's total liabilities would be: (a) $200,000, (b) $80,000, (c) $480,000, (d) $460,000.

__D__ 4. See the preceding test item. The company's total assets would be: (a) $500,000, (b) $460,000, (c) $400,000, (d) $480,000.

__C__ 5. Joplin Co. has $310,000 of liabilities and $700,000 of stockholders' equity. It issued for cash 20,000 shares of common stock for $20 per share, and purchased land and buildings for $600,000, paying $60,000 cash and signing a note payable for the balance. As a result, the company's total assets would now be: (a) $2,000,000, (b) $1,700,000, (c) $1,950,000, (d) $1,570,000.

__B__ 6. See the preceding test item. The company's owners' equity would now be: (a) $840,000, (b) $1,100,000, (c) $1,940,000, (d) $720,000.

__C__ 7. The dividends declared and paid by a corporation to its stockholders affect a corporation's financial position as follows: (a) F decrease retained income and increase cash, (b) F increase retained income and decrease cash, (c) decrease retained income and decrease cash, (d) increase retained income and increase cash. F

__B__ 8. Rampal Transport, Inc. purchased tools on account for $40,000. It also sold some of its transportation equipment at cost for $240,000, receiving $40,000 in cash and a note receivable for the remainder. As a result, there would be: (a) no change in the total amount of the company's assets, (b) an increase of $40,000 in its assets, (c) a decrease of $40,000 in its assets, (d) a decrease of $160,000 in its assets.

__B__ 9. A materials inventory account had a beginning balance of $75,000, purchase of materials was $35,000, and usage of materials was $100,000. The ending inventory balance was: (a) $140,000 credit, (b) $10,000 debit, (c) $10,000 credit, (d) $140,000 debit.

__C__ 10. During one period a corporation earned income of $40,000, received paid-in capital of $50,000, paid dividends of $30,000, and retired debt of $10,000. The retained income account: (a) increased $50,000, (b) stayed the same, (c) increased $10,000, (d) increased $30,000.

Completion

Complete each of the following statements by filling in the blanks.

1. If a company purchases merchandise inventory on account (for credit), its total assets would be __increased__, its total liabilities would be __increased__ and its stockholders' equity would be __unchanged__.

2. When unexpired or stored costs, such as merchandise inventory or equipment, are used in the production of revenue, the expired cost portions are transferred from __Asset__ accounts to __Expense__ accounts, which are summarized in __Income Statement__.

3. Gross profit is the excess of __Revenue__ over __CGS__.

4. The three tests that must be met before revenues may be recognized in the accounting records are:
   (a) __delivery__
   (b) __exchange__
   (c) __collection of revenue__

5. The balance sheet equation requires that __Assets__ equal __Liabilities__ plus __Retained Equity__ at all times.

6. Identify the following terms:
   GAAP __Generally Accepted Accounting Principles__
   APB __Accounting Principles Board__
   FASB __Financial Accounting Standards Board__
   SEC __Security Exchange Commission__
   What they have in common is __Last 3 set rules for publicly traded corps.__

7. Two accounting conventions that are critical to the measurement of operating income are __realization__ and __matching__.

8. The conservatism convention means that when in doubt __use pessimistic estimates__

9. Decreases in liability accounts are recorded by __Debit__ entries.

10. An entry on the __Right__ side of an account is called a credit and an entry to the __left__ side is called a __debit__.

Problems

1. You are given the following data (in thousands) for Gnu Co. Prepare an income statement and a balance sheet, ignoring income taxes.

Accounts payable	$12,000	Furniture and fixtures	$15,300
Accounts receivable	21,000	Inventory	14,400
Accrued interest payable	60	Notes payable	6,000
Accrued salaries payable	900	Prepaid rent	1,050
Advertising expense	600	Rent expense	2,100
Capital stock	54,000	Retained income	1,500
Cash	22,950	Salaries expense	7,500
Cost of goods sold	15,000	Sales	27,000
Depreciation expense	300	Unearned rent revenue	240

2. Given the following selected data for Eland Publishers, Inc., compute: (a) net income for 19X3, (b) retained income at December 31, 19X3.

Retained income at January 1, 19X2	$240,000
Cash dividends declared and paid to stockholders in 19X2	110,000
All other cash payments in 19X2	750,000
Total cash receipts in 19X2	825,000
Depreciation expense in 19X2	20,000
All other 19X2 expenses	815,000
Total revenues for 19X2	970,000

3. a. Complete this transaction analysis framework:

		Assets				=	Liabilities & Stockholders' Equity		
	Cash	Accounts Receivable	Merchandise Inventory	Prepaid Rent	Equipment		Accounts Payable	Paid-in Capital	Retained Income
1. Issued capital stock for cash, $100,000	100,000							100,000	
2. Issued capital stock for store equipment, $50,000					50,000			50,000	
3. Purchased store equipment for cash, $10,000	−10,000				10,000				
4. Purchased merchandise on account, $70,000			70,000				70,000		
5. Sold merchandise on account, $35,000		35,000							35,000
6. Recorded cost of merchandise sold, $20,000			−20,000						−20,000
7. Sold part of store equipment at cost on account, $2,000		2,000			−2,000				
8. Collected cash on account for previous credit sales recorded, $13,000	13,000	−13,000							
9. Recorded depreciation of store equipment, $1,000					−1,000				−1,000 Expense
10. Paid cash for six months' rent in advance, $9,000	−9,000			9,000					
11. Recorded current month's rent expense, $1,500				−1,500					−1,500 Expense
12. Paid cash for current month's salaries, advertising, utilities, and miscellaneous office supplies purchased and used, $8,500	−8,500								−8,500 Expense
13. Paid cash on account to suppliers for merchandise purchases previously made and recorded, $40,000	−40,000						−40,000		
14. Declared and paid cash dividends to stockholders, $3,000	−3,000								−3,000 Dividend
Totals	42,500	24,000	50,000	7,500	57,000		30,000	150,000	1,000

b. Compute:

Total assets _____ 181,000 _____   Total stockholder's equity _____ 151,000 _____

Total liabilities _____ 30,000 _____   Total equities _____ 181,000 _____

Net income _____ 4,000 _____

    3,000 Dividend
+ 1,000 R/I
    4K

4. End-of-Period Adjustments. Use only the words *increase, decrease,* or *no effect* to fill each of the blanks below to indicate the usual effect of these end-of-period adjustments on a company's reported assets, liabilities, revenues, and expenses:

	Assets	Liabilities	Revenues	Expenses
a. Expiration of unexpired costs	DEC	N/E	N/E	INC
b. Realization (earning) of previously deferred revenues	N/E	DEC	INC	N/E
c. Accrual of previously unrecorded expenses	N/E	INC	N/E	INC
d. Accrual of previously unrecorded revenues	INC	N/E	INC	N/E
e. Depreciation	DEC	N/E	N/E	INC

CHAPTER 18 SOLUTIONS TO PRACTICE TEST QUESTIONS AND PROBLEMS

True or False Statements

1. True — Though income and cash flow certainly are related over the long run, in a particular period, it is possible that a combination of credit sales and cash outlays for costs could result in positive income and negative cash flow.

2. False — It is possible to have a net loss yet increase the cash balance if a relatively large portion of expenses are the expiration of unexpired costs such as depreciation. Another possibility is an increase in cash from borrowing or additional paid-in capital, which do not affect income but would affect cash.

3. True — A firm can increase its total assets by acquiring them with debt, which certainly would not increase income.

4. False — Stockholders' equity is a measure of the claim stockholders have against the general assets of the firm; no dollar of stockholders' equity is traced to any specific item of property.

5. True — A firm may acquire inventory or prepaid expenses, which are assets because they have not yet expired.

6. True — When an asset is consumed or used for productive purposes (e.g., generating income), that asset becomes an expense.

7. True — Retained income is that portion of owners' equity that represents the accumulated net income of the firm that has not been withdrawn or paid to owners as dividends. It is possible to have positive retained income, but not a dime of liquid assets that could be paid to owners.

8. True — The statement of retained income describes the changes that have occurred in this section of owners' equity. Income increases the account, and dividends decrease the account.

9. False   Total assets increased by $500,000. A $600,000 asset was acquired with $100,000 cash (an exchange of assets) and $500,000 of debt. The net increase in assets is $500,000.

10. False   Though accounting logic certainly plays a role in setting GAAP, the process is quite political and depends on the strength of lobbying by affected parties as much as or more than logic.

11. False   The realization principle means that revenues may not be counted as earned unless the transaction meets three tests: goods or services delivered, exchange of resources, collectibility assured.

12. False   Though the monetary unit is not stable, users still derive significant usefulness from the financial disclosures based on that unstable monetary unit, and that is the most relevant measure of validity. It is possible that usefulness could be improved by using an adjusted monetary unit to account for inflation, but we do not have any systematic evidence of this.

13. False   The materiality convention means that an item does not need to be disclosed separately if so doing would not mislead users of financial statements.

14. True   Revenue represents an increase in owners' equity; thus a credit entry.

15. True   Though terminology can differ, it is customary to call a debit a charge when the debit is to an expense account, since it is a charge against income.

Multiple Choice Questions

1. c, d   The transaction increased merchandise inventory, an asset, and also increased accounts payable, a liability.

2. a   This transaction was an exchange of assets, with no effect on total assets.

3. a   Before the transaction total liabilities (in 000s) = $420 - $280 = $140. To analyze this with the accounting equation proceed as follows:

	Assets	= Liabilities +	Stockholders' equity
beg. bal.	420	= 140	+ 280
purchase	60	= 60	+ 0
collection	20 - 20	= 0	+ 0
end bal.	480	= 200	+ 280

4. d   See above.

5. c   Analyze this with the accounting equation:

	Assets	= Liabilities +	Stockholders' equity
beg. bal.	1,010	= 310	+ 700
issue stock	400	= 0	+ 400
purchase	600 - 60	= 540	+ 0
end bal.	1,950	= 850	+ 1,100

6. b   See above.

7. c   Dividends that are declared and paid are taken from retained income and cash.

8. b   Analyze with the accounting equation (in thousands):

Basic Accounting: Concepts, Techniques, and Conventions

	Assets	= Liabilities +	Stockholders' equity
purchase	40	= 40	+ 0
sale of equip	40 + 200 - 240	= 0	+ 0
net change	40	= 40	

9. b   Use a T-account to analyze this account:

```
      Materials
      Inventory
   ─────────────
      75  │
      35  │
          │ 100
   ─────────────
      10  │
```

10. c   Use a T-account to analyze this account:

```
      Retained
      Income
   ─────────────
          │ 40
      30  │
          │
   ─────────────
          │ 10
```

Completion

1. increased, increased, unchanged
2. asset, expense, income
3. sales revenue, total cost of goods sold
4. products or services must be delivered, there must be an exchange of resources, revenues must be collectible
5. total assets, total liabilities, total owners' equity
6. Generally Accepted Accounting Principles, Accounting Principles Board, Financial Accounting Standards Board, Securities and Exchange Commission, the last three are groups that have or had authority to set accounting policy for publicly traded corporations.
7. realization, matching
8. use the most pessimistic estimates of the values of assets, expenses, liabilities, revenues, and equities.
9. debit
10. right, left, debit

Problems

1. Gnu Co.

INCOME STATEMENT

Revenue:
  Sales $27,000

Expenses:
  Cost of goods sold $15,000
  Depreciation expense   300
  Rent expense   2,100
  Advertising expense   600   25,500
Net income $1,500

Alternative form of income statement (multiple-step form):
  Sales $27,000
  Cost of goods sold   15,000
  Gross profit $12,000
  Operating expenses:
    Depreciation expense $ 300
    Rent expense   2,100
    Advertising expense   600
    Salaries expense   7,500   10,500
  Net income $ 1,500

BALANCE SHEET

Assets		Liabilities and Stockholders' Equity	
Cash	$22,950	Liabilities:	
Accounts receivable	21,000	Accounts payable	$12,000
Inventory	14,400	Notes payable	6,000
Prepaid rent	1,050	Accrued interest payable	60
Furniture and fixtures	15,300	Accrued salaries payable	900
		Unearned rent revenue	240
		Total liabilities	$19,200
		Stockholders equity:	
		Capital stock $54,000	
		Retained income 1,500	$55,500
Total	$74,700	Total	$74,700

2. Eland Publishers, Inc.
   a. Net Income

   Revenues $970,000
   Less expenses:
     Depreciation $ 20,000
     Other expenses   815,000 $835,000
   Net Income $135,000

b. Retained income

Retained income, January 1, 19X2	$240,000
Net income for 19X2	135,000
Total	$375,000
Cash dividends for 19X2	110,000
Retained income, December 31, 19X2	$265,000

Note: The $750,000 cash payments and the $825,000 cash receipts are not relevant to the solution.

3. a. Transaction Analysis

		Assets					=	Liabilities & Stockholders' Equity	
		Cash	Accounts Receivable	Merchandise Inventory	Prepaid Rent	Store Equipment		Accounts Payable	Paid-in Capital	Retained Income
1.	Issued capital stock for cash, $100,000	100,000							100,000	
2.	Issued capital stock for store equipment, $50,000					50,000			50,000	
3.	Purchased store equipment for cash, $10,000	(10,000)				10,000				
4.	Purchased merchandise on account, $70,000			70,000				70,000		
5.	Sold merchandise on account, $35,000		35,000							35,000
6.	Recorded cost of merchandise sold, $20,000			(20,000)						(20,000)
7.	Sold part of store equipment at cost on account, $2,000		2,000			(2,000)				
8.	Collected cash on account for previous credit sales recorded, $13,000	13,000	(13,000)							
9.	Recorded depreciation of store equipment, $1,000					(1,000)				(1,000)
10.	Paid cash for six months' rent in advance, $9,000	(9,000)			9,000					
11.	Recorded current month's rent expense, $1,500				(1,500)					(1,500)
12.	Paid cash for current month's salaries, advertising, utilities, and miscellaneous office supplies purchased and used, $8,500	(8,500)								(8,500)
13.	Paid cash on account to suppliers for merchandise purchases previously made and recorded, $40,000	(40,000)						(40,000)		
14.	Declared and paid cash dividends to stockholders, $3,000	(3,000)								(3,000)
	Totals	42,500	24,000	50,000	7,500	57,000		30,000	150,000	1,000

280 Chapter 18

b. Compute: Total assets $181,000 Total owners' equity $151,000
Total liabilities $ 30,000 Total equities $181,000
Net income $ 4,000 (look at owners' equity column)

4. End-of-Period Adjustments:

	Assets	Liabilities	Revenues	Expenses
a.	decrease	no effect	no effect	increase
b.	no effect	decrease	increase	no effect
c.	no effect	increase	no effect	increase
d.	increase	no effect	increase	no effect
e.	decrease	no effect	no effect	increase

CHAPTER 19

Understanding Corporate Annual Reports: Basic Financial Statements

> **MAIN FOCUS AND OBJECTIVES**
>
> This chapter presents the construction of and the relationships among the principle financial statements prepared for external users. The major new focus of this chapter is the statement of cash flows. Your learning objectives are to:
>
> - Classify assets, liabilities, and stockholders' equity in a balance sheet
> - Identify elements of an income statement
> - Identify elements of the statement of retained income
> - Classify cash activities as operating, investing, or financing activities
> - Prepare the statement of cash flows using the direct method
> - Reconcile net income to cash provided by operations
> - Understand the role of depreciation in computing net cash flow

REVIEW OF KEY CONCEPTS

A. Corporate *balance sheets* are usually prepared in *classified form,* which means that accounts are separated according to major groups. Main groups are:

> See textbook Exhibit 19-1

1. *Assets:* the economic resources owned by the corporation:
    a. **Current assets** are the assets directly involved in the **operating cycle** (also called a **working-capital cycle**) and usually include: cash, temporary investments in marketable securities, accounts receivable less allowance for doubtful accounts, merchandise inventories, and prepaid expenses.
    b. **Property, plant, and equipment** (sometimes called **fixed assets** or **plant assets**) include the original cost of land and the original cost of other

longterm tangible assets less accumulated depreciation (cost allocated to expense since acquisition of the assets). The remainder is called **net book value.** **Leasehold improvements** and **natural resources** are often reported as plant assets.

> See textbook Exhibits 19-2 and 19-3

    c. **Intangible assets** include goodwill, patents, franchises, trademarks, and copyrights. These are reported at original cost, less accumulated amortization where applicable.

2. *Liabilities:* the monetary obligations of the corporation:
   a. **Current liabilities** are company debts falling due within the coming year or within the normal operating cycle if longer than a year. They include: accounts payable to suppliers, notes payable to banks and others, accrued expenses payable, and income taxes payable.
   b. **Long-term liabilities** fall due beyond the coming year and include mortgage bonds and *debentures.*

> See textbook Exhibit 19-4

3. *Stockholders' equity* (also called *ownership equity, capital,* or *net worth*): the owner's residual interest in the business, that is, the excess of total assets over total liabilities:
   a. **Preferred stock** is the par or stated value paid in by investors who purchased stock with a priority over common stock for periodic dividends or liquidating distributions. Preferred stock usually has a *predetermined dividend rate* with a *cumulative feature* and *no voting rights* in stockholder's meetings.
   b. **Common stock** is the par or stated value paid in by investors in common stock. Although this stock has *no predetermined dividend rate*, it typically *has voting rights,* an *unlimited potential participation in earnings,* and a *limited liability* for debts owed by the corporation to its creditors.
   c. **Paid-in capital in excess of par or stated value** was formerly called **surplus** or **paid-in surplus.** This is the excess received by the corporation over the par or stated or legal value of the shares issued.
   d. **Retained income** (also called **retained earnings** or **reinvested earnings**) is the part of stockholders' equity measured by the excess of accumulated profits over accumulated dividends distributed to stockholders since the company was formed.
   e. In addition to such **positive** elements as the above four items, the stockholders' equity section may include a **negative** item called **treasury stock,** the company's cost of reacquiring some of its own capital stock that had previously been issued.

B. In accounting, a **fund** is an asset usually composed of highly liquid cash or securities dedicated to a specific purpose, such as pensions. The term **reserve** never means a *fund* or any other kind of asset. Technically, a reserve can be used to refer to any of three quite different kinds of items often appearing in balance sheets:

1. *An appropriation or restriction of retained income* to inform the reader of the balance sheet that the intent or authority to declare dividends has been restricted by a certain amount for a specified reason. Examples include the contingencies of impending lawsuits or currency devaluations. It is merely an earmarking or segregating or subdividing of part of retained income.

2. *An asset valuation account* (or asset offset), for example, such asset deductions as allowance for uncollectible accounts or accumulated depreciation.

3. *An estimated liability* of indefinite or uncertain amount, for example, such payables as product guarantees, employee pensions, and income taxes.

C. The *income statement* reports a company's revenues (sales) and expenses and the net income or net loss that represents the difference between revenues and expenses, the change in the firm's wealth over time. The absorption form of the income statement (Chapters 4 and 16) is used for financial reporting.

> See textbook Exhibit 19-5

1. Note how this multiple-step income statement arrives at a figure called *income from operations* by deducting selling and administrative expenses from gross profit.
   a. Interest expense is deducted from this figure.
   b. The statement reflects the distinction between *operating management* and *financial management*.

2. The income statement must also show the **earnings per share of common stock**. In the simplest capital structure, the earnings-per-share figure is net income divided by the number of common shares outstanding.

3. Net income links the beginning and ending balance sheets because it is the difference between beginning and ending stockholders' equity (except as modified by dividends as discussed below).

D. The **statement of retained earnings** (also called **statement of retained income**) reports the effects of net income and dividends on the balance of retained income.

> See textbook Exhibit 19-6

1. Net income increases retained earnings.
2. Dividends to stockholders decrease retained earnings but are *not expenses* (not deductions in computing net income).

> Before going on be sure that you understand how the three foregoing financial statements are linked together. How are the income statement and the balance sheet related?

E. The **statement of cash flows** typically summarizes the sources and uses of cash and cash equivalents during a fiscal period, and it must be presented as a basic financial statement in corporate annual reports.

> See textbook Exhibits 19-7

1. The statement of cash flows is supposed to aid users of financial statements who want to:
   a. Predict future cash flows
   b. Evaluate management of cash
   c. Determine the ability of a company to pay interest, debt, and dividends.

2. *Cash equivalents* are liquid short-term investments such as money market funds and treasury bills.

3. Changes in cash are grouped into *operating, investing,* and *financing* activities to aid in understanding the sources and uses of cash.
   a. *Operating activities* include collections from customers, interest earned (both inflows) and payments to suppliers, employees, banks and the IRS (all outflows).
   b. *Investing activities* include sales of assets and investments (inflows) and purchases of assets and investments (outflows) -- other than cash equivalents.
   c. *Financing activities* include borrowing and issuing stock (inflows) and repayments and repurchases of debt or equity (outflows).

4. The statement of cash flows may be prepared using either the *direct* or *indirect* method, but the format is the same.
   a. The **direct method** *analyzes changes in balance sheet accounts* to determine their effects on cash flow.

See Exhibit 19-8

   b. First analyze the accounts that affect income to determine cash flow from operations. For example, cash inflows may be from reductions in accounts receivable, and cash outflows may be from reductions in interest payable.
   c. Next determine cash flows from investing and financing activities by analyzing all balance sheet accounts other than cash.
      - Increases in cash are from increases in liabilities or stockholders' equity (e.g., new debt or issue of securities) or from decreases in noncash assets (e.g., sales of fixed assets).
      - Decreases in cash are from decreases in liabilities or stockholders' equity (e.g., retirement of debt or payment of dividends) or from increases in noncash assets (e.g., investment in fixed assets).
   d. The **indirect method** *adjusts reported net income for all non-cash accruals* contained in net income. If this method is used, net income must be reconciled to net cash flow.

See Exhibit 19-10

   e. The general rules for reconciling net income to cash flow are:
      - Add depreciation
      - Add decreases in noncash current assets
      - Add increases in current liabilities
      - Deduct increases in noncash current assets
      - Deduct decreases in current liabilities

- Add loss (or deduct gain) from sale of fixed assets
- Add loss (or deduct gain) on retirement of debt

f. Remember that because depreciation was not a cash outflow of the period (it is an allocation of an historical cost) it is added back to income to determine cash flow.

PRACTICE TEST QUESTIONS AND PROBLEMS WITH SOLUTIONS

True or False Statements

Determine whether each of the following statements is True (T) or False (F) and enter your answer in the space provided.

__F__ 1. Depreciation accounting is both a cost allocation process and a valuation process.

__F__ 2. The usual balance sheet presentation of property, plant, and equipment shows either their resale value or their replacement cost. ACQUISITION COST

__F__ 3. Accumulated depreciation serves the purpose of a fund for replacement or expansion of plant and equipment.

__T__ 4. The intangible asset classification used in financial statements includes trademarks and goodwill. EXCESS OF PURCHASE PRICE OVER FAIR MARKET VALUE

__F__ 5. The goodwill asset should be measured by the excess of the fair value of net identifiable assets of businesses acquired over the total purchase price of the businesses acquired.

__F__ 6. When a company develops goodwill through advertising, managerial ability, and maintenance of high-quality products and services, the goodwill should be placed on the books and carried as an asset in the balance sheet.

__F__ 7. Liabilities are company debts falling due within the current year or within the normal operating cycle if longer than a year. (CURRENT)

__F__ 8. If capital stock is issued by a corporation at a price in excess of par or stated value, the excess is a gain that may be reported as part of retained earnings. ADDITION PIC.

__T__ 9. When a corporation declares and distributes periodic cash dividends to its stockholders, the results include decreases in the corporation's retained income and stockholders' equity.

__F__ 10. The cost of treasury stock held by a corporation is an asset of the corporation.

__F__ 11. When retained income is "appropriated," there is a reduction in total stockholders' equity. RELABELS IT!

__T__ 12. Whether a company buys merchandise for cash or on credit, the amount of its working capital is not affected.

__T__ 13. Financing activity inflows would include acquisition of treasury stock and issuance of capital stock.

__T__ 14. Financing activity outflows would include retirement of long-term debt and declaration and payment of dividends.

__F__ 15.   The purchase of noncurrent assets is an operating activity.

__F__ 16.   The issuance of long-term debt increases cash and increases stockholders' equity.
   LIABILITIES INCREASE, NOT STOCKHOLDERS EQUITY.

Multiple Choice Questions

For each of the following multiple-choice questions, select the best answer(s) and enter the identification letter(s) in the space provided.

__D__ 1.   Current assets include: (a) cash and land, (b) accounts receivable and payable, (c) trademarks and equipment, (d) merchandise inventories and prepaid expenses.

__C__ 2.   In accounting, a reserve may mean: (a) an asset or an estimated liability, (b) an asset offset or a liability offset, (c) an asset offset or an estimated liability, (d) an asset or a liability offset.

__D__ 3.   In a recent period Catalpa Corp. had net income of $20,000, issued additional debt of $50,000, declared dividends of $10,000, and purchased $40,000 of equipment for cash. Total assets: (a) decreased by $50,000, (b) increased by $50,000, (c) decreased by $70,000, (d) increased by $70,000.

__D__ 4.   See the previous test item. Stockholders' equity: (a) increased by $60,000, (b) decreased by $100,000, (c) increased by $10,000, (d) increased by $20,000.

__D__ 5.   In computing the amount of cash provided by operations, one should add depreciation to net income because depreciation: (a) generates funds, (b) provides cash, (c) is not an expense, (d) does not require a current cash outlay.

__C__ 6.? The cash flow statement of Tantra, Inc. showed a $50,000 increase in inventory and a $40,000 decrease in liabilities. Thus there was a cash: (a) increase of $10,000, (b) decrease of $10,000, (c) decrease of $90,000, (d) $90,000 increase.

__A__ 7.   The income statement of Naropa, Inc. reported $500,000 of sales and $400,000 of total expenses, including $30,000 of depreciation. During the same period, its accounts payable increased by $20,000, while accounts receivable decreased by $6,000, and merchandise inventory increased by $32,000. Compute the cash provided by operations: (a) $124,000, (b) $136,000, (c) $70,000, (d) $130,000

__C__ 8.   The activities of Arapahoe Corporation included (in thousands): purchase of fixed assets $360, operating income $540, income taxes $300, $30 gain on cash sale of equipment carried at $50, issuance of debt $300, cash dividends $60, depreciation $230. Cash from operating activities totaled: (a) $480, (b) $740, (c) $470, (d) $240.

__B__ 9.   See the preceding test item. Asset Acquisition, etc. Cash from investing activities totaled: (a) $360 outflow, (b) $280 outflow, (c) $140 inflow, (d) $80 inflow.

__A__ 10. See item number 8. Cash from financing activities totaled: (a) $240 inflow, (b) $300 inflow, (c) $60 outflow, (d) $40 outflow.

__A__ 11. See item number 8. Total net cash flow was: (a) $430 inflow, (b) $740 inflow, (c) $420 outflow, (d) $60 outflow.

Completion

Complete each of the following statements by filling in the blanks.

1. The four principal financial statements that appear in annual reports are:
   (a) _____
   (b) _____
   (c) _____
   (d) _____

2. The cost of plant and equipment less accumulated depreciation leaves an amount commonly called _____.

3. Goodwill, patents, and copyrights are _____ assets which means they have _____ but are not _____ in nature.

4. The operating cycle is the time span during which _____ to acquire _____ used to produce goods and services for sale to customers who _____.

5. Retained income, also called _____ or _____ is the increase in stockholders' equity from the excess of accumulated _____ over accumulated _____. since the company was formed.

6. A company's own capital stock once issued and later reacquired by the company is called _____ and is treated as _____ on the balance sheet.

7. An earmarking of retained income for financial reporting purposes may be called a _____.

8. The issuance of long-term debt is _financial_ activity; it _increases_ cash.

9. If outflows of cash from operations and investing exceed inflows for a given company during a certain period, there is _a need for borrowing_

10. The amount of cash provided by operations is _____ plus _____.

288 Chapter 19

Problems

1. Given for Kalmia Trading Company's operations for 19X3 (in thousands):

Total cash receipts	$700
Total cash disbursements	590
Total revenues earned	516
Total expenses incurred (including cost of goods sold)	455
Total dividends declared and distributed to stockholders	40
Additional capital stock issued at par	50
Treasury capital stock acquired at cost	20

   a. Compute the net income for 19X3:

   b. Compute the net change in retained income for 19X3:

   c. Compute the net change in stockholder's equity for 19X3:

2. For each of the transactions listed below for the Bosque Corporation, use plus, minus, or zero symbols to indicate the effect on net income, total owners' equity, and cash. The first is given as an example.

	Net Income	Total Owners' Equity	Cash
Issued capital stock for cash	0	+	+
Issued capital stock for plant site (land)	0	+	0
Issued capital stock for merchandise inventory	0	+	0
Paid bonds payable with cash	0	0	−
Declared and distributed cash dividends	0	−	−
Recorded bad debt expense	−	−	0
Collected accounts receivable in cash	0	0	+
Paid accounts payable with cash	0	0	−
Purchased land and buildings with cash	0	0	−
Purchased treasury stock with $900 cash	0	−	−
Sold treasury stock in (10) for $700 cash	0	+	+
Created a reserve for contingencies	0	0	0
Created a reserve for depreciation of machinery			
Increased bond sinking fund (a noncurrent asset)			
Recorded accrued salaries			
Purchased merchandise on account			
Collected rents in advance in cash			
Sold merchandise on account (for credit) at a profit			

3. From the following data, prepare a statement of 19X4 cash flows for Genessee Company. Use the indirect method similar to Exhibit 19-11. Assume changes in account balances are due to cash transactions.

	December 31	
	19X4	19X3
Inventories	$870,000	$840,000
Accounts Payable	150,000	240,000
Land	115,000	130,000
Equipment, net	435,000	440,000
Bonds payable	200,000	300,000
Capital stock	550,000	400,000
Retained income	590,000	500,000

For 19X4 Year:
Net income	$160,000
Depreciation	25,000
Dividends on capital stock	70,000
Gain or loss on sale of land	none

CHAPTER 19 SOLUTIONS TO PRACTICE TEST QUESTIONS AND PROBLEMS

True or False Statements

1. False — Depreciation is an allocation of an historical cost; it is not meant to measure the decline in economic value of an asset.

2. False — Plant, property, and equipment is shown at net book value: historical cost less accumulated depreciation. Net book value may be greater or lesser than resale value or replacement cost.

3. False — The accumulated depreciation account in no way creates an asset fund that could be used for replacement or expansion of assets. A separate *sinking* fund would be established for that purpose.

4. True — Intangible assets are resources with long lives, but are not physical in nature.

5. False — Just the opposite: goodwill is measured as the excess of the purchase price of assets over their fair market value.

6. False — Though tempting, goodwill recognized on a balance sheet results from an economic transaction, not managers' judgment.

7. False — *Current* liabilities are company debts falling due within the current year or within the normal operating cycle if longer than a year.

8. False — The amount in excess of par value is counted as additional paid-in capital, not a gain in retained earnings.

9. True — While declaring dividends merely sets aside a portion of retained income, actually paying dividends reduces cash and retained income, and thus stockholders' equity.

10. False — Treasury stock reduces the amount of traded stock and is counted as a reduction of stockholders' equity.

11. False — An appropriation of retained income does not reduce total stockholders' equity, it merely relabels it.

12. True — Working capital is the excess of current assets over current liabilities. If merchandise is acquired on credit, current assets increase the same amount as current liabilities, leaving the difference unchanged.

13. True — These activities are concerned with the external claims on the assets of the firm, and are therefore considered financing activities.

14. True — As above.

15. False — The purchase of longterm assets qualifies as an investing activity since the assets are expected to benefit more than the current period.

16. False — The issuance of longterm debt does increase cash, but liabilities are increased, not stockholders' equity.

Multiple Choice Statements

1. d   Merchandise inventories and prepaid expenses will benefit the current period, whereas the other answers are mixes of current and noncurrent assets or liabilities.

2. c   A reserve may be of three types: a retained income reserve, an offset to an asset, or an estimated liability.

3. d   This can be analyzed by the accounting equation:

	Assets =	Liabilities +	Owners' Equity
net income	20		20
debt	50	50	
dividends			10 - 10
equipment	-40 + 40		
net change	<u>70</u>	50	20

4. d   See above.

5. d   Net income understates cash flow by the amount of depreciation (and other noncash expenses); so depreciation is added back to net income to move toward cash flow.

6. c   There are two possible explanations: Acquiring $50,000 of inventory required a cash payment of $50,000 and reducing liabilities required another $40,000. Alternatively, the inventory was acquired on credit, but overall liabilities decreased by $40,000, requiring a total of $90,000.

7. a   Cash from operations equals net income plus depreciation plus net changes in current asset or liability accounts: $500 - 400 + 30 + 20 + 6 - 32 = $124

8. c   Following the same format as above: cash from operations = $540 + 230 - 300 = $470.

9. b   Investing activities include: purchase $360 outflow and sale of equipment $30 + $50 inflow = $280 outflow.

10. a   Financing activities include: issuance of debt $300 inflow and cash dividends $60 outflow = $240 inflow.

11. a   Net cash flow equals cash from operations plus investment and financing activities: $470 - 280 + 240 = $430 inflow.

Completion

1. (a) balance sheet, (b) income statement, (c) statement of retained income, (d) statement of cash flows

2. net book value

3. intangible, long lives or value, physical

4. cash is spent, resources and services, pay for them with cash

5. retained earnings, reinvested earnings, profits (or earnings, or net income), dividends distributed

6. treasury stock, a reduction of stockholders' equity

7.   an appropriation of retained income,

8.   investing, increases,

9.   a need for borrowing,

10.   net income, depreciation and net changes to current accounts

Problems

1. Kalmia Trading Company

    a. 19X3 net income:

Total revenues earned	$516
Less total expenses incurred	455
Net income	$ 61

    (Cash receipts and disbursements are not relevant here.)

    b. Change in retained income for 19X3:

Net income as above	$61
Less dividends to stockholders	40
Increase in retained income	$21

    c. Change in stockholders' equity

Increase in retained income as above	$21
Additional capital stock issued	50
Total	$71
Less treasury stock acquired	20
Increase in stockholders' equity	$51

2. Bosque Corporation

	Net Income	Total Owners' Equity	Cash
Issued capital stock for cash	0	+	+
Issued capital stock for plant site (land)	0	+	0
Issued capital stock for merchandise inventory	0	+	0
Paid bonds payable with cash	0	0	-
Declared and distributed cash dividends	0	-	-
Recorded bad debt expense	-	-	0
Collected accounts receivable in cash	0	0	+
Paid accounts payable with cash	0	0	+
Purchased land and buildings with cash	0	0	-
Purchased treasury stock with $900 cash	0	-	-
Sold treasury stock in (10) for $700 cash	0	+	+
Created a reserve for contingencies	0	0	0
Created a reserve for depreciation of machinery	-	-	0
Increased bond sinking fund (a noncurrent asset)	0	0	-
Recorded accrued salaries	-	-	0
Purchased merchandise on account	0	0	0
Collected rents in advance in cash	0	0	+
Sold merchandise on account (for credit) at a profit	+	+	0

3. Genessee Company
Statement of Cash Flows
For the Year Ended December 31, 19X4

Cash provided (used) by operations:	
Net Income	$ 160,000
Income charges (credits) not affecting cash:	
Depreciation	25,000
Charges in certain working capital components	
Increase in inventories	(90,000)
Cash provided by operations	$65,000
Cash provided (used) by investing activities:	
Sale of land	$15,000
Purchases of equipment	(20,000)*
Cash used by investing activities	$(5,000)
Cash provided (used) by financing activities:	
Reductions in long term debt	$ (100,000)
Payments of dividends	(70,000)
Issuance of capital stock	$ 150,000
Cash used by financing activities	$ (20,000)
Net increase (decrease) in cash	$ 40,000

*$435,000 + $25,000 − $440,000 = $20,000 increase in equipment (a decrease in cash).

CHAPTER 20

More on Understanding Corporate Annual Reports

MAIN FOCUS AND OBJECTIVES

The first part of the chapter explains how investments in other companies are disclosed in financial statements. When certain criteria are met, firms disclose these investments using the *cost*, *equity* or *consolidation* methods. Coverage of the last method explores the relationship between *parent and subsidiary* companies and their *consolidated corporate financial statements*. The second part of the chapter examines well-known *financial ratios* for analyzing reported corporate data and the concept of capital market efficiency. Your learning objectives are to:

- Contrast accounting for investments using the equity and the cost methods
- Understand the basics of consolidated financial statements
- Understand and account for goodwill
- Compute and use common financial ratios
- Address the implications of efficient capital markets for financial reporting

---

REVIEW OF KEY CONCEPTS

Part One

A. When one company has a long-term investment in the equity securities (capital stock) of another company, there are two methods of accounting for the investment:

1. *If the ownership is less than 20%*, the **cost method** may ordinarily be used.
    a. The initial investment is recorded at acquisition cost, and dividends received from the investee are treated as income.
    b. Thus the carrying amount of the investment is unaffected by the dividends or profits of the investee.

2. *If the ownership is 20% to 50%*, (sometimes called *investments in affiliates*) the **equity method** must ordinarily be used, because it would usually be assumed that the owner has the ability to influence significantly the operations of the investee.

a. The initial investment is recorded at acquisition cost, but this basis is adjusted for the investor's share of the earnings and losses of the investee after the investment date.
b. Dividends received from the investee are treated as reductions of the cost basis of the investment.
c. Under this method, the net income of the investor could not be directly affected by manipulating the dividend policies of the investee, because dividends received by the investor are not treated as income.

3. *When a corporation owns more than 50% of the outstanding voting shares of another corporation, there is a **parent-subsidiary relationship** that usually results in the operation of these two separate legal entities in the manner of a **single economic unit**.*
   a. Therefore the financial data of such companies would be combined into **consolidated statements.**

   > See textbook Exhibit 20-1

   b. Consolidation is required even if parent and subsidiary companies have markedly different types of businesses (for example, banking and transportation).

4. In *consolidated financial statements*, the assets and equities in the individual balance sheets of the parent and subsidiary companies are *added together* except for the *eliminations of the intercompany transfers* to avoid double-counting (e.g., sales between the parent and the subsidiary do not generate revenue for the consolidated entity).
   a. Thus the parent company's asset, investment in subsidiary, is canceled against the subsidiary's stockholders' equity (or the appropriate proportion of it).
   b. If part of the subsidiary's capital stock is *not owned* by the parent company (a **minority interest**), the consolidated balance sheet would ordinarily include this outside interest just above the stockholders' equity section.
   c. This minority interest represents the ownership interest of the minority stockholders in one or more of the subsidiary companies in which they own stock.

5. In the consolidated income statement, the expenses and revenues of the two companies are also combined, but there would be a deduction for any minority share of subsidiary net income.

   > See textbook Exhibit 20-2

6. Note two important points concerning consolidated statements:
   a. The separate legal entities continue to operate, each with its own set of accounts.
   b. For periodic reporting purposes, the accounts of parent and subsidiary are merely added together, after eliminating double-counting.

7. When one company purchases another, often called a **merger,** the purchasing company should record the assets obtained at **acquisition cost** (the agreed amount of money to be paid, or the fair value of other assets exchanged).
   a. If the total purchase price exceeds the sum of the fair value of the identifiable individual assets acquired less the liabilities, the excess, often called **purchased goodwill,** is an asset that should be reported on the consolidated balance sheet as "excess of cost over fair value of net identifiable assets of businesses acquired."
   b. Such a goodwill should be carried as a separate intangible asset on the consolidated balance sheet but should be **amortized** (systematically charged to expense similar to depreciation) over a period not greater than forty years, because the income-producing ability of goodwill is not likely to last forever.

> Before going on to the next section, be sure that you understand the principles of the different methods of combining financial statements of related companies. Work through the summary problem in the text using the balance sheet equation approach. Review the criteria for disclosure in textbook Exhibit 20-3.

Part Two

B. **Financial statement analysis** is the study of relationships contained in financial statements for the purposes of
   - evaluating past performance of the entity or
   - predicting future performance of the entity or
   - evaluating the risk of the entity.

   1. Techniques of financial statement analysis include:
      a. Comparing financial information over time (*time-series* comparisons), with that of similar companies, and against industry averages (*cross-sectional* comparisons).
      b. Measuring differences from budgets and cash-flow projections.
      c. Computing ratios and *common-size statements* to aid in *profit evaluation* and *solvency determination*.

   2. **Common-size statements** are really ratios of individual financial statement amounts to a base of sales (for the income statement) or total assets (for the balance sheet).

      > See textbook Exhibit 20-7

      a. Note how the elements in the common-size income statement are related to the dollar amount of *sales*, which is used as the *base figure* for the *common* sizes. Each dollar figure in the statement can be expressed as a percentage of sales.
      b. In the balance sheet, the *total asset* dollar amount is used as the *base* for determining the common sizes of the major balance sheet items. Each balance sheet is expressed as a percentage of total assets (or total equities, of course).
      c. These ratios may be compared over time, with competitors, and against industry averages to evaluate the entity.

3. Below are definitions of some typical ratios, but note that there are many variations in practice.

> See textbook Exhibit 20-8

a. **Short-term ratios** help in assessing a company's ability to pay its current debts on time:
Current ratio: Current assets ÷ Current liabilities
Inventory turnover: Cost of goods sold ÷ Average inventory at cost
Average collection period in days: Average accounts receivable x 365 ÷ Sales on Account

b. **Debt-to-equity ratios** help in judging the risks of insolvency and disappearance of profits:
Current debt to equity: Current liabilities ÷ Stockholders' equity
Total debt to equity: Total liabilities ÷ Stockholders' equity

c. **Profitability ratios** aid in measuring operating success and overall accomplishment:
Gross profit rate or percentage: Gross profit ÷ Sales
Return on sales: Net income ÷ Sales
Return on stockholders' equity: Net income ÷ Average stockholders' equity
Earnings per share: Net income less preferred dividends ÷ Average common shares outstanding
Price-earnings ratio: Common market price per share ÷ Earnings per common share

c. **Dividend ratios** relate profit distributions to common stock prices and earnings:
Dividend yield: Dividends per common share ÷ Market price per common share
Dividend-payout ratio: Dividends per common share ÷ Earnings per common share

d. The pretax operating rate of **return on total assets** (also called **ROI** -- see Chapter 10) helps measure operating performance:
Operating income ÷ Average total assets available
This ratio can also be computed by multiplying the two following ratios:
Return on sales: Operating income ÷ Sales
Total asset turnover: Sales ÷ Average total assets available
See the discussion on ROI in Chapter 10.

> Before going on, review the construction of these common financial ratios and just as importantly, review in the text their meaning for decision making. Be sure that you understand how to calculate the ratios in textbook Exhibit 20-8 from the data in the financial statements in Exhibits 20-4, 5, and 6. Note also how to compare these ratios to industry averages.

C. Research over the past 20 years has indicated that capital markets are reasonably efficient with respect to accounting information.

1. This means that stock market prices "fully reflect" relevant data that are publicly available. Be aware that financial statements are just one of many sources of information about the prospects of a firm.

2. Thus financial ratios and other reported data are, in effect, "translated" by or combined with other information by informed readers and analysts, regardless of the different accounting and reporting methods that may be used.

3. This assumes, of course that there are *adequate disclosures* of such methods, either in the body of the financial statements or in the accompanying footnotes (as required by the SEC).

4. Research in recent years, however, indicates that not all accounting information may be utilized by capital markets. For example, it may be that careful analysis of financial statement ratios can yield insights that others do not have. Of course, financial analysts have been making good livings doing just that for many years.

PRACTICE TEST QUESTIONS AND PROBLEMS WITH SOLUTIONS

True or False Statements

Determine whether each of the following statements is True (T) or False (F) and enter your answer in the space provided.

__F__ 1. The equity method must generally be used when the equity ownership by one company of another company is less than 20%.

__T__ 2. When two companies have a parent-subsidiary relationship, they are a single economic entity.

__F__ 3. The minority interest measures the interest of parent company stockholders in the subsidiary company.

__F__ 4. When parent and subsidiary companies have totally different types of business, the parent company should carry its investment in the subsidiary by the equity method.

__F__ 5. When a company develops "goodwill" internally, it should be placed on the books and reported as an asset in the balance sheet

__F__ 6. Purchased goodwill should be amortized over a period not to exceed 20 years.

__T__ 7. Nix Co. had a current ratio of two to one. It paid part of its accounts payable. As a result, the current ratio increased.

__T__ 8. The dividend yield multiplied by the price-earnings ratio would be equal to the dividend-payout ratio:

__F__ 9. When common-size income statements are constructed, the base figure is usually net income. (SALES)

__F__ 10. Your company's inventory turnover increased. This suggests greater risk of decline in value of inventory.

__T__ 11. The average collection period of accounts receivable increased. This suggests closer screening of credit applications from customers and greater risk of uncollectibility of accounts receivable.

__T__ 12. The carrying amount of one company's long-term investment in the equity securities of another company would be unaffected by the dividends or profits of the investee if the cost method were used.

__T__ 13. Earnings per share is the only ratio required to be disclosed in reported financial statements.

__T__ 14. Common-size financial statements are made up of component percentages.

____ 15. If a capital market is efficient with respect to accounting information, that means, for example, that if a company changes from accelerated depreciation to straight-line depreciation for its reports to stockholders, the market price of its stock will tend to fall because the market recognizes the reduced income.

Multiple Choice Questions

For each of the following multiple-choice questions, select the best answer(s) and enter the identification letter(s) in the space provided.

__C__ 1. First Company owns 30% of the voting stock of Second Company, which reported a net income in Year One of $10 million and paid $4 million of cash dividends. Compute the increase in the retained income of First Company in Year One from Second Company's operations, using the **cost** method: (a) $3.0 million, (b) $1.8 million, (c) $1.2 million, (d) $4 million.

__A__ 2. See the preceding test item. Compute the increase in the retained income of First Company in Year One from Second Company's operations, using the **equity** method: (a) $3.0 million, (b) $1.8 million, (c) $1.2 million, (d) $4 million.

__B__ 3. See item 1 above. Assume that the acquisition cost of First Company's investment was $100 million. Compute the year-end balance of First Company's investment account, using the equity method: (a) $103.0 million, (b) $101.8 million, (c) $101.2 million, (d) $102 million.

__C__ 4. Bigg Company acquired a 90% voting interest in Small Company for $150 million. The stockholders' equity of Small Company was $160 million at acquisition, and the book values of its individual assets were equal to their fair market values. Compute the consolidated goodwill: (a) $16 million, (b) $10 million, (c) $6 million, (d) negative $10 million.

__A__ 5. See the preceding test item. The minority interest is: (a) $16 million, (b) $15 million, (c) $15 million, (d) negative $15 million.

__D__ 6. The individual net incomes of a company and its 75% owned subsidiary were each $16 million. Compute the consolidated net income: (a) $32 million, (b) $20 million, (c) $24 million, (d) $28 million.

__D__ 7. Normad Co. has $12,000 current assets, $150,000 sales, $75,000 total assets, and $24,000 net income. What is the common-size percentage for $3,000 accounts payable? (a) 12.5%, (b) 2%, (c) 25%, (d) 4%.

__A/C__ 8. BankWestern is evaluating financial statements of a loan applicant. The applicant's current ratio has increased over the past two years. This signals (a) improved asset position, (b) increased risk of nonpayment, (c) decreased risk of nonpayment, (d) growth in short-term claims against the company.

__D__ 9. Farrone Company has a return on sales of 12% and asset turnover of 4 times. Its return on total assets is: (a) 12%, (b) 3%, (c) 24%, (d) 48%.

__C__ 10. Bodin Corp. has a return on total assets of 12% and return on sales of 6%. Its asset turnover is: (a) 7.2 times, (b) .5 times, (c) 2 times, (d) 9 times.

Completion

Complete each of the following statements by filling in the blanks.

1. The three methods of combining financial statements are:
   (a) _cost_
   (b) _equity_
   (c) _consolidated_

2. Under the equity method of accounting for a parent company's interest in a subsidiary, the investment in the subsidiary should be carried as __ASSET__ in the parent company's balance sheet at __COST (ORIGINAL)__ plus the consolidated group's share of accumulated __INCOME__ since acquisition.

3. An account called "minority interest" on a consolidated balance sheet measures __Third Party Interest__.

4. When one company buys another, the excess of the total purchase price over the fair values of the identifiable individual assets acquired less the liabilities is often called __goodwill__. This is an asset that should be reported in the acquiring company's balance sheet as __intangible asset__.

5. The pretax operating rate of return on total assets can be computed by multiplying the __Return on sales__ by the __total asset turnover__. This ratio can be improved by increasing either __ROS__ or __turnover of assets__.

6. The total asset turnover is __sales__ divided by average total assets available. When this ratio is less than that of a competitor it signals __assets are not being utilized as well as a competitors__.

7. The dividend-payout ratio for common stock is __earnings per share__ divided into __dividends per share__. When this ratio is lower than the industry average, it signals __firm is retaining income__.

8. The inventory turnover is _average Inventory_ divided into _CGS_.
   When this ratio increases over time, it signals _efficient (low) levels of inventory_

9. The average collection period for accounts receivable is 365 days multiplied by _Average Acc Receivable_ divided by _Credit Sales_. When this ratio decreases, it signals _aggressive collection_.

Problems

1. Company P owns 40% of the voting stock of Company S. Given in millions of dollars:

Cost of P's 40% ownership	$180
Net income of S in year one	20
Cash dividends of S in year one	10

   Compute:

   a. Year-end balance of P's investment account:

   Using the equity method $180 + .40(20-10) = \$184$.

   Using the cost method $\$180M$

   b. Increase in retained income of P in year one from S operations:

   Using the equity method $.40(20) = \$8M$

   Using the cost method $.40(10) = \$4M$

2. Tamarisk Company acquired 20% of the voting stock of Aspen Company for $60 million. During the following year, Aspen reported a net income of $25 million and distributed total cash dividends of $15 million.

   a. Assume that the **cost method** is used by Tamarisk Company. Compute:
   The carrying amount of the investment at the end of the year

   $.20 \times 15 = \$60M$

   The increase in Absorption's reported stockholders' equity because of subsidiary operations during the year

   $.20 \times 15 = \$3M$

   b. Assume that the **equity method** is used by Tamarisk Company. Compute:
   The carrying amount of the investment at the end of the year

   $= \$60M + .20(25) - .20(15) = 60+5-3 = 62$

   The increase in Tamarisk's reported stockholders' equity because of subsidiary operations during the year

   $.20(25) = +\$5M$

3. Table Mesa Company acquired Piedra Company. Before the acquisition the companies had neither debt nor preferred stock outstanding. Their annual reports before the acquisition revealed the following data:

	Table Mesa	Piedra
Net assets	$80,000	$20,000
Stockholders' equity	80,000	20,000
Net income	8,000	7,000

Table Mesa Company issued capital stock with a market value of $50,000 in exchange for all the stock of Piedra Company. Assume that the book value and the current value of the individual assets of Piedra were equal before the acquisition.

a. Compute the following for the consolidated company immediately after acquisition:
Purchased goodwill

$50 K
− 20 K
$30 K

Net assets (including goodwill)

80 + 20 + 30 = $130

Stockholders' equity

80,000
+ 50,000 Capital Stock
S/E = +130,000

b. Compute the prospective annual net income of the consolidated company, assuming that purchased goodwill is not to be amortized

INCOME TM $8,000
"   P $7,000
$15,000

c. Compute the prospective annual net income of the consolidated company, assuming that purchased goodwill is to be amortized to expense on a straight-line basis over a five-year period

Goodwill Amortization $30,000/5 = $6,000/YR

Prospective Net Income = $15,000
Amortized Goodwill   − $6,000
                       $9,000

4. Company P has just acquired a 90% voting interest in Company S for the amount shown below in the investment account (all amounts in millions of dollars):

P Co.:	Investment in S	$180
	Cash and other assets	440
	Liabilities	200
	Stockholders' equity	420
S Co.:	Cash and other assets	500
	Liabilities	300
	Stockholders' equity	200

a. Prepare a consolidated balance sheet. (No work sheet is required, but show support for all figures.) Assume that the book values of S individual assets are equal to their fair market values.

```
                    A         =      L      +     S/E      +   MII
P           440              200            220
ACQ (90%)   180                             180
S           500              300            200
ELIM       (180)                           (180)
           ─────           ─────          ─────          ─────
      ∅    $940            $500           $420           $20
```

b. Compute the consolidated goodwill, assuming that a 75% voting interest had been acquired, but use all the **same dollar numbers** shown above. Also assume that the book values of the S individual assets are equal to their fair market values. Prepare the consolidated balance sheet (work sheet not required).

```
P              440       =    200           220
ACQ (75%)      180                          180
S              500            300           200
GOODWILL        30                           30
ELIM         (180)
            ─────         ─────         ─────         ─────
      $∅    $970         $500          $420          $50
```

5. Selected data for Roaring Fork Corporation (in millions):

Sales	$800	Cost of goods sold	$500
Current assets	240	Current liabilities	120
Stockholders' equity	200	Merchandise inventory	125
Accounts receivable	80	Accounts payable	60
Retained income	150	Net income	36

Assume that all sales were on account. Compute each of the ratios indicated below. It is not necessary to compute any average amounts for balance sheet figures.

Current ratio: $\dfrac{\text{CURRENT ASSET}}{\text{CURRENT LIABILITIES}} = \dfrac{240}{120} = 2$

Inventory turnover: $\dfrac{CGS}{\text{AVG INV}} = \dfrac{500}{125} = 4$

Collection period for accounts receivable: $\dfrac{A/R \times 365}{\text{CREDIT SALES}} = \dfrac{80 \times 365}{800} = 36.5 \text{ days}$

Gross profit rate: $= \dfrac{\text{GROSS PROFIT}}{\text{SALES}} = \dfrac{800 - 500}{800} = 37.5\%$

Return on sales: $\frac{\text{OPER INC.}}{\text{SALES}} = \frac{36}{800} = 4.5\%$

Return on stockholders' equity: $\frac{\text{NET INCOME}}{\text{S/E}} = \frac{36}{200} = 18\%$

6. Given for Gunnison Corporation (in millions):
   - Operating income $54
   - Sales 900
   - Average total assets available 500

Find:

a. Operating margin percentage on sales = $\frac{\text{INCOME}}{\text{SALES}} = \frac{54}{900}$

b. Total asset turnover = $\frac{\text{SALES}}{\text{TOT. ASSET}} = \frac{900}{500} = 1.8$

c. Pretax operating rate of return on total assets = $\frac{\text{INCOME}}{\text{ASSETS}} = \frac{54}{500} = 10.8\%$

CHAPTER 20 SOLUTIONS TO PRACTICE TEST QUESTIONS AND PROBLEMS

True or False Statements

1. False — The cost method must be used when ownership is less than 20%. The equity method is used when ownership is between 20% and 50%.

2. True — Parent and subsidiary decisions are likely to be so intertwined that they are effectively a single economic unit. Thus consolidation of financial statements is required.

3. False — A minority interest measures ownership by a third party, not the parent.

4. False — Even when parent and subsidiary are in unrelated businesses, the financial statements must be consolidated.

5. False — Goodwill results from actual, "arms-length" economic transactions not internal developments.

6. False — The amortization period generally is not more than 40 years.

7. True — Though both current assets and current liabilities decreased by the transaction, because current assets are larger, they decreased proportionately less, and the current ratio increased.

8. True — Dividend yield x price-earnings ratio = (dividend per share ÷ price per share) x (price per share ÷ earnings per share) = dividend per share ÷ earnings per share = dividend payout ratio.

9. False — The base is usually sales.

10. False	Greater inventory turnover means that inventory is in the warehouse less; thus there is less chance of inventory obsolescence.
11. True	An increased collection period means that customers are slower to pay for their purchases. This definitely reduces cash flow and could signal greater bad debt expense as more uncollectible accounts are written off.
12. True	In the cost method, the investment is carried at cost and any dividends received are treated as income.
13. True	This ratio is so widely used (apparently) that its disclosure (often in multiple forms) is required.
14. True	Each line or component of a common-size financial statement is a percentage of the base (sales or total assets).
15. False(?)	Most early research (e.g., 1970s) indicated that this switch would not affect stock prices because it is perceived to be a "cosmetic" change; that is, it only changes reported income. However, more recent research (late 1980s and early 1990s) indicates that the switch to straight-line depreciation, for example, might signal lower expected future profits or some other adverse event. Thus the switch could result in a stock price decline. We know very little for sure about the effects of alternative accounting disclosures on stock prices. It seems fair to expect that managers do not choose or change accounting disclosure methods at random; there must be an underlying reason, and that reason, when understood by the market, could result in stock price changes.

Multiple Choice Questions

1. c	First's share of Second's dividends is .3 x $4 million = $1.2 million. Because the cost method is used, Second's income does not affect First.
2. a	Using the equity method, First's retained income increases by its share of Second's income: .3 x $10 million = $3 million. Dividends are treated as a reduction in the cost basis of the investment.
3. b	The new cost basis is adjusted by income and dividends: $100 + $3 - $1.2 = $101.8.
4. c	The goodwill is equal to the purchase price less Bigg's share of the stockholders' equity: $150 - .9 x $160 = $6 million.
5. a	The minority interest is .10 x $160 million = $16 million.
6. d	The consolidated net income is the parent's net income plus its share of the subsidiary's income: $16 + .75 x $16 = $28 million
7. d	The component percentage of this balance sheet account is $3 ÷ $75 = 4%
8. a, c	The current ratio is current assets divided by current liabilities. An increase in this ratio (other things equal) indicates an improvement in assets and a greater ability to pay short-term obligations.
9. d	The return on assets is equal to the product of these two ratios: 4 x 12% = 48%.

10. c   Turning the above calculation around means the asset turnover is equal to return on assets divided by return on sales: 12% ÷ 6% = 2 times.

Completion

1. the cost method, equity method, consolidation
2. an asset, original cost, retained income
3. a third party's investment in a subsidiary.
4. purchased goodwill, excess of cost over fair value of net identifiable assets of businesses acquired
5. return on sales, total asset turnover, return on sales, total asset turnover
6. sales, that the firm's assets are not being utilized as well as a competitor's
7. common earnings per share, common dividends per share, that the firm is retaining more income for internal investment than the industry norm (assuming income and cash levels are comparable)
8. average inventory, cost of goods sold, efficient (low) levels of inventory
9. average accounts receivable, sales on account, that collections are being pursued aggressively

Problems

1. Company P and Company S (in millions of dollars)

    a. Year-end balance of P's investment
    Equity method: $180 + 40%(20 - 10) = 180 + 4 = $184
    Cost method: $180

    b. Increase in P's retained income
    Equity method: 40%($20) = $8
    Cost method: 40%(10) = $4

2. Tamarisk Company

    a. Cost method:
    Investment carrying amount: $60 million
    Increase in stockholders' equity: 20% x $15 million of dividends = $3 million

    b. Equity method:
    Carrying amount of investment: $60 million + (20% x $25 million) - (20% x $15 million)
        $60 million $5 million - $3 million = $62 million
    Increase in stockholders' equity: 20% x $25 million = $5 million

3. Table Mesa Company and Piedra Company

a.
Market value of capital stock exchanged	$50,000
Less current *value* of individual assets of Piedra	20,000
Goodwill	$30,000
Net assets of Table Mesa before acquisition	$80,000
Individual assets of Piedra before acquisition	20,000
Goodwill, as above	30,000
Net assets after acquisition (including goodwill)	$130,000
Stockholders' equity of Table Mesa before acquisition	$ 80,000
Market value of additional Table Mesa capital stock issued	50,000
Stockholders' equity after acquisition	$130,000

b.
Net income of Table Mesa before acquisition	$8,000
Net income of Piedra before acquisition	7,000
Prospective annual net income after acquisition	15,000

c.
Prospective annual net income before goodwill amortization, as above	$15,000
Less goodwill amortization: $30,000/5 yrs	6,000
Prospective annual net income after goodwill amortization	$9,000

4. Company P and Company S

a.

Assets		Liabilities and Stockholders' Equity	
Cash and other assets (440 + 500) =	$940	Liabilities (200 + 300)=	$500
		Minority interest (10%)(200) =	20
		Stockholders' equity	420
Total assets	$940	Total equities	$940

b.

Assets		Liabilities and Stockholders Equity	
Cash and other assets (400 + 500)	$940	Liabilities (200 + 300)	$500
		Minority interest (25%)(200)	50
Consolidated goodwill*	30	Stockholders' equity	420
Total assets	$970	Total equities	$970

*Consolidated goodwill: 180 - 75%(200) = 180 - 150 = $30

5. Roaring Fork Corporation

Current ratio: 240 ÷ 120 = 2 to 1, or 2
Inventory turnover: 500 ÷ 125 = 4 times
Collection period: (80 x 365) ÷ 800 = 36.5 days
Gross profit rate: (800 - 500) ÷ 800 = 37.5%
Return on sales: 36 ÷ 800 = 4.5%

Return on stockholders' equity: 36 ÷ 200 = 18%

6. Gunnison Corporation
   a. 54 ÷ 900 = 6%
   b. 900 ÷ 500 = 1.8 times
   c. 54 ÷ 500 = 10.8%

   alternative calculation:

   6% x 1.8 = 10.8%

CHAPTER 21

Difficulties in Measuring Net Income

> **MAIN FOCUS AND OBJECTIVES**
>
> The first part of the chapter explains four different ways of measuring the *flow of costs* from inventories to cost of goods sold. These inventory measurement methods are: specific identification, weighted average, first-in, first-out (FIFO), and last-in, first-out (LIFO). The second part of the chapter examines various ways for measuring the effects of *changing price levels* on balance sheets and income statements. Your learning objectives are to:
>
> - Understand the four inventory methods
>
> - Compare LIFO and FIFO
>
> - Explain the lower-of-cost-or-market rule
>
> - Distinguish between financial and physical capital maintenance
>
> - Use four methods for measuring income based on alternative concepts of capital maintenance

REVIEW OF KEY CONCEPTS

Part One

A. When identical or similar goods are purchased at different times and prices, four alternative methods are generally accepted accounting practice for measuring the cost of inventory: *specific identification, weighted average, FIFO,* and *LIFO*.

    1. Essentially, these methods model assumptions of the sequence of cost flows; that is, the method chosen directly affects the *timing* of the transfer of costs from assets (inventories) to expenses (costs of goods used or sold).
        a. Over the life of the firm, total cost of goods sold will be the same regardless of the inventory method.
        b. However, given the corporation's indefinite life, the differences may persist indefinitely.
    2. When prices fluctuate over time, these assumptions can result in strikingly different amounts reported in financial statements, affecting both:

　　　　a.　　Inventory assets in the balance sheet
　　　　b.　　Cost of goods sold in the income statement

> See textbook Exhibit 21-1

3. In general the chosen inventory method must be used *consistently* from year to year.
   a. In the U.S. the IRS requires firms to use the same method of inventory accounting for both tax reporting and financial reporting.
   b. Because switching methods can affect income dramatically, the IRS does not allow switching methods without prior approval.

4. **Specific identification** requires a tracing of the actual inventory items through the inventory and into cost of goods sold.
   a. This is usually not feasible except for high-unit-value types of goods, for example, automobiles and expensive jewelry.
   b. Thus the *flow of costs* coincides with the *physical flows* of inventory items.

5. However, the other three methods do *not* require that the flow of costs coincide with the actual sequence of the physical flow of inventory.

6. The **weighted-average** method requires a computation of the **weighted-average unit cost** of goods available for sale.
   a. Such an average is not a simple average; it is the total cost of beginning inventory plus purchases divided by the total number of units purchased and in the beginning inventory.
   b. This average unit cost is then multiplied by units to arrive at the cost of goods sold, and the cost of the ending inventory.

7. The **first-in, first-out method** (FIFO) assumes that the costs of the *earliest*-acquired goods are used *first*, whereas the **last-in, first-out method** (LIFO) makes the opposite assumption -- the last acquired goods are used first.

8. Compared with the LIFO method, the FIFO method leaves the ending inventory valuation nearer to current replacement costs, but the FIFO method tends to mismatch *old* costs with *current* revenues (sales).

9. In contrast, LIFO values the inventory on an old-cost basis but tends to match current costs more closely with current revenues, and therefore LIFO measures a net income that more closely represents the efficiency of *current* activities.

10. Compared with FIFO, the use of LIFO tends to show lower inventory measurements during periods of rising prices (and higher inventory figures when prices are falling).
    a. If prices are rising, LIFO therefore tends to show less income than FIFO, and thus it often *minimizes current income taxes*. This is the main reason many companies have adopted LIFO.
    b. The use of LIFO also permits management to influence the measurement of net income by deciding on the *timing* of purchases.

11. Regardless of the inventory method, if an inventory's market price drops below its historical cost, accountants must decrease the inventory's book value to market value.
    a. This helps prevent overvalued inventories from appearing on balance sheets.
    b. This is another example, though, of accountants' conservatisim; they are willing to write-down assets when the market value drops, but they generally will not write them up if their market value rises. This issue is covered in the next part of the chapter.

Part Two

B. In concept, net income is the measurement of change in wealth between two periods of time. For example, accountants can compute net income as the difference between owners' equity at the beginning and at the end of a year. Management is charged with maintaining the wealth or capital of the firm. But the way net income is measured depends on how one defines wealth -- *financial* capital or *physical* capital.

   1. **Financial capital** means capital is measured in terms of the **money invested** in the firm.
      a. This meaning reflects the traditional **historical-cost** view, the owners' or stockholders' equity section of the balance sheet shows the effectiveness of the business in maintaining or improving the historical value of the financial capital invested.
      b. This view ignores the effects of an unstable monetary unit and relative changes in specific asset prices (e.g., due to changes in technology).

   2. **Physical capital, is the physical operating capability** in terms of inventory, plant assets, and so forth.
      a. Maintenance of physical capital means that the firm has the ability to perform in current economic conditions, that is, it has created enough wealth to be able to replace its inventory and other, long-term assets at current prices.
      b. This implies that the values of the firm's assets should be restated to their current values in order to measure the change in wealth over time.
      c. If sales prices for products and services sold to customers have not kept pace with prices the firm *currently* must pay for inputs then the firm is not better off, even though it may show a profit based on the *historical* costs of inputs.

C. Although net income is a widely accepted indicator of the performance of a company for a given period of time, there is considerable disagreement as to how net income should be measured in an inflationary environment. There are four major ways to measure income and capital.

> See textbook Exhibit 21-3

   1. The conventional *accrual method* of measuring net income matches realized revenues with the expired costs of assets (Method 1 of Exhibit 21-3). This is the generally accepted *historical-cost approach using nominal dollars*. However, it has two alleged weaknesses:

a. The reported data for income and capital *do not reflect changes in current replacement costs* of goods sold and goods in the ending inventory.
b. The reported data *ignore general price inflation:* the increase in the general price level (decrease in the purchasing power of money).
c. The result is that a historical cost measure of income mixes monetary units with different values and purchasing power.

2. The *current-cost approach* using nominal dollars focuses on income from continuing operations (Method 2 of Exhibit 21-3).
    a. Excluded from this income are **holding gains** from goods sold and unsold, these being reported as part of *revaluation equity* (excess of *current* replacement costs over historical costs).
    b. Holding gains cannot be distributed as dividends without impairing the invesited capital needed to maintain *physical capacity*.

3. A different way of coping with the measurement distortions of the conventional accrual method is to use **general price indexes** to adjust the nominal dollars of *historical costs to constant dollars* (Method 3 of Exhibit 21-3).
    a. These adjusted amounts measure **current purchasing power.**
    b. Be sure to note that these are merely *restated historical costs* and that they are not intended to reflect specific current values.

4. A fourth approach to measuring income and capital is to use general price indexes to convert *current costs* to **constant dollars** (Method 4 of Exhibit 21-3).
    a. Advocates of this method claim that it is theoretically best way to measure income and capital.
    b. They reason that the financial statements should reflect the *total change in wealth measured in constant dollars, including both realized and unrealized elements.*

5. Although the use of price indexes and current costs might help accountants measure income more realistically and determine whether invested capital has been maintained, it is not a common practice in the U.S. to prepare and issue financial statements on these bases.

6. SFAS 33 required supplemental disclosures of the effects of inflation, but due to declining inflation and intense lobbying by firms that opposed the standard, SFAS 33 was rescinded eight years later. However:
    a. High inflation may return to the U.S.
    b. High inflation is a fact in many developing countries
    c. Knowledge of the alternative methods for coping with inflation are useful in managing mulitnational companies that operate in areas with high inflation.

PRACTICE TEST QUESTIONS AND PROBLEMS WITH SOLUTIONS

True or False Statements

Determine whether each of the following statements is True (T) or False (F) and enter your answer in the space provided.

__T__ 1. The FIFO inventory method assumes that the cost of the most recently acquired inventory items is represented by the unsold items.

__T__ 2. Compared with the FIFO method, LIFO tends to match current costs more closely with current sales.

__T__ 3. During a period of rising prices, the use of the LIFO method, in comparison with FIFO, will tend to produce lower reported net income and higher reported cost of goods sold.

__T__ 4. The main reason many companies have adopted LIFO is its appeal in minimizing current income taxes.

__F__ 5. The specific-identification inventory method would probably be more appropriate for a grocery store than a yacht dealer.

__F__ 6. When the historical costs of assets are adjusted by the use of general price indexes, the resultant figures are current costs of assets.

____ 7. The current-cost approaches exclude accumulated holding gains from retained income and stockholders' equity.

____ 8. Accumulated holding gains are not available for dividends without impairing invested capital.

____ 9. Holding gains would be identified in financial statements based on historical costs adjusted by general price indexes.

__T__ 10. The current-cost concept of income is based on the concept of maintenance of physical capital, as opposed to the concept of maintenance of financial capital.

____ 11. The traditional historical-cost view is consistent with physical capital maintenance but not financial capital maintenance.

____ 12. If capital markets are efficient, then ordinary investors should not try to "beat the market," but should rely on the expertise of professional market analysts.

____ 13. If capital markets are efficient, then managers are mistaken if they think they can influence stock prices by manipulating their reported earnings by making accounting changes.

____ 14. If capital markets are efficient, then managers have no incentives to manipulate earnings with accounting changes.

____ 15. If capital markets are efficient, that means that all information is already available to investors, so formal reporting of financial statements is not necessary.

Multiple Choice Questions

For each of the following multiple-choice questions, select the best answer(s) and enter the identification letter(s) in the space provided.

Use the following data for all of these questions:

A company had the following inventory transactions:

	Units	Total Cost	
Beginning inventory, Dec. 31, 19X2	100 units	$ 400	$4/EA
Purchase, Feb. 20, 19X3	200 units	1,000	$5/EA
Sales, Mar. 17, 19X3	250 units	?	

__B__ 1. Using a FIFO approach, the cost of goods sold on Mar. 17 was: (a) $1,200, (b) $1,150, (c) $1,000, (d) $1,400.
  100×4 = 400
  150×5 = 750 }$1,150

__A__ 2. Using a LIFO approach, the cost of goods sold on Mar. 17 was: (a) $1,200, (b) $1,150, (c) $1,000, (d) $1,400.
  200×5 = 1,000
  50×4 = 200 }$1,200

__C__ 3. Using a weighted average approach, the cost of goods sold on Mar. 17 was: (a) $1,200, (b) $1,125, (c) $1,167, (d) $1,033.
  1400÷300 = 4.66 × 250 = $1166.67

__C__ 4. Using a FIFO approach, the cost of inventory on hand after the Mar. 17 sale was: (a) $100, (b) $200, (c) $250, (d) $225
  50×5 = $250

__B__ 5. Using a LIFO approach, the cost of inventory on hand after the Mar. 17 sale was: (a) $100, (b) $200, (c) $250, (d) $225
  50×4 = $200

__D__ 6. Using a weighted-average approach, the cost of inventory on hand after the Mar. 17 sale was: (a) $167, (b) $267, (c) $225, (d) $233
  4.66 × 50 = $233

__D__ 7. The tax effect of using LIFO instead of FIFO would be (assume a 40% tax rate): (a) $30 tax savings, (b) $30 tax increase, (c) $20 tax increase, (d) $20 tax savings
  50×.40 = $20

__D__ 8. Assume on March 17 that the company received a notice from its only supplier that the cost of the inventory item had just increased to $6 per unit. Cost of goods sold was: (a) $1,200, (b) $1,150, (c) $1,300, (d) $1,500.
  250×6 = 1500

__A__ 9. See item 8 above. Using a current replacement cost approach, the Mar. 17 cost of ending inventory was: (a) $300, (b) $250, (c) $200, (d) $275.
  50×6 = $300

__B__ 10. Suppose the government's general price level index was constant at 220 until March 17 when it rose to 250. In dollars adjusted for general inflation, the March 17 cost of goods sold was: (a) $1,526, (b) $1,326, (c) $1,426, (d) $1,226.
  200 × 4.67 × 250/220

Completion

Complete each of the following statements by filling in the blanks.

1. The three inventory methods that do *not* require that cost flows coincide with the actual sequence of physical flows are
   (a) __LIFO__
   (b) __FIFO__
   (c) __Weighted average__

Difficulties in Measuring Net Income 315

2. The inventory method that assumes that the cost of the oldest inventory items acquired is represented by the current inventory is ___LIFO___.

3. During a period of rising prices, the inventory asset will tend to be reported at the highest cost by the ___FIFO___ method.

4. The generally accepted accrual method for measuring net income values assets on the ___historical cost___ basis.

5. General price indexes are used to restate _____ costs in terms of _____.

6. Business managers would naturally tend to favor the treatment of holding gains as _____.

7. Maintenance of _____ means that the firm's wealth is restated to current replacement costs in order to compute _____.

8. The ___lower of cost or market___ rule states that if current market prices of inventory are ___less___ than historical cost, the value of the inventory should be ___written down___. This is an example of accounting ___conservatism___.

9. Two methods for determining the amount of inventory on hand are ___perpetual___ and ___periodic___.

10. If a capital market is efficient with respect to accounting information, then _____ ; that is if the accounting information is good news, stock prices move _____.

Problems

1. Compute for Webster Co. the total cost of the ending inventory by each method indicated. Given: 140 - 80

    Beginning inventory: 30 units at $ 8 each
    Purchases: May 40 units at $ 9 each
    August 20 units at $10 each
    September 50 units at $12 each
    Ending inventory: 60 units
    SOLD: 80 "

    (a) FIFO 140 - 80 = 60   50×12 + 10×10 = 600 + 100 = $700

    (b) LIFO 30×8 + 30×9 = 240 + 270 = $510

    (c) Weighted average
    30×8 = 240
    40×9 = 360
    20×10 = 200
    50×12 = 600
    140 | 1400 = $10 × 60 = $600

2. Given for Roget Company:

	Units	Price	Total
Inventory, January 1, 19X3	100	$200	$20,000
Purchases in 19X3	200	300	60,000
Sales in 19X3	180	500	90,000
Inventory, December 31, 19X3	120		*
Operating expenses in 19X3	---	---	16,000

*to be computed

a. Complete the following income statements and cash summaries, assuming that all transactions are for cash:

INCOME STATEMENTS

	FIFO Method	LIFO Method
Sales	90,000	90,000
Less cost of goods sold:		
Beginning inventory	20,000	20,000
Purchases	60,000	60,000
Cost of goods available for sale	80,000	80,000
Less ending inventory:	120×300 = 36,000	100×200 = 20,000 ⎫ 26,000 20×300 = 6,000 ⎭
Cost of goods sold	44,000	54,000
Gross profit on sales	46,000	36,000
Less operating expenses	16,000	16,000
Income before income tax	30,000	20,000
Less income tax at 40%	12,000	8,000
Net income for 19X3	18,000	12,000

b. Cash Summaries

	FIFO Method	LIFO Method
Cash payments:		
Purchases	60,000	60,000
Operating expenses	16,000	16,000
Income tax	12,000	8,000
Total cash payments	88,000	84,000
Cash receipts	90,000	90,000
Cash increase (decrease) for 19X3	2,000	6,000

c. Which method would tend to provide the greater ability of the company to pay cash dividends in 19X3? Why?

LIFO. MORE CASH AVAILABLE DUE TO LOWER INCOME TAX PAYMENTS

3. The Moving Horizon Corporation has just been formed, having issued $10,000 of capital stock for cash. It immediately purchased 1,000 units of inventory for cash at $10 per unit. During the first year of operations, it sold 700 units for $20 cash each. At the end of the year, the replacement cost of the inventory was $15 per unit, and the general-price-level index had increased 20% from the beginning of the year. Compute the following amounts for each of the four methods of reporting income and capital. Assume no other transactions, and ignore income taxes.

	Nominal Dollars		Constant Dollars	
	Method 1 Historical Cost	Method 2 Current Cost	Method 3 Historical Cost	Method 4 Current Cost
a. Income from continuing operations				
b. Ending inventory				
c. Retained income				
d. Original paid-in capital				
e. Holding gains on units sold				
f. Holding gains on units unsold				
g. Total assets (cash and inventory)				
h. Total equities (items c, d, e, f)				

CHAPTER 21 SOLUTIONS TO PRACTICE TEST QUESTIONS AND PROBLEMS

True or False Statements

1. True — Under FIFO cost of goods sold is drawn from the earliest purchased goods, leaving (if anything) the most recently purchased goods.

2. True — Under LIFO cost of goods sold is drawn from the most recently purchased goods, which more closely match current costs than earlier purchased goods.

3. True — Since LIFO draws from the most recent purchases for computing cost of goods sold, in times of rising prices LIFO-cost of goods sold will be higher than it would have been under FIFO, reducing reported income.

4. True — Since LIFO is allowed for tax purposes, in times of rising prices it reduces tax liabilities and increases cash flow relative to FIFO. Even though reported income is lower, the increased cash flow is attractive.

5. False — Just the opposite is more likely. Tracing the cost of every can of soup or head of lettuce would be virtually impossible for a grocer, yet this approach would be possible, even necessary for a yacht dealer.

6. False — Adjusting for *general* changes in prices may not be the same as adjusting for *specific* prices. For example, the costs of computing equipment (of a specific type) have dropped steadily over the years though in general prices have increased.

7. False — Since the effect of revaluing assets to current costs would generally result in debits to asset accounts, the credits have to go somewhere. Since the revaluation

represents adjustments in the measure of capital, the appropriate place for the credits would be stockholders' equity. Some believe the difference should go to retained income, however others believe that this should go to a reserve called *revaluation equity* to make it less likely that dividends would be paid from it.

8. True — Holding gains represent the increase in the current costs of assets. If holding gains are paid out as dividends, the firm has begun to liquidate its assets and does not have sufficient capital to replace those assets.

9. False — Holding gains would be determined by adjusting historical costs for specific price changes, not general price changes.

10. True — Proponents of current cost believe that the best measure of income is based on increases in wealth over and above the amount necessary to retain the firm's productive capacity.

11. False — Just the reverse is the case. Historical-cost-based net income measures the amount of wealth created over the period that is in excess of invested financial capital.

12. True — Unless one is prepared to devote considerable time and talent to studying the prospects of various firms, one should not expect to do better than the experts on a consistent basis.

13. True — Managers probably cannot mislead the market into thinking the prospects of the firm are better than they really are just by changing accounting methods to inflate income. However, markets may react favorably if changing accounting methods does avoid some costs, such as taxes, government regulation, or debt foreclosure.

14. False — Managers may be able to make relatively small adjustments to income with accounting changes to, say, benefit their bonus compensation plans or to avoid violating debt covenants that require maintenance of certain financial ratios.

15. False — Considerable research has shown that accounting numbers are consistent with market valuations of firms, which means that the numbers reflect other information available in the marketplace. That is not to say that elimination of financial reporting would not be missed. Many believe that one of the major effects of requiring audited financial statements is that investors are more confident that investment is a relatively safe endeavor. That is why so many are calling for auditors to explicitly search for management fraud.

Multiple Choice Questions

The following table can be used to answer these questions:

Method	Cost of goods sold	Ending inventory
FIFO	400 + 150 x 5 = 1,150(1b)	50 x 5 = 250(4c)
LIFO	1,000 + 50 x 4 = 1,200(2a)	50 x 4 = 200(5b)
Weighted Average, $1,400÷ 300 = $4.67	200 x 4.67 = 1,167(3c)	50 x 4.67 = 233(6d)
Current cost	250 x 6 = 1,500(8d)	50 x 6 = 300 (9a)
Price-level adjusted $4.67 x (250/220) = 5.303	200 x 5.303 = 1,326(10b)	50 x 5.303 = 265

7. d   The tax savings is the difference between LIFO and FIFO cost of goods sold multiplied by the tax rate: $50 x .4 = $20 tax savings because LIFO net income is $50 less than FIFO income. Note this is similar to the tax saving effect of using accelerated depreciation rather than straight-line depreciation (see Chapter 12).

Completion

1. LIFO, FIFO, weighted average
2. LIFO
3. FIFO
4. historical cost
5. historical costs, general purchasing power
6. operating income
7. physical capital, net income and asset values
8. lower of cost or market, less, written down to market, conservatism
9. perpetual inventory, periodic inventory methods
10. stock prices fully reflect that information, upward

Problems

1. Webster Co.
   (a) (50 x 12) + (10 x 10) = 700
   (b) (30 x 8) + (30 x 9) = 510
   (c) (30 x 8) + (40 x 9) + (20 x 10) + (50 x 12) = 1400;
   1400 ÷ (30 + 40 + 20 + 50) = 1400 ÷ 140 = 10; 10 x 60 = 600

2. Roget Company

   a.

   INCOME STATEMENTS

	FIFO Method	LIFO Method
Sales	$90,000	$90,000
Less cost of goods sold:		
Beginning inventory	20,000	20,000
Purchases	60,000	60,000
Cost of goods available for sale	80,000	80,000
Less ending inventory:		
120 x $300	36,000	
100 x $200		
20 x $300		26,000
Cost of goods sold	44,000	54,000
Gross profit on sales	46,000	36,000
Less operating expenses	16,000	16,000
Income before income tax	30,000	20,000
Less income tax at 40%	18,000	12,000
Net income for 19X3	$12,000	$ 8,000

320 Chapter 21

	FIFO Method	LIFO Method
Cash payments:		
Purchases	$60,000	$60,000
Operating expenses	16,000	16,000
Income tax	18,000	12,000
Total cash payments	94,000	88,000
Cash receipts	90,000	90,000
Cash increase (decrease) for 19X3	$ (4,000)	$ 2,000

    b.   LIFO, because more cash would be available as a result of lower income taxes.

3.   Moving Horizon Corporation

	Nominal Dollars		Constant Dollars	
	Method 1 Historical Cost	Method 2 Current Cost	Method 3 Historical Cost	Method 4 Current Cost
a. Income from continuing operations:				
Sales: 700 x $20 = $14,000;				
Deduct 700 x $10 = $7,000	$ 7,000			
Deduct 700 x $15 = $10,500		$ 3,500		$ 3,500
Deduct 120$ x $7,000 = $8,400			$ 5,600	
b. Ending Inventory:				
300 x $10	3,000			
300 x $15		4,500		4,500
300 x $10 x 120%			3,600	
c. Retained income (same as a)	7,000	3,500	5,600	3,500
d. Original paid-in capital	10,000	10,000		
10,000 x 120%			12,000	12,000
e. Holding gains on units sold:				
700 x ($15 - $10)		3,500		
700 x ($15 - 120% of $10)				2,100
f. Holding gains on units unsold:				
300 x ($15 - $10)		1,500		
300 x ($15 - 120% of $10)				900
g. Total assets:				
Cash (700 x $20)	$14,000	$14,000	$14,000	$14,000
Inventory (item b above)	3,000	4,500	3,600	4,500
Total Assets	$17,000	$18,500	$17,600	$18,500
h. Total equities				
Original paid-in capital (d)	$10,000	$10,000	$12,000	$12,000
Retained income (c)	7,000	3,500	5,600	3,500
Holding gains (e)	-	3,500	-	21100
Holding gains (f)	-	1,500	-	900
Total equities	$17,000	$18,500	$17,600	$18,500

Difficulties in Measuring Net Income   321

APPENDIX

Introduction to Journal Entries and T-Accounts

> **MAIN FOCUS AND OBJECTIVES**
>
> The purpose to this appendix is to introduce the primary means of recording data in double-entry accounting systems -- *journal entries*. As an aid to explaining the effects of journal entries, the appendix uses so-called *T-accounts*, which are useful conceptual devices and which represent actual balance sheet and income statement accounts.

REVIEW OF KEY CONCEPTS

A. Most accounting systems are designed to record data simultaneously to all *accounts* affected by a single transaction. Though more than two accounts may be affected, these systems are called **double-entry systems** because at least two entries are required to record every transaction.

1. The double-entry system is built on the accounting equation (discussed in Chapter 18) for every privately owned company, which is:
   Assets = Liabilities + Owners' Equity

2. Every economic transaction affects this equation, and at all times the equation must be balanced.

3. The continual balancing of the accounting equation is what makes accounting systems such effective control devices: if the system is designed with appropriate accounts and tended by competent (and honest) personnel, it is almost impossible lose track of costs and revenues. In addition, the system almost automatically produces useful (and required) financial statements.

4. The accounting equation is balanced by recognizing that an increase or a decrease in one account *must* be accompanied by an offsetting increase or decrease in another account (hence the double-entry designation).

   a. For example, purchase of materials results in an increase in the material inventory account. The offsetting or balancing entry would show where the resources were obtained to purchase the material: either by decreasing *cash* (another asset) or by increasing the *accounts payable* account (a liability, or promise to pay cash in the future).

   b. As another example, application of labor to the construction of a custom-built house results in an increase of an asset, *work* (or construction) *in process* accomplished by either a decrease in *cash* (another asset) or an increase in *wages payable* (a liability).

c. As a third example, credit sales of products result in the increase of the asset account, *accounts receivable*, and a corresponding increase in *owners' equity* (an equity account; though many systems funnel revenues through *temporary* accounts, such as *sales* or *income* in order to have a ready means of computing periodic income).

5. In every case, an increase in an asset account must be accomplished by (1) a corresponding decrease in another asset or (2) a corresponding increase in a liability or equity account, or (3) a combination of the two effects.
   a. Likewise, a decrease in an asset is accompanied by an increase in another asset, a decrease in a liability or equity, or a combination of the two.
   b. Similarly, an increase in a liability or equity is accompanied by a decrease in another liability or equity, a decrease in an asset, or a combination of the two.
   c. How is a decrease in a liability balanced?

B. Most accounting systems accomplish the double-entries by means of making *journal entries* as transactions occur and by *posting* these entries to the affected accounts (also called *ledger accounts* after the large books or ledgers in which these accounts used to be kept in manual systems of not too long ago).

1. A **journal entry** is the means of recording (at one time literally in a daily journal, but now of course mostly via computer input) the amounts of a transaction and the identity of all accounts affected by the transaction.
   a. The journal entry would identify which accounts were increased or decreased and by how much.
   b. For example, to record the purchase of materials, the journal entry would record that material inventory was increased, and that either or both cash and accounts payable were decreased or increased, respectively.

2. For many, many years accountants and bookkeepers have employed logical devices to help them keep track of which accounts were increased and which were decreased by transactions. Most computerized accounting systems retain this logic, if not the physical devices.
   a. *Ledger accounts* exist for every balance sheet account and temporary account (used primarily to record income statement items). There also may be *subsidiary* ledgers, such as job-cost records that are subsidiary to work in process accounts (see Chapter 14 -- many of the examples of this appendix reflect the context of Chapter 14 and job-order costing).
   b. Ledger accounts for assets record *increases* in *assets* on the *left* side (or **debit** side, from a Latin word meaning "what is owed") of the account.
   c. Likewise, *decreases* in *assets* are recorded on the *right* side (or **credit** side, which is just an accounting term for "the other side") of the account.
   d. Because liability and equity accounts are on the other side of the accounting equation, the designation of increases and decreases is reversed for these accounts:
      • *Increases* in *liabilities* or *equities* result in *credit* entries to those accounts.
      • *Decreases* in *liabilities* or *equities* result in *debit* entries to those accounts.

e. The probably familiar phrase "debits equal the credits" explains that in order to keep the accounting equation balanced, all debit entries (e.g., increases in assets) must be accompanied by an equal amount of credit entries (e.g., reductions in other assets or increases in liabilities or equities).

3. Journal entries for every separate transaction, by convention, list the debit entry first and the credit entry second (indented to the right), accompanied by a brief explanation of the transaction.

    a. For example, a transaction to record the purchase of $14,000 of materials on credit would be recorded in the journal as:

Accounts	Debit	Credit
July 22, 19X3 Purchase of materials:		
Materials inventory	$14,000	
Accounts payable		$14,000

    b. Issuing $10,000 of this material to a job would be recorded as follows:

Accounts	Debit	Credit
July 23, 19X3 Issuance of material		
Work in process inventory	$10,000	
Materials inventory		$10,000

    c. Use of $8,000 direct labor (half cash and half payable at the end of the month) on a job would be recorded as:

Accounts	Debit	Credit
July 23, 19X3 Application of labor:		
Work in process inventory	$8,000	
Cash		$4,000
Wages payable		$4,000

    d. Recording incurrence of a $2,000 utilities bill, part of factory overhead, would be recorded:

Accounts	Debit	Credit
July 23, 19X3 Factory utilities:		
Factory overhead control	$2,000	
Utilities payable		$2,000

    e. Applying factory overhead at 150% of direct labor cost would be recorded:

Accounts	Debit	Credit
July 23, 19X3 Application of factory overhead:		
Work in process inventory	$12,000	
Factory overhead control		$12,000

  f. Credit sales of products resulting in revenues of $45,000:

Accounts	Debit	Credit
July 24, 19X3 Sales of products:		
Accounts receivable	$45,000	
Sales (or Owners' equity)		$45,000

4. Each journal entry is *posted* or written to the debit or credit sides of the affected ledger accounts, so that at virtually any time a glance at a ledger account shows its current balance, much as you are able to do with your balanced checkbook, or more likely these days as you are able to do at the mini-teller.
 a. Ledger accounts can be represented by T-accounts (in fact many manual ledgers look just like T-accounts), which are so-called because of their T shape.
 b. The account title goes on top of the T, and debit entries (and beginning positive balances for assets) go on the left or debit side. Likewise, credit entries (and beginning positive balances for liabilities and equities) go on the right side of the T. For example, a T-account for work in process inventory would look like this before any entries:

```
            Work in process
           ─────────────────
                  │
                  │
```

 c. The journal entries above that would be posted to the work in process ledger account can be shown on the T-account as:

```
                                    Work in process
                                   ─────────────────
July beginning balance                     0  │
7/22/X3 Application of material       $10,000 │
7/23/X3 Application of labor            8,000 │
7/23/X3 Application of overhead        12,000 │
7/23/X3 balance                       $30,000 │
```

 d. As shown above, at any time an account balance can be determined by totaling all the entries (debit and credit).
 e. In the above example, when goods are completed, the journal entry for the cost of goods completed would *debit* (increase) *finished goods* inventory and *credit* (decrease) *work in process*. Assume that products costing $20,000 were completed on July 24; the T-accounts would look like:

```
                                    Work in process
                                   ─────────────────
July beginning balance                     0   │
7/22/X3 Application of material       $10,000  │
7/23/X3 Application of labor            8,000  │
7/23/X3 Application of overhead        12,000  │
7/24/X3 Completion of products                 │   $20,000
7/24/X3 Balance                       $10,000  │

                                     Finished goods
                                   ─────────────────
July beginning balance                     0   │
7/24/X3 Completion of products        $20,000  │
```

f. When those goods are sold, say in a single transaction, you would debit cost of goods sold (a temporary income account), and credit finished goods:

Finished goods	
July beginning balance	0
7/24/X3 Completion of products	$20,000
7/25/X3 Sale of products	$20,000
7/25/X3 Balance	0

Cost of goods sold	
7/25/X3 Sale of products	$20,000

C. This appendix has been a brief introduction to the mechanics of recording accounting transactions. Though real accounting systems can be very complex and the transactions they record can be even more complex, be assured that every transaction can be recorded by balancing the accounting equation, by insuring that the debits equal the credits. The real accounting problem can be deciding where the debits and credits *should* go!